W9-DIR-684

# The SECOND
# RUSSIAN
# REVOLUTION

*By arrangement with BBC Books,*
*a division of BBC Enterprises Ltd.*

# The SECOND RUSSIAN REVOLUTION

## The struggle for power in the KREMLIN

ANGUS ROXBURGH

**PHAROS BOOKS**
A SCRIPPS HOWARD COMPANY
NEW YORK

TO MY FATHER,
IN MEMORY OF MY MOTHER

Copyright © 1992 by Angus Roxburgh.
English version © 1991 by Angus Roxburgh.
All rights reserved. No part of this book may be reproduced
in any form or by any means without written permission of
the publisher.

First U.S. edition.

Library of Congress Cataloging-in-Publication Data
Roxburgh, Angus.
The second Russian revolution : the struggle for power in the
Kremlin / Angus Roxburgh. — 1st U.S. ed.
p.    cm.
Includes bibliographical references and index.
ISBN 0-88687-683-4
1. Soviet Union—Politics and government—1985–  2. Perestroïka.
I. Title.
DK288.R69  1992
947.085′4—dc20        92-1201        CIP

Printed in the United States of America.

Pharos Books
A Scripps Howard Company
200 Park Avenue
New York, N.Y. 10166

10 9 8 7 6 5 4 3 2 1

Pharos Books are available at special discounts on bulk purchases
for sales promotions, premiums, fundraising or educational use.
For details, contact the Special Sales Department, Pharos Books,
200 Park Avenue, New York, NY 10166.

# Contents

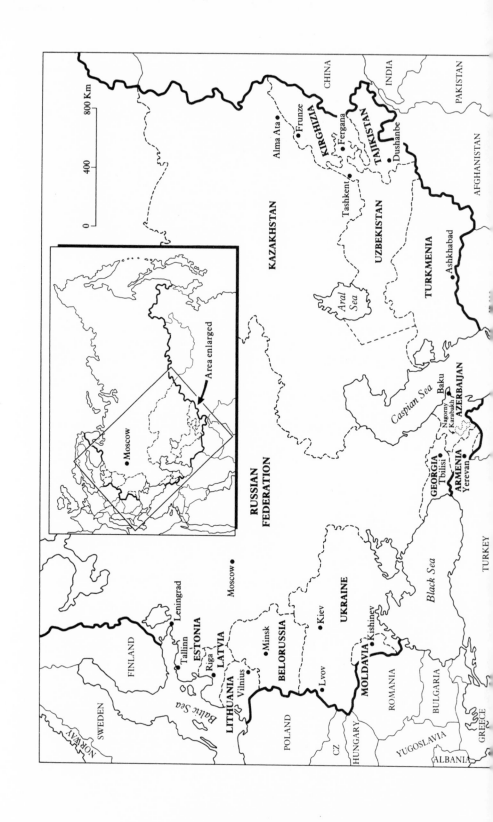

# Introduction

'What is the good of a road if it does not lead to a temple?'

*From the film* Repentance *by Tengiz Abuladze*

WHEN I wrote the Introduction to the first edition of this book, in January 1991, I felt obliged to justify the use of the word 'Revolution' in the title. *Perestroika* ('Restructuring'), I suggested, was too modest a word to describe what had happened in the Soviet Union since 1985. The policies initiated by Mikhail Gorbachev had already changed the face of Europe. Very little remained of the communist system under which the people of the USSR and Eastern Europe had lived.

Since the events of August 1991, few people would dispute that the word 'revolution' is appropriate. Gorbachev's attempt at evolutionary change was thrown aside, and the Communist Party that seized power in the 'first' revolution of 1917 was swept away, precipitating the disintegration of the Soviet Union itself.

But even before then the basic features of communist rule had been undermined. The one-party state, with its rubber-stamp parliament, had been replaced by a rudimentary multi-party system, pluralism, a real parliament. A totalitarian dictatorship had given way to civil society. Instead of a centralised, Russified state, there were plans for a loose federation of nations. Instead of the centrally planned, over-bureaucratic economy, moves towards a market economy had begun. Tight censorship and control of all information had been replaced by press freedom and openness about Soviet history; all taboos had been broken, and almost all banned books had been published. The police state, with its intimidation, closed borders, lawlessness and KGB rule, had virtually gone; Soviet citizens could travel abroad, only a handful of prisoners could be classified as 'political', and the foundations of a 'law-based state' had been laid. The fear had gone out of Soviet life. Finally, in foreign policy, the Soviet Union was no longer an isolated country peering suspiciously and threateningly at the West from behind a stockade of missiles; it was

1

becoming integrated into the world community, cutting its arms and desperately keen to be 'accepted'.

Above all, there had been a revolution in the sense that an entire system of values – the inhuman, Stalinist version of 'socialism', which degraded millions of human lives in many countries for much of the twentieth century – had finally been exposed as worthless. In the Soviet Union, Alexander Solzhenitsyn once wrote, 'the lie has become not just a moral category but a pillar of the state'. When the lies were exposed, the communist state crumbled.

Indeed, it was precisely because Gorbachev's reforms had gone so far that the Old Guard mounted its counter-revolution in August 1991; and precisely because the reforms were already so deep that the coup was defeated.

The makers of the television series which this book accompanies also worried about the words 'second' and 'Russian' in the title. Russians pointed out to us that there had been at least three revolutions in Russian history, in 1905 and in February and October 1917, and that the 'Gorbachev revolution' was really number four. Calling this the 'second' was, we felt, justified because the only revolution which crucially changed both Russia and the world was the Bolshevik one in October 1917. Moreover, it is the results of *that* revolution which have been overturned by the events of the Gorbachev period.

Non-Russians rightly objected to our use of the word 'Russian' to describe events in which some of the other Soviet nations – Lithuanians, Georgians, Armenians and many others – played at least as large a part as the Russians. The fact remains that for most Westerners, 'Russian' is useful shorthand for 'Soviet' – though given the current disintegration of the USSR, that usage will have to change.

THIS book tells the story of the political struggles behind these six years of revolution. My account has benefited from one of the side-effects of *perestroika* – the unprecedented willingness of present and former members of the top leadership to spill the beans, or at least some of them. In exclusive interviews for the television series, twelve Politburo members and many of their closest advisers spoke for the first time about arguments and struggles that have never before been reported in the Soviet or Western press.

In all, about one hundred of the most senior decision-makers in the USSR were willing to spend time with us, sharing their personal memories of the past six years. Among those who spoke to the *Second Russian Revolution* team – many of them at great length – were Nikolai Ryzhkov (prime minister throughout most of this period), Alexander Yakovlev (Gorbachev's closest liberal ally), Yegor Ligachev (the leader of the Politburo conservatives until 1990), Boris Yeltsin (the most radical thorn in Gorbachev's flesh), Viktor Grishin (the former Moscow Party boss and Gorbachev's one-time rival for power), Vitaly Vorotnikov (the former Russian prime minister) and six other former Politburo members: Geidar Aliyev, Vladimir Dolgikh, Anatoly Lukyanov, Viktor Nikonov, Yuri Solovyov, and Mikhail Zimyanin. We also interviewed Gorbachev's personal aides Anatoly Chernyayev, Ivan Frolov, Nikolai Petrakov and Georgy Shakhnazarov; his economic advisers Leonid Abalkin, Abel Aganbegyan, Oleg Bogomolov and Stanislav Shatalin; the influential sociologist Tatyana Zaslavskaya; senior politicians such as Ivan Laptev, Anatoly Sobchak, Mikhail Nenashev, Yuri Prokofyev, Arkady Volsky, Vadim Pechenev, Vytautas Landsbergis, Vadim Bakatin, Ivan Polozkov; and dozens of other politicians, military men, economists, senior *apparatchiki*, journalists and writers who have played important parts in the history of *perestroika*.

Traditionally, writing about Soviet politics has been based on two sources, both unreliable. The first was the official press, whose aim was as much to deceive as to inform, and which deliberately tried to conceal the cut and thrust of decision-making inside the Kremlin. The second source was the gossip, informed speculation and leaks gleaned by Western journalists and diplomats, which were often wildly inaccurate.

In this book I have relied wherever possible on 'insider' accounts, rather than on the traditional skills of Kremlinology. Gossip and second-hand accounts which could not be substantiated have been ignored or – where no better version was available – clearly indicated by the use of turns of phrase such as 'probably' or 'it is thought'. (Direct quotations used in the book, unless attributed in the Notes to published sources, generally come from interviews given to the *Second Russian Revolution* team.) Of course, memories can be faulty, and also affected by political expediency. Different witnesses recalled different aspects of some events, and occasionally their accounts clashed. Sometimes they lied (pointlessly, when so many other witnesses of the same events were also being interviewed). In sifting through the evidence, I have doubtless made some mistakes, though I hope my account is reasonably close to the truth.

It remains, of course, only a part of the story – not least because, even when Politburo members were willing to be interviewed, the truth still had to be prized out of them. A typical answer to the question, 'Tell us about the most furious row you witnessed at the Politburo?' was a chuckle, followed by the words, 'Oh, there were so many of them, so many . . . .' Most Politburo members were willing to part with only one or two of their secrets – though almost all of them jumped at the chance to expose what appears to have been the most divisive issue in the early years of *perestroika*, the ill-fated attempt to stamp out alcoholism. Many other missing parts of the jigsaw have been found. Others will be recovered only when the Kremlin archives are finally opened.

Since this is a political history, it concentrates on what went on in the corridors of power, and I make no apologies – though many Soviet people would disagree – for concentrating on the central role played by Mikhail Gorbachev.

At the same time, the central thesis of this book is that the tumultuous events of the past six years are the product of many influences – other politicians such as Boris Yeltsin, Alexander Yakovlev and Yegor Ligachev, and, above all, the Soviet people, whose flourishing social and political awareness stole the initiative from the men in the Kremlin. Their role, too, is described in these pages.

I WOULD like to thank Brian Lapping and Norma Percy for inviting me to join their television team as series consultant and to write this book.

My thanks also go to the other members of the production team from whose research skills and advice I have benefited: Mark Anderson, David Ash, Kate Clark, Oren Jacoby, Angus Macqueen, Paul Mitchell, Daphne Skillen and Masha Slonim. Jessy Kaner and Vicky Goodden provided much assistance, as did the ever willing staff of CARIS (the Current Affairs Research and Information Section of the BBC World Service): Nancy Reynolds, Susan Eastwood and Jonathan Rowe.

I am indebted to Andrew Neil, editor of *The Sunday Times*, for appointing me as the paper's Moscow correspondent in 1987 – for this book is very much a product of my time working there.

Robin Cameron, Philip Hanson, Alex Pravda and Stephen White kindly read an early draft of the book and helped to steer me clear of some blunders.

Above all, thanks to Neilian, my wife and constant companion in our Russian adventures, for her advice and help during the writing of the book, and to my sons Ewan and Duncan for their constant interruptions, without which my study would have been too lonely a place.

Angus Roxburgh

# CHAPTER ONE

# *'We cannot go on living like this'*

THE Second Russian Revolution began on Sunday 10 March 1985, at 7.20 in the evening. There was no theatrical cannon-shot, like the one fired from the cruiser *Aurora* to signal the start of the Bolshevik Revolution in October 1917; just the wheezing last gasps of an old white-haired man dying in a hospital for Kremlin leaders, hidden from sight in the woods of Kuntsevo, in the western outskirts of Moscow.

Konstantin Chernenko had ruled the Soviet Union for just thirteen months, desperately ill with cirrhosis and emphysema for much of that time. During his illness the Kuntsevo hospital became a second Kremlin. Mikhail Gorbachev, the youngest member of the ruling Politburo and Chernenko's deputy, shuttled between the two – as much to inform the old man of what was going on as to obtain his instructions.

It was Gorbachev who first received the news of Chernenko's death that Sunday evening from Yevgeny Chazov, the Kremlin physician. Gorbachev replaced the receiver and took some of the quickest decisions of his life. The following story of what happened over the next crucial twenty-four hours has been pieced together from eye-witness accounts by members of the Politburo.

Gorbachev immediately instructed the head of the central committee's general department, Klavdii Bogolyubov, to call a meeting of the top leadership (see diagram, on page 211). Speed was of the essence, for Gorbachev had a rival for the Party leadership – Viktor Grishin, the seventy-year-old Moscow Party chief, and one of the Old Guard from the days of Leonid Brezhnev. Support for the two among the ten full Politburo members was evenly divided. But luckily for Gorbachev, two of Grishin's supporters were far from Moscow – Vladimir Shcherbitsky, the Ukrainian Party boss, was in the United States, and Dinmukhamed Kunayev, the Kazakhstan leader, was at home in Alma Ata, five hours' flight from the capital. One of

Gorbachev's supporters, Vitaly Vorotnikov, was also absent, in Yugo-slavia. But by calling the others together immediately, Gorbachev could still ensure a majority – of one – in his favour.

Gorbachev's supporters were Andrei Gromyko (the foreign minis-ter), Geidar Aliyev (deputy prime minister) and Mikhail Solomentsev (head of the Party Control Commission); Grishin's were Nikolai Tikhonov (the prime minister) and Grigory Romanov (a central com-mittee secretary).

Over the next two hours, black Zil limousines ferried the country's rulers to the Kremlin, mostly from their weekend dachas outside Mos-cow. Apart from the seven full Politburo members, the leadership included six candidate members, and five central committee secretaries (ranking just below the Politburo). At first, the 'inner core' of seven full members met separately in the Walnut Room, adjoining the main Politburo meeting room, where the others were waiting.

Officially, the only business that night was to choose a commission to organise Chernenko's funeral, but the question of who was to head the commission was crucial: by tradition that job went to the man who would become the next leader of the Party. Gorbachev immediately put Grishin on the spot by suggesting that he should head the funeral commission. Grishin, realising his main supporters were absent, declined, saying that Gorbachev himself should do it, as he had been Chernenko's deputy.

At 9.30 the seven went through to join their colleagues. Their meet-ing lasted just over an hour and a half. Gorbachev opened it, formally announced Chernenko's death and said they would have to choose a funeral commission. Next to speak was Andrei Gromyko, the foreign minister and one of the most senior members of the Politburo. He immediately proposed that Gorbachev should head the commission. But others demurred. Gorbachev's opponents pointed out that by naming him they would effectively be choosing the next general secre-tary of the Party, and urged that the matter therefore be decided by the full Politburo and central committee. Gorbachev went along with this, and said they should 'think it over' until next day, when both bodies could meet and take a 'conscious decision'. But Gromyko was firm: the question was clear, he said, it had to be Gorbachev. No other name was proposed, and no vote was taken.

They decided to hold a meeting of the funeral commission at 11 a.m. the following day, and to agree on the new Party leader at a Politburo meeting at 3 p.m., before putting their choice to a full session or ple-num of the 300-member central committee. They instructed the gen-eral department and the organisation department, headed by a central committee secretary, Yegor Ligachev, to summon the committee members. They also gave orders for Chernenko's obituary, an address to the nation and the new general secretary's speech to the plenum to be written by morning. Even though no formal decision had been made on who the new general secretary would be, the group of functionaries who went back to the central committee headquarters on Old Square to work through the night on the new leader's speech all understood that it was Gorbachev who would read it.

Word of Chernenko's death was sent to Moscow Radio, which from one o'clock replaced its night-time light music and comedy shows with classical music. Soviet television closed down – ironically, after showing *The Merry Widow* – without its customary preview of the next day's programmes. Those were the only outward signs that the Soviet Union had lost its third leader in two-and-a-half years, after Leonid Brezhnev and Yuri Andropov.

In the next few hours Gorbachev, Ligachev and KGB chief Viktor Chebrikov worked closely together. Ligachev was a junior member of the Secretariat, the body in charge of day-to-day affairs in the Party, and second only to the policy-making Politburo. His job, as head of the organisation department, was to liaise with the scores of provincial Party bosses, most of whom were on the central committee. He had been in touch with many of them and knew they would support Gorbachev at the next day's plenum. Indeed, some let it be known in the next few hours that if any other choice was put to the central committee, they would take the unprecedented step of speaking up and voting against it. There was a strong feeling that the country could not afford another old and infirm leader. Chebrikov arranged tightened security measures, and special transport for central committee members from distant parts of the country.

Gorbachev, Ligachev and Chebrikov left the Kremlin together at 3 a.m., still not entirely sure, according to Ligachev, of what the next day would bring. Grishin could count on Kunayev's vote (he would arrive from Kazakhstan within hours), but not on Shcherbitsky's: as luck would have it (or was it intentional?) news of Chernenko's death reached Texas too late to prevent Shcherbitsky from boarding a plane bound for San Francisco. Vorotnikov's vote for Gorbachev was essential, but he was held up by blizzards at Belgrade airport. If he failed to get back in time, Grishin might still be tempted to put his name forward.

Raisa Gorbachev was waiting up for her husband. Five years later, speaking at a private reunion with his old university classmates, Gorbachev recalled how he and Raisa went outside to discuss things that night – presumably to avoid the microphones in their flat. As they strolled in the dimly lit streets, he told Raisa that it looked as though the Politburo would propose him as Party leader the next day, and he suddenly felt nervous at the thought of taking on such a burden. They discussed how Gorbachev had tried to make things work when he was Party chief in the big agricultural region of Stavropol, in the south of

7

Russia, from 1970 to 1978. It had been hard, though he had achieved a lot. Then he had been promoted to Moscow, and had quickly risen to a commanding position. After a year as central committee secretary in charge of agriculture, he was made a candidate member of the Politburo as well, and in just one more year he became a full member. But even with such power he had found it impossible to do what he wanted.

Gorbachev's version of his conversation with Raisa that night went on: 'That brought me to the thought that if they proposed me [for general secretary], I should take it. After all, our country is huge, and the people were full of hope – so what right did we have to disappoint them? We have to think about the people, when it comes down to it, and about the country, and when the time comes, throw away all our doubts.

'It was then that I said: "We cannot go on living like this, we must change." And in order to change things, it seemed I would have to agree if the other comrades proposed it.'[1]

By next morning, Vorotnikov had reached Moscow, and he spoke to Gorbachev by telephone at 10 a.m. Shcherbitsky was only just learning the news of Chernenko's death from the Soviet consul in San Francisco. Kunayev had left Kazakhstan, but would arrive only in time for the afternoon Politburo and central committee meetings.

The funeral commission met at eleven o'clock in the Secretariat's conference room. It discussed organisational details – the timing of Chernenko's lying-in-state, how long the period of mourning would be, when to hold the funeral, and so on. Since Gorbachev had chaired the funeral commission meeting, there could now scarcely be any doubt about his selection as leader. In the afternoon he went up in the lift to the Politburo room together with Vladimir Dolgikh, a candidate Politburo member. Dolgikh asked him if he had prepared a speech. 'Yes,' replied Gorbachev, tongue in cheek. 'I have given instructions just in case. I don't know what will happen, but a speech is being prepared.'

Gorbachev, who had run the Politburo in Chernenko's periods of illness, again opened the meeting. There was only one point on the agenda, he said: the country could not remain without a leader; the question had to be decided.

Gromyko again forcefully made the case for Gorbachev. There was no dissent. Every person present spoke, and they all supported Gromyko's proposal.[2] A formal vote was taken by a show of hands, and all were in favour.

Then Gorbachev made a short speech of thanks. Nothing of the proceedings at these crucial meetings has ever been published, but what Gorbachev said now was of great importance. Dolgikh wrote down a summary of his remarks: 'Gorbachev thanked the Politburo. Noting that they had been united in their point of view, he thanked them for their trust and said he was very moved by the atmosphere that had been created, and thought highly of collectivism and unity. The Communist Party of the Soviet Union had huge potential, and he saw his task in supporting continuity. Collectivism of leadership was the most important thing. The course had to be maintained, especially since we had no need to change our policy: policy is not worked out every day [anew].'

The stress Gorbachev laid on continuity – implying no change of personnel or of policy – was an olive branch to those who had for years resisted his elevation, including the prime minister, Nikolai Tikhonov. Asked if he had ever imagined at this time that Gorbachev would eventually introduce sweeping reforms to the Soviet system, Dolgikh spread his hands and laughed: 'Of course not. We didn't have a clue.'

That afternoon the central committee was presented with the Politburo's 'recommendation'. Gorbachev opened the meeting, but then allowed Romanov to chair it. Again it was Gromyko who made the nominating speech, which was published eventually, but not in the national press, probably because it included lavish praise of Gorbachev's personal qualities, not at all in the restrained and jargon-filled style of most official speeches of that time. Gromyko said Gorbachev had performed 'brilliantly, without any exaggeration' when running the Secretariat and the Politburo in Chernenko's absence. He had a 'sharp and profound mind', and was a man 'of broad erudition', capable of analytical thinking, of breaking problems down into their parts before coming to conclusions. Gromyko said he had often been struck by Gorbachev's abilities in foreign affairs, and noted – lest any of the military had doubts – that the 'holy of holies' for the new man was 'to fight for peace and maintain our defence at the necessary level'. He pointed out that Gorbachev always expressed his position directly, 'whether or not it is to the liking of his interlocutor', but the published version omitted Gromyko's well-known comment, that Gorbachev had a 'nice smile but iron teeth'.[3]

There was no discussion. Gromyko cleverly included in his remarks a long passage about how the West was always looking for signs of 'cracks in the Soviet leadership', and warned the central committee not to 'give our ideological opponents any satisfaction on that count'. His call for the plenum to support his proposal was greeted with prolonged applause. Gorbachev was elected by a unanimous vote. It was the swiftest transition ever, accomplished within twenty-four hours, compared to the two days needed to elect Andropov after Brezhnev's death, and almost four days to choose Chernenko.

At two o'clock, shortly before the start of the meeting, radio and television had finally told the nation of Chernenko's death. Four hours later they revealed the name of the new leader. The country moved swiftly into a new era, even before the brief period of mourning for Chernenko had ended.

The style of the mourning and funeral seemed calculated to send a message of change to the people. The period of mourning lasted only two full days – half the time decreed for Andropov and Brezhnev. A decision to close schools on the day of the funeral was rescinded just a few hours after being announced. Chernenko's portrait was relegated to page two of Tuesday's newspapers, page one being given over to Gorbachev. Diplomatic business carried on as usual: Gromyko met the French foreign minister on the Monday, in between nominating Gorbachev at the Politburo meeting and the central committee plenum. In Geneva, new arms talks with the Americans started as scheduled. Television coverage of the funeral lasted less than half the time given to Brezhnev's in 1982. The cameras lingered on Chernenko's wife grieving over the coffin, as if to stress that his death was a personal but not a national tragedy. To cap it all, as soon as the coffin was out of sight, the brass band struck up the Soviet national anthem at the brisk tempo normally reserved for sports festivals.

To the outside world, the transition had gone like clockwork. But the Old Guard had struggled against it to the end. The victory of Gorbachev and a new generation was the reward for several years of waiting and frustration.

SINCE the late seventies a succession of elderly, ailing leaders had come to symbolise the Soviet Union, as it too slipped into senility and stagnation.

Leonid Brezhnev had come to power in 1964 as a relatively sprightly fifty-seven-year-old. In 1965 he and his prime minister, Aleksei Kosygin, introduced reforms aimed at decentralising the Soviet economy – not dissimilar to those that Gorbachev would try out twenty years later – but they were soon killed off. The rate at which the economy was growing fell steadily, until it scarcely kept pace with the growth of the population. Ordinary consumers derived little benefit from economic policies overwhelmingly biased towards heavy industry. As real economic achievements dwindled, so propaganda grew in importance, becoming the hallmark of the later Brezhnev period. The principle was simple: if the system was not producing the goods, you just pretended it was. That quintessential Soviet concept – 'ideology' – became more important than economics, and the man in charge of it in the Politburo was regarded as second only to the general secretary.

During the Brezhnev years, Alexander Yakovlev, later to become Gorbachev's closest liberal ally, worked in the propaganda department of the Party's central committee. He was always aware of the dangers of the job: 'When dogmatism prevails,' he later explained, 'it is always the ideologists who get the blame for everything. If our transport system is the worst in the world, it is the ideologists who carry the can, for failing to "explain properly" that it is the best transport system in the world.'

To mask the inadequacies of the lumbering centralised economy, Brezhnev went in for grandiose schemes intended to impress, both at home and abroad. A command economy can do this. It is less tricky than providing consumer goods, which annoyingly keep changing with the fashion. 'BAM', the Baikal–Amur Railway, was dubbed the 'Project of the Century'. Billions of roubles were thrown at this second Trans-Siberian line, and countless hours of propaganda told of the selfless exploits of Soviet youth, 'taming Siberia'. Work began on another multi-billion-rouble project which would reverse north-flowing Siberian rivers to irrigate arid cotton-growing land in Soviet central Asia. Western scientists warned of calamitous consequences for the world's climate. But the planners in Moscow were carried away with their monumental project, and the propagandists were in their element: 'the triumph of man over nature' had long been held up in schoolbooks as the pinnacle of human achievement, especially under socialism. Now they could really prove their point.

Nobody in power seemed to care that most of the population watched only the foreign news on television, ignoring the bombast and boasting in the home news section where what counted as 'news' was reports of work collectives, towns or whole republics 'fulfilling the Five-Year Plan ahead of schedule', or of a milkmaid 'overfulfilling her socialist obligation', of 'further improvement' of this or that, of 'shock-workers' increasing yields and receiving 'challenge red banners'. And, of course, of the latest pronouncements of (or medals received by) the Soviet leader, never referred to by anything less than his full title: 'General-Secretary-of-the-Central-Committee-of-the-Communist-Party-of-the-Soviet-Union, Chairman-of-the-Presidium-of-the-Supreme-Soviet-of-the-USSR, Leonid-Ilyich-Brezhnev'. Mind-numbing and meaningless, all of it. An obsession with secrecy meant that no real facts about the growing crisis – the economic stagnation, the crime and corruption, even straightforward social problems – ever leaked out.

Ideological purity was taken to absurd extremes. In 1980, shortly before the Communist Party's Twenty-sixth Congress, an artist friend of mine in Moscow did a humorous illustration that accompanied an article on genetic engineering in a popular science magazine. It showed a column of lorries loaded with amino-acids, being driven by the animals whose growth they were intended to hasten – pigs, ducks, cows and so on. The drawing appeared under the general heading 'Towards the Twenty-sixth Congress'. The propagandists were outraged at this mild irreverence towards the Party leadership. The Party's chief propagandist and the President of the Academy of Sciences severely reprimanded the editor 'for irresponsibility' and ordered that the offending page be torn out of almost half-a-million printed copies of the magazine.[4]

Direct critics of the regime were punished less subtly: dissident writers, artists and human rights campaigners found themselves in prisons, labour camps, or exiled to Siberia or the West. Senior Party officials who refused to toe the line were also 'exiled', as ambassadors to foreign countries: Yakovlev spent ten years in Canada. His erstwhile boss, Mikhail Suslov, the chief ideologist, ruled supreme, crushing unorthodox thought and earning himself the title of 'Grey Cardinal'. The Soviet military, meanwhile, was given almost unlimited resources to defend this quagmire – one-quarter of the entire budget, Eduard Shevardnadze revealed in a speech in 1990.

It was in this atmosphere that Mikhail Sergeyevich Gorbachev became a politician. In 1966 he became first secretary of the Stavropol city Party committee, and four years later of Stavropol province. During his eight years in this post, he apparently created a good impression among the 2.5 million inhabitants of the province, while diligently following every swing of the Kremlin pendulum.

Gorbachev's speeches in the early seventies show him to have been an enthusiast even then for the kind of incentive schemes which he later implemented when he became Soviet leader, particularly the 'team contract' system, under which small teams, or brigades, of farmers were allotted land, materials and resources, freed to organise their own labour, and were paid by results.

But in 1977 he became associated with a very different kind of farming experiement which, though of dubious value, helped propel him to the highest echelons of power. The experiment was conducted in the district of Ipatovo, in Gorbachev's Stavropol province. It was apparently the brainchild of Fyodor Kulakov, Gorbachev's predecessor as Stavropol Party chief and by then agriculture secretary in Moscow, but it was clearly inspired by Leonid Brezhnev himself, with his love of grand showpieces of communist 'innovation'.

The 'Ipatovo method' of grain-harvesting was classic Brezhnevism. The idea was that great teams of some fifteen combine harvesters, working in perfect harmony and backed up by a support group of mobile canteens, health services and 'ideological workers', would zip round the fields in record time before the grain spoiled, their efforts co-ordinated by walkie-talkies. The result was the kind of pictures that became famous in the late Brezhnev period: armies of machines advancing in step-like formation over great plains of yellow farmland. Most important of all was the date: the scheme was introduced in 1977, so the harvest (which, thanks to the excellent weather, turned out to be a bumper one) could be dedicated to the sixtieth anniversary of the October Revolution.[5]

The Ipatovo method was recommended for widespread application throughout the country, and Gorbachev took all the laurels coming his way. He was interviewed about it in *Pravda*, made speeches about it, and was awarded the Order of the October Revolution.

But it was not long before he began to distance himself from the scheme, which had a nasty smell of *pokazukha* – showiness – and was also inconsistent with his own preference for smaller teams working on a 'contract system'. In May 1978 the young provincial leader took what appears to have been a conscious and risky step to attract attention in Moscow: he sent a long memorandum on farming policy to the central committee. The memo – not published until after he became Soviet leader – only briefly mentioned the Ipatovo method (without suggesting it was any kind of panacea), and included a hard-hitting critique of farming policy under Brezhnev. It proposed raising the prices paid to farms for their produce to a realistic level, increasing investment in the social infrastructure of the villages, and – most importantly – it suggested that 'administrative methods' would never raise food production, only 'material and moral incentives' and 'economic stimuli and levers' would do that. Gorbachev vehemently criticised the central planners for interfering in farmers' work instead of concentrating on long-term problems, and continued: 'enterprises must be given more independence in deciding questions of production and finances'.[6]

Gorbachev also displayed the sycophancy required of an up-and-coming leader. When Brezhnev turned author, and produced several books of inane memoirs, Gorbachev was among the bootlickers. In May 1978 – the same month he wrote his critique of Brezhnev's farming policies – he waxed lyrical about the 'ideological profundity' of Brezhnev's potboilers, insisting that 'the communists and all the workers of Stavropol express limitless gratitude to Leonid Ilyich Brezhnev for this literary work'.

He had the good luck to be Party chief in a region full of health spas visited with increasing regularity by the ageing leadership. In September 1978 Brezhnev stopped there on his way to Azerbaijan. (By coincidence, two other future Party leaders, Yuri Andropov, who was on holiday, and Konstantin Chernenko, who was accompanying Brezhnev, were also there.) The Azerbaijan Party chief, Geidar Aliyev, recalls that Brezhnev was pleased with what he had seen in Stavropol – 'He liked the mood, the atmosphere, there.'

Two months later, apparently on the strength of Brezhnev's impressions and Gorbachev's memo on farming – Gorbachev was appointed to the Party's Secretariat in Moscow, to be in charge of agriculture.

Within a year, Gorbachev added candidate membership of the Politburo to his posts. In October 1980 he was promoted again: at the age of forty-nine he was now both a central committee secretary and a full member of the Politburo. Under his guidance Soviet agriculture went from bad to worse: after a record grain harvest of 240 million tonnes in 1978 – the year Gorbachev took over – it fell to 158 million tonnes in 1981 and recovered only slightly thereafter. Yet this appeared to have no effect on his political progress. He successfully conveyed the impression that he was less the brains behind Soviet farming policy than an administrator of Brezhnev's ideas. He did not even speak during the debate of a major ten-year Food Programme which was adopted by the central committee in May 1982, perhaps because it paid scant attention to the kind of wage incentive schemes he had advocated earlier. His silence may also have indicated disagreement with the Programme's central plank, the creation of so-called 'agro-industrial associations' in all districts and regions. These were intended to improve co-ordination between suppliers, farms, distributors and processors, but turned out to be little more than an extra layer of bureaucracy. Shortly before the Programme was adopted, Gorbachev asked six academics, including a radical sociologist, Tatyana Zaslavskaya, to comment on it. She recalls suggesting that the new co-ordinating bodies were a good thing, but only if they *replaced* the large number of ministries dealing with various aspects of agriculture rather than supervising them. Gorbachev indicated he agreed but could do nothing about it. He turned to an aide and said: 'Do you think if I wrote that into the Programme I would still be sitting in this office?'

In November 1982 Brezhnev died. Russians suddenly found themselves jerked out of the poor-but-comfortable rut into which they had settled during the 'years of stagnation', as the Brezhnev period became known. The new leader was Yuri Andropov, formerly head of the KGB. As leader, he applied policemen's tactics to the economy. Russians who were accustomed to standing in queues for food during working hours suddenly found the shops being raided by police, who demanded their identity papers and threatened to report them for being absent from work. Andropov's campaign for shop-floor discipline was accompanied by a crackdown on corruption at higher levels of the Party and state.

Andropov came to power admitting that he had 'no ready recipes' for improving the economy, but he did introduce some experiments, primarily intended to give enterprises more autonomy from the ministries. And Gorbachev was now able to get his 'collective contract' system in agriculture adopted by the Politburo.[7] This was a revival of the scheme he had favoured in the seventies: it allowed small teams of farmers to sign a contract with their collective farm,

14

under which they undertook to deliver a certain amount of produce for an agreed payment, in exchange for which they were free to decide for themselves how to organise their work, how to distribute the earnings, and what to do with any surplus. Earnings were thus closely linked to results.

Gorbachev was clearly a favourite, and Andropov increased his responsibilities to include the whole economy and also 'cadres', i.e. personnel policy. Together, the two men started replacing corrupt and inefficient officials, eventually firing some 20 per cent of government ministers and regional Party bosses. Andropov also promoted younger, more energetic men to the central leadership. In June 1983 he brought the Leningrad Party chief, Grigory Romanov, to Moscow to join the Secretariat; Romanov thus became one of the small number of 'senior secretaries', like Gorbachev, who combined membership of the Secretariat and the Politburo. This dual qualification was essential for a future Party leader, and Romanov clearly had his eyes on this goal.

In November 1982 Andropov promoted fifty-three-year-old Nikolai Ryzhkov, formerly managing director of the huge Uralmash engineering complex and a typical representative of the new 'technocratic' generation of leaders. In the Secretariat, Ryzhkov was put in charge of economics, directly under Gorbachev. The following spring Andropov brought Yegor Ligachev (then aged sixty-two), a career Party worker from Siberia, to head the Secretariat's organisation department, where he also worked under Gorbachev, vetting all important Party appointments in Moscow and the provinces. After a few months, in December 1983, Ligachev was promoted to the Secretariat itself.

This new group of leaders started, with Andropov's encouragement, to explore ways out of the country's growing crisis, the extent of which was not yet clear even to them. Ryzhkov remembers: 'There were a number of us, secretaries of the central committee, who started a profound analysis of what was going on in the country. No one obliged us to do this – on the contrary! Often, when we began to penetrate some economic or political issue, we were told to go easy. We were saved by the fact that Andropov trusted us. He himself was not a great expert on the economy, but he trusted us.'

Ryzhkov describes his work with Gorbachev in those days as 'not exactly underground work, but it was semi-legal'. Many of the older generation in the leadership were suspicious of them: 'They saw us as reformers, poking our noses in, analysing, when according to them everything was fine.'

The 'Establishment' attitude to reform was demonstrated by an incident at an economics institute in Novosibirsk, run by the radical professor, Abel Aganbegyan. In April 1983, Tatyana Zaslavskaya, the head of the sociology department, presented a paper at a seminar on economic reform for about a hundred invited academics from other institutes. Her basic thesis was that the centralised administrative system in the economy – unchanged since Stalin introduced it in the thirties – alienated workers from the results of their work and encouraged sloth, negligence and wastefulness, instead of efficiency. By analysing the factors that influenced people's behaviour at work – what she termed the 'social mechanism' of the economy – she came to the conclusion that only 'economic methods' of management (i.e. the market) could act as an incentive for better performance.

The ideas were too hot for the censor, who refused to let her even photocopy the paper for the participants at the seminar, even though it contained only arguments, and nothing that could be called a state secret. Aganbegyan used his position as director of the institute to authorise the duplication of a limited number of copies. They were all marked 'For official use only', individually numbered and signed out to the participants. The participants were not allowed to take such classified documents away with them, however. They had to be sent by special mail to the security departments at their places of work. Despite all the precautions, two copies went missing.

When a leaked version of the paper appeared later in the Western press, there was an uproar.[8] Zaslavskaya remembers: 'For months our institute was turned upside-down by a KGB commission. They scoured the country to find those missing documents.'

Aganbegyan and Zaslavskaya were hauled before the Novosibirsk Party committee, which had drafted a severe reprimand for their alleged seditious activity to undermine Soviet power. 'I wasn't too worried,' says Aganbegyan, 'because it was the fourteenth time I had been called in, but Zaslavskaya wasn't experienced in these things. She was terribly upset. She cried, and fell ill. I said to her: "Tanya, this is very good for you. It is only the beginning, you'll have to get used to it."' In the end the charge was lessened to one of 'lax security with regard to official documents'.

The system's inbuilt aversion to change took the upper hand as Andropov's capacity for work dwindled and he slowly succumbed to a fatal kidney disease. He spent more and more time attached to a dialysis machine, while Gorbachev became his political lifeline, conveying messages to and from his hospital bed, much as he was later to do for Chernenko. Andropov wanted Gorbachev to succeed him as leader.

But Andropov's experiments and clear-out of Party personnel had already terrified the Old Guard, and at the end of 1983, with Andropov bed-ridden, they took steps to ensure that Chernenko, not Gorbachev, would succeed him. Chernenko was seventy-two and already a sick man, but as Brezhnev's protégé he would restore 'stability'. He had the support of the prime minister, Nikolai Tikhonov, and the defence minister, Dmitry Ustinov. Arkady Volsky, Andropov's personal aide, describes how they plotted against Gorbachev.

A central committee plenum was scheduled for 26 December 1983. Andropov prepared for it on the assumption that he would be well enough to attend, but in the event he could not leave hospital. It was decided that the text of his speech would be typed up and distributed to those attending the plenum. On 24 December he called Volsky to his bedside and gave him six additional paragraphs, which he wanted appended to the speech. The last one read: 'For reasons which you understand, I will not be able to chair meetings of the Politburo and Secretariat in the near future. I would therefore request members of the central committee to examine the question of entrusting the leadership of the Politburo and Secretariat to Mikhail Sergeyevich Gorbachev.' It was an official request to the central committee to transfer the duties of general secretary to Gorbachev for the duration of Andropov's illness. As Volsky recalls, it was a bombshell. Until then Chernenko had been considered number two in the Party.

Volsky consulted two other aides. All three were stunned by what they read. They took the precaution of photocopying Andropov's handwritten 'testament', then gave the original to Klavdii Bogolyubov, head of the central committee's general department, to be typed and included in the red folder containing the rest of Andropov's speech. When Volsky arrived at the Kremlin for the plenum two days later he leafed through the text, and was horrified to discover that the final passage was missing. He leapt to his feet and dashed off to speak to the three men who were effectively running the country at the time, Chernenko, Tikhonov and Ustinov. Volsky recalls: 'They told me: "Mind your own business. In general you're getting too active. Just hold your tongue." I'll never forgive myself for not phoning Andropov immediately from the Kremlin. He would never have forgiven them for it. That troika had simply removed the paragraph from the speech. As a result it was Chernenko who chaired the Politburo and became *de facto* second man in the country.'

When Volsky got back to his office he received a furious phone-call. 'Yuri Vladimirovich was normally very restrained. I had never heard him speak so sharply. He cursed me for not getting up at the plenum and telling the central committee that his speech had been cut.' Rumours were already out: Ryzhkov soon appeared in Volsky's office and demanded to know what had happened. 'Out of weakness,' Volsky says, 'I said I knew nothing. That was my second mistake.'

Gorbachev then went to the hospital to calm Andropov. 'It was a noble gesture,' says Volsky. 'Andropov could have done something drastic. It took Gorbachev two days to calm him down.' Volsky assumes that Gorbachev reassured Andropov that the time for change would come eventually.

Six weeks later, on 9 February 1984, Andropov died. As the Polit-buro members filed into their meeting-room in the Kremlin to choose his successor, Volsky waited next door in the Walnut Room. He overheard a conversation between Ustinov and Tikhonov: 'The min-ister of defence put his hand on the prime minister's shoulder and said: "Kostya [Chernenko] will be more amenable than Misha [Gorbachev]." That is how the leader of our great country was chosen.'

It was no easy transition, however. It took almost four full days before a central committee plenum was called to approve the Polit-buro's choice. This may have been connected with difficulties in securing unanimous support for Chernenko. For although his election was greeted with some relief by ordinary workers, who realised they would be allowed to shop and drink during working hours again, it caused dismay among progressive Party people. Their numbers in the central committee were small, so they could not have changed the out-come. But the Party liked its votes to be unanimous.

Given Gorbachev's prominent position under Andropov, it was log-ical that, having failed to gain the general secretaryship, he should at least move into the position of 'second secretary', as the Party's dep-uty leader was informally known. The second secretary traditionally chaired the meetings of the Secretariat, and also, in the leader's absence, the Politburo[9]. At the first Politburo meeting after his acces-sion, on 23 February, Chernenko proposed Gorbachev for this post. But some of the Old Guard, notably prime minister Tikhonov, objected even to this. Volsky, who attended the meeting, recalls Tikhonov saying: 'I am absolutely against this, because there will be deviations and disorder in the country.'

There was a long and stormy debate. Grishin and Romanov also opposed Gorbachev's elevation to the deputy leadership. Tikhonov suggested that all the secretaries should take it in turn to chair ses-sions of the Secretariat. But Chernenko, the new Party leader, stood up for Gorbachev, apparently sensing that he had to make a conces-sion to the reform-minded element in the leadership. 'For once,' says Volsky, 'Chernenko showed firmness.' Vadim Pechenev, Chernenko's aide who was also present, says that Ustinov, though he had shown no fondness for Gorbachev, supported Chernenko's proposal. Gromyko finally broke the deadlock and suggested that Gorbachev, who already had experience of chairing the Secretariat under Andropov, be allowed to continue for the time being. This solution soon became per-manent.

But Tikhonov still objected to the proposal that Gorbachev should also run the Politburo in Chernenko's absence. Another Politburo member of the time, Vitaly Vorotnikov, says that Tikhonov argued, 'Why should the agriculture secretary chair Politburo meetings?'

Apparently Tikhonov himself wanted to do this, because he argued that Lenin (who, he pointed out, was – like himself – prime minister but not a secretary of the central committee) used to preside at Politburo sessions. Others also objected: 'Gorbachev is already in charge of the Secretariat. Why should he chair the Politburo as well?' The matter was left unresolved until the first occasion when Chernenko was ill, and the chairmanship of the Politburo fell to Gorbachev by default.

Gorbachev now had enormous power. He was in charge of the economy and cadres, and ran the Secretariat and hence the Party apparatus – all the traditional functions of the Party's deputy leader apart from ideology, which Chernenko clung to.

Gorbachev's reformist colleagues were not so lucky. Nikolai Ryzhkov, who had felt exhilarated under Andropov, says he suddenly felt redundant. 'Andropov had confidence in us and was always asking me what we were up to, but Chernenko wasn't interested in anything.' Ryzhkov complained to Gorbachev: 'There's no point in my working here if things go on like this. I'm not needed. My abilities are just wasted.' Gorbachev told him to be patient: it would all come in useful in the end.

Ligachev, too, saw his pet campaigns – against indiscipline and corruption – grind to a virtual halt, although some of the anti-corruption cases begun under Andropov were carried through. His organisation department was no longer overseeing massive changes in personnel: in Chernenko's thirteen months only seven regional Party leaders were replaced.

Instead of trying to tackle the country's problems, even in Andropov's fainthearted way, the leadership once again tried to ignore them, as Alexander Yakovlev discovered. Gorbachev had made a week-long trip to Canada in May 1983, and soon afterwards brought Yakovlev back from 'exile' to become director of a prestigious think-tank, the Institute for World Economy and International Relations (IMEMO). The two men met 'almost every day' according to Yakovlev, and in 1984 Gorbachev asked him, together with other leading academics, to carry out a feasibility study on joint business ventures with the West. Their report to the central committee came out strongly in favour of such ventures, but, with Chernenko in charge, the idea was instantly buried.

Also in 1984, Yakovlev's institute was asked by Gosplan, the state planning committee, to prepare a scientific projection of where the country would stand economically by the year 2000. They wrote ninety pages, and argued, with detailed figures, that if the system of management, the structure of industry and the economy, investment policy and foreign economic links all remained unchanged, then by the year 2000 the Soviet Union would be an underdeveloped country, somewhere between seventh and twelfth from the bottom of the world league. 'The first deputy chairman of Gosplan was so terrified,' says Yakovlev, 'that he came and told us not to show the report to anyone. He said he himself could have his head chopped off just for asking us to write it.'

Such was the state of Chernenko's Russia as his health began to deteriorate. He disappeared from public view for such long periods that the authorities had to resort to ruses to assure people he was still alive. Statements were issued in his name, and *Pravda* carried ambiguous reports about Politburo meetings which gave the impression, though they did not exactly state, that Chernenko had been present. Many Russians remember a television news item which showed Chernenko, aided by Grishin, fumbling to pin medals to the lapels of a group of authors. What they did not realise was that the writers had received their awards earlier, when Chernenko was too ill to present them. When the old man recovered sufficiently to remember he had this important duty to perform, his aides arranged for the ceremony to be repeated specially for the television.

THE contenders for the succession began jockeying for positions. Grigory Romanov was an outsider, not particularly popular in the central committee offices. He was tainted by rumours (probably untrue) that he had allowed priceless Tsarist crockery to be used and smashed at his daughter's wedding, and by reports (undeniably true) that he had a drink problem. Romanov's best hope was to support the Old Guard's candidate, Viktor Grishin, in order to be better placed to defeat Gorbachev the next time round.

Grishin, the Moscow Party boss and a thoroughbred Brezhnevite, attempted to improve his own chances by presenting himself as Chernenko's chosen successor – though one of the leader's aides says that in fact Chernenko looked on Grishin's supposed closeness with irony: 'Grishin never belonged to the group of close people whom Chernenko trusted to give advice.' In any case, it was scarcely a clever move, as a close association with Chernenko could be more of a liability than an advantage. The country, including large sections of the Communist Party, was growing desperate for change. Most people realised that if Grishin became leader the country could look forward to several more years of bumbling gerontocracy. He was almost certainly supported by his peers – Tikhonov, Shcherbitsky and Kunayev – who evidently regarded Gorbachev as a dangerous upstart. But support for Gorbachev was growing within the middle and upper ranks of Party officials.

Boris Yeltsin, then first secretary in Sverdlovsk region, confirms the role played in the struggle for the leadership by Party leaders of his rank: 'A large group of first secretaries concurred with the view that of all the Politburo members, the man to be promoted to the post of general secretary had to be Gorbachev. He was the most energetic, the best educated and the most suitable from the point of view of age. We conferred with several Politburo members, including Ligachev. Our position coincided with his, because he was as afraid of Grishin as we were. Once it had become clear that this was also the majority view, we decided that if any other candidate were to be put forward – Grishin, Romanov, or anyone else – we would oppose him *en bloc*.'[10]

Gorbachev skilfully built up his own position, and at the same time undermined Grishin's. In August 1984 some journalists on the government paper *Izvestiya* brought their new, liberal-minded editor, Ivan Laptev, an explosive article. It was about corruption in Moscow – Grishin's territory. Andropov's anti-corruption drive had already led to the arrest of Yuri Sokolov, manager of Moscow's best-known foodstore, Yeliseyev's on Gorky Street. Sokolov, who had served as a back-door purveyor of fine foods to Brezhnev's family and the Moscow élite, had been found guilty of embezzlement on a massive scale and sentenced to death. He was executed in the summer of 1984 (while Chernenko was seriously ill in hospital), but Moscow was full of rumours that he had been set free under Chernenko's more tolerant regime. Now Laptev had in his hands an article which confirmed that the sentence had been carried out, and took the story even further, suggesting Sokolov also had patrons at a higher level.[11] When the censors forbade Laptev to print it, he turned to Gorbachev for advice. Gorbachev asked him whether he was sure of the facts in the story. 'Yes,' said Laptev. 'Publish it,' said Gorbachev.

As soon as the story appeared, Laptev was bombarded with furious calls from the central committee. One was from Grishin, who demanded: 'Why are you rubbing Moscow's face in the mud? Who authorised that publication?' Laptev kept his mouth shut.

In December 1984 Gorbachev pushed forward his quiet campaign on two fronts, both at home and abroad. On the 10th he gave a major speech at an ideology conference in which for the first time he sketched out his vision of change, albeit encrypted in the opaque jargon of the time. Interested intellectuals, inside and outside the Party, noticed his unusual emphasis on the social sciences (the kind of thing Zaslavskaya had been reprimanded for), his awareness of market relations (known by the Soviet euphemism 'commodity-money relations'), and his call for 'openness' – *glasnost* – which he described as an 'inalienable part of socialist democracy'. 'Broad, timely and frank information,' he said, 'is evidence of trust in people, of respect for their reason and feelings, and for their ability to understand various events by themselves.' According to Vadim Pechenev, a Chernenko aide, 'it was seen in the Party as a declaration of Gorbachev's programme, not just of his ideology, but of his candidacy for the leadership of the country'. But Gorbachev's opponents in the leadership were shocked by the speech, particularly by one heresy – Gorbachev's criticism of 'dogmatic views', which he said were shackling progress. Volsky says there were heated arguments over this in the Politburo: 'They reproached him with it, and demanded: "What do you consider to be dogmatism? And what's wrong with dogmatism anyway?"' They wrongly saw his use of the word as an attack on Marxist theory. With the help of Richard Kosolapov, then editor of the Party's main theoretical journal, *Kommunist*, the conservatives ensured that Gorbachev's message reached as few people as possible. The speech appeared in full only in book form, while a long theoretical article by Chernenko, which was supposed to be published in the January issue of *Kommunist*, was brought forward to the December issue, and the mass media were instructed to analyse it, thereby sidelining both the conference and Gorbachev's speech.

A week later Gorbachev made a highly successful trip to Britain. For the first time he (and Raisa) received worldwide media exposure – all of it positive, most of it ecstatic. His stature as an international statesman was quickly established, and Mrs Thatcher's now celebrated accolade – 'I like Mr Gorbachev; we can do business together' – enhanced his prestige back home, too. Whatever views there might be inside the Kremlin, the world's media had decided that Russia was soon to have a young, energetic and personable leader, with an elegant First Lady for good measure.

Gorbachev had to cut short his trip. The defence minister, Dmitry Ustinov, had died at the age of seventy-six. According to Arkady Volsky, Ustinov was the strongman in the leadership of the time: 'His word was always decisive. It was enough for him to declare, "The Soviet Army considers that it should be so!" for all other arguments to wither away.' Volsky had witnessed many arguments between Ustinov and Gorbachev over the presence of Soviet troops in Afghanistan, especially when the death toll began to rise. According to Volsky, Andropov had also spoken 'with anguish' about Afghanistan at Politburo meetings, but the hawks, led by Ustinov, had insisted that 'to withdraw would mean a loss of prestige for a great power'.

With Ustinov dead, Gorbachev's chances of succeeding Chernenko improved. The day could not be far off: Chernenko was too ill even to attend his old friend's funeral. Vadim Pechenev says that an 'uneasy equilibrium' then established itself in the Politburo, not always in Gorbachev's favour. 'But Gorbachev struck an alliance with Gromyko and thus broke through the inner circle of elderly rulers.'

The last leg in the leadership race came in January and February 1985, during the 'campaign' for elections to the Supreme Soviet (the rubber-stamp parliament) of the Russian Federation, the country's largest republic. Such elections were always a farce, since there was no choice of candidates, and the result was invariably a 99 per cent vote for the 'indestructible bloc of communists and non-Party candidates'. But this year there was the additional spectacle of Chernenko being paraded, half-dead, before television cameras, accompanied by Viktor Grishin.

On election day, 24 February 1985, Grishin appeared with a frail Chernenko to cast his vote, apparently in a hospital room rigged up to look like a polling station. A few days later Soviet television showed him propping the old man up as he received his credentials as a member of parliament. The public was shocked. Georgy Arbatov, director of the US and Canada Institute, remembers his impressions: 'The two looked awful, the whole country saw a man in agony. I couldn't believe that Grishin could do this. But it was Grishin's initiative; there was no decision in the leadership as a whole to put on such a show.'

Earlier there had been a big meeting of Moscow voters to hear Chernenko's eve-of-poll speech. A cursory reading of *Pravda*'s long report on the event could have given the impression that Chernenko had actually attended it; he was even chosen as head of the gathering's 'honorary presidium'. But a closer reading of *Pravda*'s curious wording revealed that this had been a 'meeting . . . devoted to a meeting' with Chernenko. In fact, the candidate was in hospital. At the end of the report, as a reward for marathon readers, *Pravda* admitted Chernenko's speech had been read out by Grishin.

Gorbachev, by contrast, apeared at his eve-of-poll meeting flanked by Ryzhkov and Ligachev, the core of his future leadership team. No other Politburo member was accompanied when making his election speech. It was an intentional breach of protocol designed to demonstrate that Gorbachev was already effectively leader of the Party and of the country.

So Grishin had all but lost the fight by the time Chernenko died and the Politburo met to choose a successor. With Gromyko firmly on Gorbachev's side, with Ligachev warning of a central committee revolt if Grishin was chosen, and – it is said – Chebrikov and Solomentsev making dark hints about the 'Moscow mafia' which had proliferated with Grishin's connivance, his supporters did not even dare to nominate him.[12] Gorbachev was not lying when he later claimed that talk of a power struggle on the night of 10 March was nonsense, and that it had all passed 'without drama'.[13] There *had* been a power struggle, but by then it was all over.

SOON the Western press was writing excitedly about the 'new broom' in the Kremlin. The catchwords for his policies – *perestroika* ('reconstruction' or 'restructuring') and *glasnost* ('openness') – became known worldwide. Yet Gorbachev's early moves were really only breathtaking in comparison with what went before. In retrospect, the first twenty months of *perestroika* saw only a cautious stirring. Russia was like a bear waking from a long hibernation, beginning to sniff around and explore.

That the West already saw it as something more than this was largely due to Gorbachev's charisma and talent for public relations. He demonstrated these gifts during his first state visit abroad in October – to France – where Raisa's fashions were perceived as no less symbolic of the new Russia than Gorbachev's affability in the streets. In November he attended his first summit with President Reagan in Geneva, where their fireside chats began to break the ice of the Cold War.

At home, however, the image was slower in forming. Gorbachev's first factory visit and walkabout in Moscow was in the Chernenko/Andropov mode. (Both previous leaders had made similar visits a month or so after coming to power.) There was no television coverage, only a TASS report, accompanied by a few photographs. It came just a week after *Pravda* had published an editorial urging Party officials to get closer to the masses.[14] Gorbachev's attempt to do this is said to have failed. When he dropped in at a working family's apartment for a cup of tea he thought he was seeing real life – until he spotted a 'Central Committee' stamp on the teacup! His aides had set up this 'spontaneous' visit in advance. Gorbachev, so the story goes, was furious.

The event that first brought home to Soviet citizens that there was something different about Gorbachev was his visit to Leningrad in May 1985. Television showed him in a crowd on Nevsky Prospekt, talking about his plans, answering their questions, and parrying criticism that he should 'get closer to ordinary people' with a good-humoured retort: 'How can I get any closer than this?' Gorbachev had chosen Leningrad for his first trip outside Moscow because, according to his colleagues, he wanted to visit the 'Cradle of the Revolution'. His first major televised speech – delivered in a Lenin-like pose from the white balustrade of the Smolny Institute, where the Bolsheviks had plotted their coup in 1917 – caused a sensation. Nikolai Ryzhkov recalled: 'A whole generation of people in the Soviet Union had grown used to seeing their leaders reading speeches from a sheaf of papers. For twenty years they had all read like that. At Smolny, Gorbachev got up and spoke just like a human being. It was like a bomb exploding: for the first time we had a leader who could speak without notes!'

The content was equally astonishing. It was a blunt assessment of the mammoth task facing the country, delivered with feeling and humour. He declared that everyone, 'from worker to minister, to secretary of the Party's central committee, to the head of the government', was going to have to 'restructure themselves'. There was no time to relax; a great deal had to be done in a short time. The country was 'swimming in resources', but this had merely corrupted them. No one suffered if a factory worked badly: 'In a family you feel it when something is taken from your pocket, but if it's the state's pocket nobody feels it directly.' This was accessible language of a kind that Russians had not heard from their leaders for a long time. Gorbachev also revealed that he knew the problems of ordinary citizens: 'We have a plan for housing repairs, but just try to repair your flat yourself, and you will certainly have to find a moonlighter. And he will steal the materials from a construction site, so they end up coming out of state funds anyway.' To change things, he said, would require the 'psychological restructuring' of officials. And his message to the Old Guard was blunt: 'Those who don't want to restructure themselves, or try to put a brake on the solution of new tasks, will just have to get out of the road and not be a hindrance.'[15]

This speech had a much greater impact than his earlier address to a central committee plenum in April, though it is the April speech which Soviet commentators regard as the starting-point of *perestroika*. The difference was television. Gorbachev is often seen as a natural performer, but at first he was suspicious of the medium and worked hard to polish his performances – aware, perhaps, of the skills of Ronald Reagan, America's actor president.

Soviet television filmed the Smolny speech without forewarning him. Leonid Kravchenko, a senior official at state television, says he told Gorbachev afterwards that if he would let them screen the speech 'from that evening the whole nation would see that the USSR, a great nation, finally had a great leader'. Gorbachev told Kravchenko not to flatter him but agreed to take a look at the recording. Four days later it was broadcast.

Gorbachev gradually realised that television was an asset, and began to think about how to project himself. Kravchenko says he hated reading from an autocue: it was 'too mechanical'. During rehearsals for a broadcast from his Kremlin office the crew tried putting big cue-cards on the antique chairs, but he did not like that either because his eye movements were too obvious. Eventually, says Kravchenko, 'we gave up and just relied on his phenomenal memory. All he needed was a sheet of notes in front of him. Once he asked someone to stand across from him, next to the camera, so that he could see some sort of human response to what he was saying. He would practise his delivery and intonation, and was happy to retake sections to get them right.' He took particular care over his first New Year's address to the American people. It was recorded on a Saturday, and the recording was sent to his country dacha for approval. At 11.30 that night he called Kravchenko and said he wanted to re-record the entire thing the next morning. Kravchenko explained that they would have to install a lot of equipment, including big studio cameras, in the Kremlin, and it would be difficult in the middle of the night. Gorbachev insisted.

AT THE April 1985 central committee plenum Gorbachev began the long process of putting his own team together. Unlike a new American president, he could not name an entire cabinet of his own, especially not after promising his colleagues that his prime concerns were 'continuity' and 'collectivity of leadership'. There were no sackings at this first Gorbachev-era plenum, but he was able to promote Ligachev and Ryzhkov straight into the Politburo (bypassing the normally obligatory candidate stage) and to elevate Chebrikov from candidate to full membership. These were his principal allies from the Andropov period. Together, they now took charge of the key sectors of Soviet life – ideology (Ligachev), the economy (Ryzhkov), and state security (Chebrikov).

The promotions brought with them a return, after the neo-Brezhnevism of 1984, to Andropov's priorities: rejuvenating the *nomenklatura* (i.e. leading officials in the Party and state apparatus), clamping down on corruption and indiscipline, and introducing experiments in the economy. Within a year Gorbachev would have replaced forty-seven regional Party bosses and thirty-nine ministers.[16]

The first provincial appointment came just eleven days after Gorbachev came to power. Vadim Bakatin, a vigorous and radically-minded man (later to become interior minister), was made party chief in Kirov region, where, he says, 'the old first secretary had been in place for twenty years: the whole region was in a state of stagnation'. Like many of the appointments of this period he had worked in Siberia, Ligachev's home territory. Ligachev had brought him into the central committee bureaucracy – the *apparat* – in 1984, to work as an 'inspector'. This is a curious title given to Party functionaries who are in effect themselves being 'inspected' during a short tour of duty in the central offices on Moscow's Old Square, prior to being sent out to work in the provinces. Many of the new regional appointees went through this process.

In some areas the replacement of officials was closely bound up with the fight against corruption, no more so than in the central Asian republic of Uzbekistan. In March 1985 some 9000 extra police were drafted in, and a huge number of officials were sacked as investigators closed in on what would come to be known as the 'Uzbek mafia', which had exaggerated cotton production figures and pocketed payments for imaginary deliveries on a colossal scale.[17]

The campaign brought a new departure in the way dismissals were announced. Usually, no reason was given. But when a deputy prime minister of the republic of Moldavia was sacked in April he was accused of 'abusing power for his own interests'.[18] This announcement was a warning of a big clean-up.

The campaign for shop-floor discipline, started under Andropov but relaxed under Chernenko, now took a radical turn which did not endear Gorbachev to the public. A massive assault on drunkenness and alcoholism was mounted – the very first new policy announced under Gorbachev – and earned him his first nicknames: 'Lemonade Joe' and 'Mineral Secretary'. Gorbachev was certainly an active supporter of the policy, but the driving forces behind it were the puritanical Ligachev and Solomentsev. Ligachev had previously tried to ban alcohol in the Siberian city of Tomsk, when he was Party leader there. Solomentsev, by contrast, pursued the cause with the radicalism of a reformed drinker. The policy soon caused some of the most serious rifts in the Politburo.

It was at their meeting on 4 April that the Politburo decided to take action on alcoholism. Gorbachev told a gathering of writers later that his mission was to 'save the people, especially the Slavic people', from drink. A campaign was started in the media, under the title: 'Sobriety – the norm of life'. Newspapers began publishing statistics about drinking and its harmful consequences; they reported the setting-up of sobriety clubs, and weddings where the guests drank toasts in lemonade or mare's milk; television ran public service announcements with harrowing scenes of domestic brutality caused by drink. The details of the campaign were finally published in a central committee decree on 7 May. It denounced films and books which depicted 'cultured', moderate drinking as attractive, and banned the consumption of alcohol at all places of work, at holiday resorts and at official banquets and receptions. The decree raised the legal age for drinking to twenty-one, and demanded the 'total elimination of alcohol consumption among students and in young people's hostels'. Alcohol production was to be reduced every year starting from 1986, and an 'All-Union Voluntary Society for Sobriety' was to be set up with its own periodical. More clubs, libraries and sports facilities were to be built. Liquor stores were forbidden to trade before 2 p.m., and *carte blanche* was given to the prohibitionists by a clause which banned sales *near* any of the following places: industrial enterprises, building sites, educational establishments, hostels, children's institutions, hospitals, sanatoria, rest homes, railway stations, ports, airports, cultural and sports arenas, and 'places of mass recreation'. A further decree, a week later, stipulated stiff fines for anyone caught drunk in the streets, and corrective labour or prison sentences of up to fifteen days for second-time offenders.[19] Not even Andropov had gone so far – indeed, under his rule a new, cheaper brand of vodka had appeared, which a grateful public soon dubbed 'Andropovka'.

Nikolai Ryzhkov was one of the fiercest opponents of the campaign: 'I was in favour of taking measures against alcoholism, and agreed that the nation was going to ruin, but I was categorically against the methods being proposed. At first I thought they were joking when they said that "drunkenness would continue so long as there was vodka on the shelves". Then I realised they were dead serious.' Ryzhkov argued it would end in tears, as had attempts to introduce dry laws in other countries. He proposed only prohibiting drinking in public places and at work, and using 'economic methods' (i.e. higher prices) and education to combat the evil. He warned that if they were going the way of prohibition they had better introduce sugar rationing, because there would be an upsurge of moonshining. His advice was ignored. They started closing down shops, punishing people, sacking officials if sales of cognac or of wine and beer went up somewhere.

Ryzhkov was supported by Vitaly Vorotnikov, prime minister of the Russian Federation, who pointed out to his colleagues the unpopularity of the campaign: 'The people were outraged. You couldn't visit a factory without being shoved into a corner and shouted at, "What are you doing? You can't do this to us!"' Vladimir Dolgikh, a candidate member of the Politburo, recalled driving through a village in his Zil limousine, past a long queue waiting for a liquor store to open. The crowd shook their fists and whistled as he sped past.

But in the Politburo, where it mattered, the opponents of the campaign were in a minority. Solomentsev would come to meetings armed with thick files of information on how alcoholism had been combated through the ages – from Peter the Great onwards – and delivered lengthy lectures on the subject. Ligachev used his good contacts with the provinces to whip regional leaders into action, telephoning them to check progress and order more cuts in sales. In his native Tomsk only two out of forty-seven liquor stores remained open. Geidar Aliyev, a Politburo member and deputy prime minister, protested in vain when a champagne factory, which he had set up in his native Azerbaijan with West German equipment, was closed down. He claimed that there was no great problem in Azerbaijan because wine-drinking was different from vodka-drinking, and that in any case 95 per cent of Azerbaijan's wine was exported to other republics. As a result, says Aliyev, 'Ligachev went to Azerbaijan and carpeted the republic's leaders, accusing them of poisoning the rest of Russia with their drink'. The 'prohibitionists' did not distinguish between types of alcohol. Whole vineyards in the Caucasus were ripped up, and wineries turned over to producing fruit juice. When Aliyev, as deputy prime minister, was ordered by the central committee to close down breweries he protested that beer was 'not really alcohol'. Solomentsev replied by saying that he would send Aliyev a report proving that people got more drunk from beer than from vodka. Vorotnikov had just bought equipment from Czechoslovakia for several dozen breweries to be installed in the Russian Federation – he went behind his colleagues' backs and got them built anyway.

Reviewing progress in September 1985, a central committee decree declared that the campaign had met with 'the full approval and support of the Soviet people', and responded to their 'hopes that the struggle . . . should take on an even greater scale and concreteness' by intensifying the campaign. There were further price rises that autumn, and even more a year later. 'It was a reign of terror,' remembers Vorotnikov.

THE original anti-alcohol decree stipulated that Party leaders 'with a weakness for spirits' should be dismissed and even expelled from the Party. The highest-level drunkard to go was Gorbachev's erstwhile rival, Grigory Romanov. In Finland the previous winter the Soviet embassy doctor had been required to restore him to a condition suitable for making a speech,[20] and he is said to have disgraced himself with drink at the Hungarian Party Congress in March 1985. He was dismissed in mid-May.[21] His was the first Politburo sacking since Gorbachev came to power and was achieved while Romanov was on holiday. He 'did not accept at once the need for his retirement,' a colleague said. Romanov had been in charge of the defence industries, but 'he proved to be incompetent, his prestige was not high among the military intelligentsia, and his style showed traces of *vozhdizm* [authoritarianism]'.

Other top personnel changes followed throughout 1985. Ligachev's position as 'second secretary' – and Gorbachev's right-hand man – was soon established.[22] This put him in overall charge of ideology and personnel, and meant that he ran the Secretariat, the Party's 'civil service' which prepared policy options for the Politburo and ensured that decisions were carried out. The Secretariat was served by twenty departments, covering all the main areas of economic and political life. These departments both duplicated and supervised the work of government ministries (no government minister would take a crucial decision without referring to his 'minder' in the central committee). It followed that the departments were crucial instruments for the implementation of Party policy, and any new leader chose his department heads with care. Andropov had already replaced nine of these important functionaries, and Gorbachev continued the process, quickly bringing in four men who would eventually play key roles in the history of *perestroika*.

On a trip to Sverdlovsk in September 1984, Ligachev had met the local Party boss, Boris Yeltsin, and came back – in the words of an aide – 'ecstatic' about him. 'Ligachev is the kind of person who gets enthusiasms for people. He called the department together and told us about this great person he'd found, the first secretary in Sverdlovsk.' Soon after Gorbachev came to power Ligachev rang Yeltsin and offered him a job in Moscow, as head of the central committee's construction department. Yeltsin hesitated – he felt the job was a step down for a Party chief in a region of almost five million people. But Ligachev reminded him of Party discipline and Yeltsin accepted his orders. He was fifty-four, just one month older than Gorbachev. He came to Moscow on 12 April – just a month after Gorbachev became general secretary – and within two-and-a-half months was promoted to the Secretariat itself.

Next to move to Moscow was Georgy Razumovsky, who was forty-nine. He took over the organisation department which Ligachev had just vacated. It was a key job, overseeing personnel appointments, and also the selection of delegates to a Party Congress, due within the year. Razumovsky was known to Gorbachev both as an agriculture specialist and through having worked in leading positions in Krasnodar province, near Stavropol.

In July, Alexander Yakovlev, whom Gorbachev had 'rescued' from exile in the Soviet embassy in Ottawa, was made head of the propaganda department, working under Ligachev, though the two were destined rarely to see eye to eye.

Anatoly Lukyanov became head of the general department, the central committee's 'chief of staff'. He was a character from Gorbachev's more distant past. They had been at university together, and had both been office-bearers in the Komsomol, the young communist league. Indeed, Gorbachev, who was one year Lukyanov's junior, had been his deputy at one point.[23]

So by midsummer Gorbachev had considerably rejuvenated his central committee apparatus. Changes in the Politburo itself, however, were rather more troublesome.

One of Gorbachev's priorities was to improve relations with the West, and one of the obstacles to that was the Cold War image of the seventy-six-year-old Soviet foreign minister, Andrei Gromyko, 'Mr Nyet', as the West had dubbed him, because of his constant use of the Soviet veto in the United Nations Security Council. But Gromyko was the man who had ensured Gorbachev's election as general secretary. It would be tactless to sack him, although, according to his son, Gromyko understood that the change of leadership meant that older men would have to step aside. Gorbachev found a brilliant way out. Gromyko moved into the honorary position of head of state, while still remaining in the Politburo.

Gorbachev's choice as his new foreign minister was so unconventional that even Eduard Shevardnadze himself did not know the reason he was being summoned to Moscow that June. He had been

Party chief in the republic of Georgia for thirteen years and had no foreign affairs experience. But the two men were well acquainted. They had joined the top leadership together in 1978, and met not only at Politburo meetings but also during Gorbachev's frequent holidays in Pitsunda, a resort on the Black Sea coast of Georgia. Gorbachev recalls a conversation they had while strolling there in the last winter of Chernenko's rule, which showed they were on the same wavelength: 'Everything,' said Shevardnadze succinctly, 'has turned rotten.'

Gorbachev's next task was to move Nikolai Ryzhkov into the prime minister's office, which had been occupied by Nikolai Tikhonov since 1980. Tikhonov was eighty, a former crony of Brezhnev's, and in love with uneconomic 'stagnation period' projects such as the diversion of Siberian rivers.[24] He had also opposed Gorbachev's elevation at every step. A colleague says that Tikhonov could not come to terms with Gorbachev's innovations: 'They cut right across his position.' His manner of departure was odd. In September 1985 he sent a letter of resignation to Gorbachev, which the general secretary read out at a meeting of the Presidium of the Supreme Soviet. In it he praised the new 'warm and comradely' atmosphere which Gorbachev had created in the Politburo, and lamented: 'At a time like this one would like just to go on and on working', if only his health would allow it. This could be taken as a subtle hint that his departure was not entirely voluntary. But Gorbachev's decision to read out the letter was also a sign that he wanted to break the custom whereby retiring leaders always appeared to be in disgrace; Tikhonov was allowed to retire with honour.[25]

Viktor Grishin was not. The seventy-year-old Moscow Party chief's removal was, according to a fellow Politburo member, 'a very painful process'. Grishin found Gorbachev and his new team hard to stomach. His aide says that he 'clashed' with Ligachev by temperament', considering him an upstart. Grishin himself says: 'We immediately felt Ligachev's negative attitude towards the Moscow Party organisation. He started finding fault with us, criticising us for no good reason.' But Moscow, which Grishin for years had advertised on red billboards as 'the model socialist city', was in a mess. Its trade network was riddled with corruption, and the administration, headed for twenty-two years by mayor Vladimir Promyslov, was the epitome of stagnation. During the summer the newspaper *Sovetskaya Rossiya* ran a series of articles about Moscow's housing situation, which Grishin says were part of a campaign to discredit him, inspired by Ligachev. The paper wrote that the authorities were registering new housing estates a whole year before they were ready so that the city government could claim it was fulfilling its housing target. Promyslov wrote a reply insisting that all was well, but the paper responded with an article by a state prosecutor, warning that the affair was now a criminal matter.[26] Ironically, all the incriminating information had been given freely to *Sovetskaya Rossiya*'s reporters by officials in the Moscow construction department, in the belief that the editor, Mikhail Nenashev, would refuse to publish it. Gorbachev rewarded him for his daring by promoting him to head the Soviet publishing committee.

Even on a personal level, Grishin was not popular in the Politburo, and lower levels of the Moscow Party organisation were also indicating that they wanted him replaced. Gorbachev and Ligachev chose Boris Yeltsin – who just eight months earlier had been insulted at the level of the post being offered him in the Party apparatus – to take charge of the capital city, with its nine million people. This time, Yeltsin writes in his memoirs, he felt the job was too great for him. But the Politburo produced weighty arguments: 'Grishin had to be replaced; the Moscow Party organisation was in a state of decrepitude; its working style and methods were such that not only did it not set an example but it was also trailing behind the other Party organisations in the country. Grishin, they declared, gave no thought to people and their pressing needs; he had let the work slide, being only concerned with outward show and putting on spectacular events – noisy, carefully rehearsed and organised. All in all, a rescue operation on the Moscow Party organisation had to be mounted.'[27]

In December Gorbachev called Grishin to his office: 'He told me there was a lot of criticism and discontent among the people,' recalls Grishin, 'and said maybe I should think about giving someone else a chance to try working in Moscow.' Grishin reluctantly agreed, but asked to be allowed to stay on until the city Party conference which was four or five weeks away. He wanted a last chance to clear his name. 'I was not allowed to do that, however,' he says. That very day Gorbachev announced to the Politburo that Grishin had asked to be relieved of his post.

The transfer was then swiftly effected at a meeting of the Moscow Party committee, at which Gorbachev said a few pleasant words about Grishin's work, and introduced Yeltsin as the new leader. At the next central committee plenum, in February, Grishin was formally removed from the Politburo too, and Yeltsin moved in as a candidate member. Looking back at Yeltsin's earlier appointment as a department head and quick promotion to the Secretariat, Grishin admits: 'I did not realise that he was being groomed for my job.'

A GORBACHEV 'cabinet' of sorts was now in place. Its members were younger, but necessarily co-opted from the existing pool of Party functionaries. In choosing a team of personal advisers, by contrast, Gorbachev cast his net in fresher waters.

During the sixties and seventies two highly unusual centres of progressive Soviet thinking developed, both of them far from Moscow.

Many leading intellectuals, mainly offspring of the Khrushchev period, gravitated to Prague or to Novosibirsk. In Prague they worked on an international communist periodical, *Problems of Peace and Socialism*, and discussed their vision of an undogmatic, humane social-ism, a vision they saw flowering and being crushed before their eyes in Czechoslovakia in 1968. In Novosibirsk they worked in the Siberian Division of the Academy of Sciences, including Akademgorodok, a purpose-built 'intellectuals' city' created by Khrushchev, where aca-demics found they could do research in conditions of freedom unavailable elsewhere in the Soviet Union. Whether consciously or not, Gorbachev plundered these two powerhouses of relatively untrammelled thought, for advice and guidance.

From Prague came Gorbachev's close political aides: Georgy Shakhnazarov, Anatoly Chernyayev and Ivan Frolov. All three used to work on *Problems of Peace and Socialism*. So did Georgy Arbatov, the well-known head of the US and Canada Institute (who is often unfairly laballed a conservative). So too did economist Yevgeny Ambartsumov, who, under Chernenko, published a daring article advocating a market economy and private enterprise as the only way to avoid the kind of crisis that occurred in Hungary in 1956, Czecho-slovakia in 1968 and Poland in 1970 and 1980.

Gorbachev turned to Akademgorodok principally for economic advice. When working on the new Food Programme of 1982 he had consulted Tatyana Zaslavskaya on the immense social problems of Soviet village-life. Then in November 1983 – just months after she and the director of her institute, Abel Aganbegyan, were accused of being 'anti-Soviet' because of the leaked 'Novosibirsk report' – Gorbachev invited both of them to a seminar of academic economists in Moscow. Aganbegyan recalls the contrast with the unproductive meetings held by previous political leaders. 'People would come in, read their paper, nobody was interested. But this [with Gorbachev] was a normal meeting. He didn't make you feel he was a big leader and you were small. We all sat around the big table in his office. He was interested in what I had to say. Zaslavskaya had obviously told him about me and he seated me next to him and asked me to speak first.'

Later, Gorbachev effectively made Aganbegyan his economics adviser. Under Chernenko, Gorbachev had proposed holding a cen-tral committee plenum on scientific and technical progress – he was acutely aware of the Soviet Union's backwardness in computers and automation, and saw them as the key to reviving the economy. Aganbegyan had spent the summer of 1984 working on Gorbachev's major speech for the proposed plenum. The two men met regularly for detailed discussions. Aganbegyan says the draft 'was full of ideas about how we had to change our strategy, pay attention to the individ-ual, change our methods of accounting, about the need for technical reconstruction, machine-building, education reform, and so on'. The ideas, in other words, went far beyond the remit of normal economic debate within the Party at the time. The stress on the individual was revolutionary, and was clearly influenced by Zaslavskaya, whose constant refrain – 'the human factor' – was to enter into the early vocabulary of *perestroika*. It implied that the whole emphasis of the Soviet economy was wrong: that overcentralisation had alienated the workforce, both in factories and on the land, and that the key to change lay in giving people incentives and material interest in their work. 'People must feel themselves to be their own masters' was to become one of Gorbachev's key phrases.

It was all too revolutionary for Chernenko, though. In January 1985 he called off the plenum on science and technology. Aganbegyan felt all his work had gone to waste.

Two months later, Chernenko was dead, and Gorbachev called in the same group of speech-writers, including Aganbegyan, to work on his famous April address. In June, all the work that had gone into preparing for the non-plenum under Chernenko came into good use at a special Kremlin conference on 'intensifying scientific and technological progress'.

It was Gorbachev's first major meeting about the economy as general secretary, and it was indicative of his style that he widened it from a plenum (of communist officials) into a conference at which specialists could put forward their views. He and Ryzhkov prepared for it in their shirt-sleeves. They had received over a hundred different documents from various institutes, academics and ministries. Ryzhkov remembers: 'We worked on them for about ten days, in his office. There were so many papers we had to spread them all over the floor, and walked about on them trying to pick out ideas and thoughts. I remember it well. We took off our jackets and literally crept about over the papers. We had a secretary sitting there, we dictated things to her, argued about things, worked things through, trying to convince each other.'

Meanwhile Aganbegyan's team was working at a central committee dacha in the woods to the west of Moscow. Gorbachev would visit to check progress. Aganbegyan recalls one weekend when Gorbachev arrived in a good mood, and armed with a lot of new ideas. 'He took out his notes and said: "Yesterday I was walking in the woods, thinking all the time, and I wrote it all down when I got home. And last night I kept waking up, worrying about how best to approach this economic problem." Then he opened his notebook, and we went to work.'

It was the perfect place for productive work, but there was one drawback: since the anti-alcohol campaign started there was nothing to drink at official dachas. Aganbegyan complained: 'Mikhail Sergeyevich, good documents aren't written on water alone. Couldn't we at least have some beer?' The next day they got a delivery of *kumiss* – faintly alcoholic fermented mare's milk.

During the coming months Aganbegyan pushed for radical change. He tried to convince Gorbachev of the need for price reform, to reduce the burden on the exchequer of enormous food subsidies. But he got no support at that time (although Gorbachev seemed to be testing public opinion with a hint in a speech in September that price rises were necessary). The country was due to start a new five-year plan from 1986, but the plan had been prepared by Tikhonov and his ancient Gosplan chief, Nikolai Baibakov. Aganbegyan wrote a note to Gorbachev criticising the plan for its low growth targets, especially in high-technology development. The Politburo rejected the first draft of the plan, and in November 1985, shortly after Tikhonov and Baibakov had retired, the Politburo met to discuss a new version. Gorbachev asked Aganbegyan for his opinion of it. Aganbegyan replied that as it was it would never work – the figures were wrong. It would need to be radically revised. He heard later that the Politburo had gone ahead and adopted the plan. When Gorbachev came to the dacha the next day, Aganbegyan demanded an explanation. Gorbachev said: 'What can you do? They've got me surrounded.'

Gorbachev was surrounded not only by Brezhnevites on the Politburo, but by an intensely conservative Party and state apparatus. Much of the history of *perestroika* was to be a struggle between the reformists and the *apparat*.

At this stage, though, Gorbachev himself did not talk of 'reform', but of *uskorenie* (acceleration), which meant making the old command economy work better. There was no indication that he saw anything worth emulating in the Western system. In Kiev in June 1985, Gorbachev said: 'Not the market, not the anarchic forces of competition, but above all the plan must determine the basic features of development of the economy . . . We have to determine precisely what is to be planned at union level, and what at the level of the republic, region, ministry and enterprise.'[28]

The economic policies of the first year or so were fairly modest and simple. First was the emphasis on new technology, described earlier. One of Gorbachev's notable early moves was to appoint a new head of the central committee's department for machine-building (or engineering). He chose a bright middle-aged man, Arkady Volsky, who had worked as an aide to Andropov and Chernenko ('not that Chernenko noticed', says Volsky). But there was little point in diverting resources to high-tech engineering, computers and automation if they were going to be wasted by a hopelessly inefficient system of economic management. At his science and technology conference Gorbachev argued that the 'ground must be prepared' first, through both tighter discipline and 'restructuring' (*perestroika*). (The word 'reform' was, as yet, out of bounds.) The changes he proposed here and in the coming months would 'tighten up' central planning but increase the rights of enterprises, while cutting out some of the middle levels. 'Super-ministries' would be created to co-ordinate administration better. Thus, a new 'bureau', or super-ministry, for machine-building was set up in October 1985, and Gosagroprom, amalgamating several agricultural ministries, a month later. 'Economic methods of management' meant principally *khozraschot*, or self-financing. Under this scheme, introduced without much success under Brezhnev, enterprises were meant to be responsible for their own costs, revenues and outgoings. Previously they had been totally ruled by their parent ministries, which simply appropriated all revenue earned by an enterprise, while providing it with funds, equipment and money to pay the workforce. Gorbachev regularly referred to experiments in management at the Volga Car Factory, at another factory in Sumy in the Ukraine, in the Belorussian Railways and at the Shchokino chemical plant (an experiment which dated back to 1967). In each case, with minor variations, the management was required to keep a stable wage fund but allowed to dispose of it as it wished, such as by cutting the workforce and paying more to the remaining workers. Some aspects of the more streamlined East German system, with its *Kombinate* – large amalgamations straddling several industrial branches – were also seen as a model. 'Acceleration' – raising growth rates and the speed of technological change – was the priority, though some commentators questioned how output could be raised *at the same time* as factories were restructured and retooled.

All this was a fresh wind, but a far cry from the kind of revolutionary moves that were to come eventually – towards the market economy, democracy and a reduction of the Communist Party's role. On the contrary, the emphasis was on economic planning, and thoughts of diluting the Party's powers, or even of transferring them to the selected soviets or councils, probably never entered Gorbachev's head. This could be seen when he gave the state presidency to Gromyko, rather than taking it himself as previous general secretaries had done, saying he needed to concentrate all his energy on the Party leadership – the job with the real authority and power.

The fact that the first two years of *perestroika* were principally a period of analysis and cautious experimentation cannot all be blamed on the Old Guard in the Politburo. After all, Gorbachev and the 'new men' were products of the same system and determined to make it work.

Even the much-praised policy of *glasnost* did not mean unrestricted freedom of speech. Rather, it meant the right to criticise whatever got in the way of Gorbachev's reforms. However, Gorbachev said he envisaged *glasnost* as a 'wider concept' than freedom of speech. It included, he said, not just the right of a citizen to express his opinions but also the duty of the ruling party and organs of state to be open about their activities.[29]

Ligachev, as guardian of ideology, soon realised that such a policy contained the seeds of destruction. In the first months *glasnost* in the press had been restricted to revelations of mismanagement, false accounting, embezzlement, bribery and nepotism; it had also introduced a broader discussion of economic alternatives. Ligachev found all this perfectly tolerable. But in February 1986, as part of the general discussion leading up to the Twenty-seventh Party Congress, *Pravda* published an article which broke new ground. A review of readers' letters contained outspoken criticism of the privileges enjoyed by the Party élite: 'We must not close our eyes to the fact that Party, government, trade union and even Komsomol leaders sometimes objectively exacerbate social inequality by using all sorts of special canteens, special shops, special hospitals, and so on . . . Let the boss go to an ordinary shop and stand in a queue the same as everyone else. Maybe then the queues, that everyone is so fed up with, would be eliminated more quickly. The trouble is, the beneficiaries themselves are hardly likely to give up their privileges of their own accord. What is needed is the force of law, and a fundamental purge of the [Party] apparatus.'[30] At the Congress Ligachev reprimanded *Pravda* for taking things too far. But in his speech Ligachev's protégé, Boris Yeltsin, took the *Pravda* line. The Congress was not televised, but those who bothered to read the speeches in the Party paper saw the first signs of an acrimonious split in the leadership.

The Congress – a five-yearly gathering of some 5000 Party delegates – was an important event, not least because only a Congress has the right to elect a new central committee, the Party's 300-strong top policy-making body. But the Congress came too early for Gorbachev to be able to ensure the election of a majority of reform-minded delegates. As a result the Congress elected only ninety-four entirely new members to the central committee (30 per cent), and they, of course, had all made their careers under Brezhnev. This was the body Gorbachev would have to work with for the next five years. Persuading it to accept the need for change would clearly not be easy.

In his speech to the Congress Gorbachev signalled that he meant business. For the first time he used the words 'radical reform', and he gave a hint of innovations which at last went beyond Andropov's.

Immediately after the Congress the Politburo took an iconoclastic decision, to legalise small-scale private enterprise for the first time since the twenties. It was such a controversial decision that it took eight months to work out the details of a law governing such 'individual labour activities', as they were termed. The law itself did not come into force until May 1987, and was hedged around with qualifications, lest anyone suspect that this was back-door capitalism. In effect, only pensioners, students, disabled people, housewives and men with a job in the state sector could start up businesses. A working man could not leave his factory and set up a full-time business, though he could pursue one in his spare time. The activities legalised included tutoring, translating, taxi-driving, repair work and small cottage industries. These were precisely the sort of things that went on already in the shadow economy or black market.

But if this was a victory for the reformers, it was gained only in exchange for a simultaneous crackdown, agreed upon at the same Politburo meeting, on those who continued to operate illegally in the shadow economy.[31] This move was typical of the Andropovite element in the leadership, punitive rather than permissive. Unlike the law on individual businesses, no one opposed the ban on illicit earnings and a decree on 'non-labour income' was issued on 15 May 1986. It was aimed against 'income acquired through illegal activities, embezzlement, bribery, speculation, and using state-owned transport without permission for purposes of profit'. But like the anti-alcohol campaign of the previous year it was implemented with an excess of enthusiasm – effectively stamping on private enterprise a whole year before it was legalised.

An article in *Literaturnaya gazeta* described a 'wave of absurdities' that crossed the country that summer as a result of the crackdown, which 'perceptibly worsened our lives for at least a month and a half'. Private car owners stopped giving lifts, truck drivers stopped helping peasants to transport their produce to market, where prices spiralled, typists were afraid to take work home, and moonlighting craftsmen stopped going round blocks of flats offering to build cupboards, hang wallpaper, install TV aerials and fix locks – all things which the state repair service did badly or not at all. In a Caucasian spa-town a famous bazaar suddenly emptied as the police closed off the roads to it in order to put an end to 'profiteering'. A cobbler near Moscow, who manufactured waterproof soles for ladies' shoes, was exposed and 'rooted out'. The policy generated a spate of denunciations, like the exposure of rich peasants under Stalin. A collective farmer who had built a greenhouse beside his house was 'visited' and ordered to demolish it; it was five metres bigger than permitted. A neighbour – whose garden contained nothing but weeds and dandelions – had alerted the authorities . . . 'I honestly fail to understand,' exclaimed the *Literaturnaya gazeta* writer, 'why many cucumbers is worse than few cucumbers.'[32]

Collective farmers with private plots provided over a quarter of the country's food from only 3 per cent of its land. Moscow radio reported in 1986 that the country's 34 million plots produced 'about 30 per cent of our vegetables, milk, meat and eggs, 60 per cent of our honey and almost the same proportion of our potatoes'.[33] Gorbachev encouraged private plot holders. But he was more interested in finding ways to make the collective farms themselves produce more. In March the government adopted a major agricultural reform package which Ligachev announced had been worked out 'on the initiative and with the most direct participation of Comrade Gorbachev'.[34] Gorbachev described the reform's main element as an attempt to apply to modern conditions one of the features of the New Economic Policy (NEP) of the twenties, when Lenin had allowed some capitalism to re-emerge in the young communist state. Under Lenin's 'food tax' (*prodnalog*) peasants had paid a tax in kind (grain, meat or whatever) to the state and been allowed to sell the rest of their produce on the free market. In Gorbachev's curious new corporate version of *prodnalog*, entire collective farms would have the right to sell above-plan produce in the free markets. Within the farms Gorbachev's old idea of collective contracts was to be made universal, and families were to be encouraged to take out such contracts with the farms.

Gorbachev's policy for industry was also based on a desire to make state enterprises respond to consumer needs, rather than on encouragement for any large-scale private enterprise or the free market. At the Party Congress he had insisted that ministries must stop issuing detailed instructions to enterprises; and at a central committee plenum in June 1986 he let fly at 'wretched planners and ministerial officials' whose red tape hampered the initiative of enterprises (which he seemed to assume were just dying to flood the market with fashionable goods if only they were let off the rein a little).[35] In another speech he gave a vivid example of what he meant. In the city of Chelyabinsk, he said, a team of young shoe-manufacturers and shoe-sellers from separate enterprises had got together in an excellent independent venture, cutting out the red tape and producing high-quality, fashionable shoes which were in great demand. 'But the ministry officials saw in this only one thing – that it did not correspond to the instructions of Gosplan, the finance ministry and the state committee for labour affairs.' The bureaucrats soon put a stop to the young people's initiative. 'That happened just recently, comrades,' Gorbachev said. 'It must not happen again.'[36] He went on to say that a proposal was being prepared which would allow enterprises producing consumer goods to draw up their plans purely on the basis of what shops and trading organisations requested. From January 1987 there would be no more central planning in light industry, and prices for fashion goods were to be allowed to fluctuate according to demand. Workers' wages in these industries would depend on how much the factory sold – and therefore on the quality and stylishness of the goods.

The theory sounded all right, but in practice it never worked out, partly because Gorbachev and his colleagues could never totally overcome their inbred antipathy towards the market and their faith in the state's ability to decide things on behalf of the consumer. The most graphic illustration of this was another 'major' innovation, launched with loud fanfares in November 1986: a new 'State Acceptance Service' (*Gospriyomka*), whose officers would monitor the quality of every factory's products, and have the right to impose fines for poor quality. This was the old system re-establishing itself. As before, the state, not the consumer, was to decide whether Soviet factories were producing the right kind of goods. Gorbachev himself admitted that in the few months that the new service had been tried out experimentally it had got bogged down in red tape. The solution, he said, was to take more care in selecting the right personnel for the job. Quality control of the quality controllers, in other words – anything but the market.

IF SOVIET nuclear power planners had read the Bible they would have thought twice about building an atomic power station at a place called Wormwood ('Chernobyl'). The tragedy of April 1986 was predicted in uncanny detail:

> A great star shot from the sky, flaming like a torch; and it fell on a third of the rivers and springs. The name of the star was Wormwood; and a third of the water turned to wormwood, and men in great numbers died of the water because it was poisoned. (*Revelation 8*)

Just as *perestroika* seemed to be getting into its stride, the Apocalypse came to the Ukraine. The accident at Chernobyl cost Gorbachev prestige abroad and trust at home, made a huge hole in the country's already strained budget, and scattered radioactive poisons whose consequences for the land and people of the Ukraine and Belorussia will be felt for decades.

The appalling facts are now well known: the power station's fourth reactor blew up at 1.23 on the morning of Saturday 26 April, when an unauthorised 'experiment' went wrong. A radioactive cloud spread over the Ukraine, Belorussia, part of Russia, and into eastern and western Europe and Scandinavia. Two dozen firemen, soldiers and tunnellers lost their lives sealing off the reactor and preventing a meltdown of its core. Hundreds of thousands of people were evacuated from the power-station town of Pripyat and from a contaminated zone around it. The full effects of the radiation – congenital defects in animals and humans, and permanent damage to the food chain – are only becoming known in the 1990s.

It was the worst nuclear accident in history. Yet the Russians forfeited much of the sympathy they deserved because of their 'stagnation-era' reaction, a knee-jerk relapse into lying, as the result of fear, panic, ignorance and sheer incompetence on the part of the leadership. The prime minister, Ryzhkov, says he was telephoned at six in the morning by the energy minister, got to his office at nine, and at eleven set up a government commission, headed by a deputy premier, Boris Shcherbina, which arrived in Chernobyl that evening. At least there was some urgency in these measures. The authorities in the Ukraine and at the reactor, however, showed little awareness of the damage the accident could cause.

The evacuation of 50 000 people from Pripyat and a 10-kilometre zone around the blazing reactor did not begin until 2 p.m. the next day, a full 36 hours after the explosion. A wider, 30-kilometre area was not evacuated until a week later, when Ryzhkov himself flew out, with Ligachev, to take charge. During that week children continued to play outside in radioactive dust, cattle grazed on contaminated grass, and in the Ukrainian capital, Kiev (100 kilometres to the south), children were paraded through the streets for May Day celebrations in an area many in authority knew was dangerously contaminated. Five days later Kiev radio started warning parents to keep their children indoors, and decontamination measures (washing walls, windows and streets) finally went into operation. Life in most Ukrainian and Belorussian markets went on as normal, long after the authorities in Poland and many other countries had banned sales of leafy vegetables and warned children not to drink milk (indeed, no such instructions were ever issued except in the most heavily contaminated areas of the Soviet Union).

This slowness in reacting properly was due partly to the novelty of the situation and the unpreparedness of the authorities. But mostly, it was deception. The Politburo – which met only on the Monday, two days after the accident – 'discussed the question of how much information to release', according to one of its members, Geidar Aliyev, 'and a majority were against the idea of releasing any. I said we should release some, but Ligachev was totally against it. The decision was taken that only TASS would issue reports.'

Consequently, when Swedish and Finnish diplomats went later that day to the state committee for the use of atomic energy, and asked about the causes of the radiation cloud sweeping over their countries, they were told that the committee had no information. The fact that there had been an accident at all came out only on the Monday evening, and even then it was a bland statement which did not reveal when it had happened. (The time of the accident was first revealed *ten* days after the event; and the fact that the Politburo had set up an emergency commission on 28 April came out only when Gorbachev finally appeared on television to speak about the affair, on 14 May.)

The authorities in Kiev had begun their own cover-up even without instructions from Moscow. On the day of the accident Geiger counters at the Kiev Institute of Botany showed a sharp rise in radioactivity. When scientists there tried to establish the reasons for this, KGB men arrived and *sealed* the Geiger counters 'to avoid panic and the spreading of provocative rumours'.[37] Panic, however, was precisely the reaction to the lack of detailed information – especially as the Western press and radio were speculating about 'thousands of dead'.

Worst of all, it appears that the local authorities were taking care of their own kith and kin while pretending to the population as a whole that there was nothing to worry about. The writer, Yuri Shcherbak, recalls finding a long queue for iodine tablets, on 30 April, at a chemist's in the district of Kiev inhabited by Party and government officials. The 'fourth administration' of the health ministry, which looks after the *nomenklatura*, had warned them – the day before 'ordinary children' were sent out on the May Day demonstration.

Vladimir Gubarev, *Pravda*'s science editor, went to Kiev at the beginning of May, after a meeting with the central committee propaganda secretary, Alexander Yakovlev, who encouraged him to describe everything he saw. Gubarev's article on 6 May was the first publication on the accident other than the bald TASS reports; at first *Pravda* wanted to spike it, and it appeared only after Yakovlev's intervention. Gubarev says he became convinced while working in the area that many of the people in charge of the operation – including Shcherbina and others in the commission Ryzhkov had appointed – 'did not understand where they were or what was happening'. As a result the information being supplied to the Kremlin itself was unreliable. Yakovlev summoned Gubarev back to Moscow on 9 May to give him and Gorbachev a briefing. He then wrote them an eight-page brief which he says dealt bluntly with the behaviour of the Ukrainian leadership, the current situation, the cover-up and the probable long-term consequences, and also criticised Gorbachev's failure to explain the disaster on television. Politburo member Vladimir Dolgikh remembers the 'advice' proffered by octogenarian nuclear experts such as Anatoly Aleksandrov, the president of the Academy of Sciences, and Yefim Slavsky, minister of medium machine-building (the nuclear weapons industry) since 1957: 'What are you panicking for? We have both received 200–300 roentgen in our lives and we're both over eighty and don't feel anything.'

When the Soviet leader did finally address the nation he looked like a man bereaved. His face showed that he knew he had lost credibility. His efforts to regain some were desperate: he extended a unilateral moratorium on nuclear testing and offered to meet President Reagan (in Hiroshima!) to negotiate a complete test ban. But there was no apology to the Soviet people or the West for the attempted cover-up, or for the damage done. As a result there was a hollow ring to his arms initiatives. His call for an international 'procedure' for the swift notification of nuclear accidents was simply laughable, as if it was some other country, not the Soviet Union, which had just been withholding information.

For the first time, Gorbachev bungled a public relations opportunity. It was a sad sight, because he looked genuinely humbled – not by the West's protests, but by a sinister and abstract force, which he called the 'terrible power of the uncontrolled atom'.

The Chernobyl accident exposed many of the evils that Gorbachev had been railing against. Two years later *Pravda* revealed that the reactor managers had employed unqualified staff, that drunkenness was rife at Chernobyl, that lack of discipline and disregard for internal instructions were widespread, and that safety was sacrificed for the sake of higher output. Moreover, the article stated, the management was still continuing to behave as if nothing had happened.[38]

Above all, the accident showed how the policy of secrecy could backfire on the leadership itself. In the West, official information available to governments is supplemented by investigative journalism, and this keeps such matters as the dangers of nuclear power in the public eye. The Soviet press, by contrast, had never been allowed to discuss them, and the official agency set up to take care of nuclear safety was hardly likely to draw attention to shortcomings in its own work. As a result, Soviet leaders presumably seldom thought about the problem, and were balefully uninformed. When disaster struck, they totally failed to understand its implications.

Despite the slight opening up of the press in Gorbachev's first year, the Soviet mania for secrecy remained. Every newspaper had a fat directory of forbidden topics, issued by Glavlit, the state censorship agency. In effect Glavlit had the right to ban publication of anything it considered sensitive, from political observations to 'state secrets', which were broadly enough defined to include details of Party privileges. All published maps and even town plans were intentionally distorted, right up until the autumn of 1988. Libraries had 'special repositories' with restricted access as well as their public collections. Even they were graded according to different levels of 'security': some people could read complete copies of *The Times*, others could see only copies with articles about the Soviet Union cut out of them. The precise functions and responsibilities of members of the Politburo were unknown to the public. Photocopiers – those few that existed – were kept under lock and key. It was officially maintained that things like prostitution, venereal disease and homosexuality 'did not exist' in the Soviet Union. Nor could any statistics about drug abuse, crime or corruption be published, far less any details about real defence spending or military capabilities. American negotiators in Geneva were once ticked off by the Russian generals for revealing statistics about Soviet defence in front of civilian Soviet negotiators.

Mocking the country's 'spy-mania and ultrasecretiveness', the newspaper *Argumenty i fakty* reported that the Moscow telephone directory contained no mention of the Kurchatov Atomic Energy Institute, nor of the Ministry of the Radio Industry, 'even though some newspapers had "blurted out" the appointment of a new minister there'. The paper added wryly that in New York anyone could buy a plan of Moscow for ten dollars which even showed the flower-bed in front of the Kurchatov Institute.[39]

The pitiful coverage of the Chernobyl disaster came just as some newspapers were beginning to suggest it was time to pull back the curtains of secrecy. In February, *Sovetskaya Rossiya* had called for prompt reporting of accidents and disasters so that Russians would hear about them from domestic media rather than from foreign radio stations. At meetings with editors later, Gorbachev more than once raised the question of how the accident had been reported, and 'there were many complaints and regrets' according to one editor. Thereafter, coverage of accidents improved.

Throughout 1986 the press grew stronger. In February the liberal propaganda chief, Alexander Yakovlev, had been promoted to the central committee secretariat, sharing some of Ligachev's responsibilities for ideology. In the following months, the editors of a large number of newspapers and journals were replaced, mainly with Yakovlev's nominees. Some of the transformations were astounding. The weekly magazine *Ogonyok* had been a dreary illustrated propaganda rag for decades; under its new editor, Vitaly Korotich, it became a flagship of *glasnost*, probing the underbelly of Soviet life and history. Its boldness was rivalled only by that of *Moscow News*, a weekly newspaper edited by Yegor Yakovlev (same name, no relation). *Moscow News* started off with the advantage of being printed in several languages and intended chiefly for foreigners. It soon became so popular among Russians that those who could not get hold of the Russian version, *Moskovskie novosti*, would read the English one or get friends to translate it. Newspapers like these became important opinion-formers, and broke more and more taboos.

In the summer of 1986 Glavlit was ordered to give up the role of political censor, which it had never *legally* been given. All printed matter continued to be censored prior to publication – Glavlit's head maintained as late as November 1988 that this was 'the most effective and least "painful" method of protecting state secrets in the press'.[40] But it was now up to editors to exercise their own judgment on political and social matters, to take risks, to 'publish and be damned'.

Officials also caught the *glasnost* bug. Self-criticism became almost a fetish. The playwright Alexander Gelman told of one 'quickly restructuring' manager who before a big meeting assembled the so-called 'triangle' (the heads of his enterprise's Party, trade union and young communist organisations) and instructed them: 'There must be criticism of me in every, I repeat, every speech!' Then he called in each of the proposed speakers and gave them precise instructions as to which of them should criticise him for what.[41]

*Glasnost* also finally came into the cultural sphere. Vasily Shauro, aged seventy-two, had been suffocating Soviet culture ever since he was fifty-two, when Brezhnev had made him head of the central committee's culture department. Finally he was ousted, and replaced by a man who actually wrote poetry. Pyotr Demichev's ten-year reign as culture minister – whose main achievements were the imprisonment, exile or banning of almost every writer and artist of note – came to an end too. His replacement, it is true, was an economist and propaganda expert, not a poet, but he remained a junior figure, never promoted to the Politburo and responsible mainly for arts administration. Policy was in the safe hands of Alexander Yakovlev.

It seems tame now, but at the time it was a newsworthy event when the poet Andrei Voznesensky went into print with a call for the publication of Boris Pasternak's *Doctor Zhivago*. The film-maker Yuli Raizman wrote in *Pravda* that for too long only mediocre works had been supported 'up there' just because they were ideologically sound; it was time to encourage talented artists 'even if they are controversial'. In April it was announced that an 'experiment' in theatre independence would begin from 1987, under which sixty-nine theatres would have the right to set their own repertoires. Not exactly earth-shattering events, but in early 1987 these moves were stretching the limits of *glasnost*.

A congress of the Film-Makers' Union in May was a watershed. Elem Klimov, who was elected the first secretary in a secret ballot (itself an epoch-making event), looks back with relish: 'You could write a whole novel about it. The KGB guys guarding the doors told us they had never seen anything like it in the Kremlin . . . Whistling, shouting, rushing the podium, not letting ministers speak – this sort of thing hadn't happened before.' Although theoretically about the cinema, the speeches in fact touched on the rawest nerves of Soviet society – censorship, control of the media, artistic freedom. The rebellion had started earlier, when the old leadership of the union proposed a list of 130 'candidates' for 130 places as delegates to the congress. Radicals suggested having 200 candidates – a real choice – and managed to get their proposal accepted. The rebels then went on to win a majority among the delegates, and were thus able to control the proceedings, and win a majority on the governing board of the union. Yakovlev attended the congress throughout, quietly watching *glasnost* run riot.

Gorbachev's own attitude to all this was unequivocal. In June he told staff on the central committee apparatus that they had to stop 'ordering the intelligentsia about, since this was harmful and inadmissible'. He told those who disliked the debate at the film-makers' congress, and at later congresses of writers, journalists and others, that 'they should not be surprised or become indignant, that these congresses should be accepted as a normal, albeit new phenomenon'. When someone objected, in true *apparatchik* style, that it would be hard to work in an environment 'where everyone was his own philosopher', Gorbachev retorted that it would be worse dealing with a passive intelligentsia, with indifference and cynicism.[42]

One of the first decisions of the new film-makers' leadership was to set up a 'conflict commission' to examine banned films – some 200 of them – which had lain on the shelves since they were made. One by one, they began to be released. The literary monthlies, known as 'fat journals', started publishing more interesting work, and rehabilitating writers such as the poet Nikolai Gumilyov, who had been shot in 1921 as an alleged counter-revolutionary, and the novelist Vladimir Nabokov, until then unpublished in his native land. By the end of the year the films of Andrei Tarkovsky – considered a traitor because he had decided to live abroad – were being shown again in Moscow, and when he died in January 1987 there were even official wreaths from Soviet organisations on his grave.

A careful balance had to be struck. When Western politicians or journalists were interviewed on television or wrote in the Soviet press (unheard of before Gorbachev) they were accompanied by a comment giving the 'Soviet view'. But the progress went on. The public – especially the intelligentsia – were exhilarated. And Gorbachev was popular, despite the common perception that he talked too much – 'like an old maid' – and despite criticism of his southern accent and (less forgivable) grammatical mistakes.

More important than the visible achievements of *glasnost* was its unseen effect: the unshackling of the Soviet mind. Alexander Gelman summed it up in September 1986, just a year and a half after Gorbachev came to power: 'We already scarcely recognise ourselves sometimes. Are we really the same people? Yes, we are. The same people who yesterday accepted things we won't accept today. The same people who yesterday were silent about things we refuse to keep silent about today. The same people who yesterday quivered before people of whom we have no fear today. The same people who yesterday did not even dare think about things we now write about in the papers. Yes, it's us, the same people.' And he added, in warning: 'So tomorrow we may again put up with things we don't put up with today, and we may again be afraid to write in the papers the kind of thing we write today. That, too, will be us, the same people.' The lesson, he concluded, was the need to work hard to make *perestroika* irreversible.[43] One thing that had changed was that people had stopped having to lead a double life, saying one thing among friends and another at work or in public. That at least was irreversible: the genie could not be put back in the bottle.

For the first time since the twenties, public opinion began to play a role in Soviet life. The first victories were small. A few streets in Moscow were given back their old names: Metrobuilders Street (*Metrostroyevskaya*) reverted to Hay Meadow (*Ostozhenka*). The construction of an ugly and massive war memorial was halted, even though a hillside in Moscow had already been razed for it and half of the complex erected, and a competition was opened to find a better design.

Then in August 1986 public opinion scored its first major victory. The Siberian rivers diversion scheme was suspended 'pending further study of the ecological and economic aspects of this problem'. The Politburo decided 'to concentrate attention on and direct material resources to the more efficient use of existing water resources'.[44]

This reversal of a major policy which had been reconfirmed only a few months earlier (and had already cost millions of roubles) clearly corresponded to Gorbachev's own priorities, but it was achieved only as a result of public pressure, something which had not happened for decades. The pressure came from a broad coalition of forces – scientists, writers, ecologists, doctors, historians, engineers, and ordinary people – all of whom spoke out in the liberalised press. Some warned of the dangers for the climate, others proved that whole villages, including historic Russian cultural sites and churches, would be swamped. Their victory was the more impressive because the ministry in charge of the project was one of the most bloated and powerful in the government. Minvodkhoz, or the ministry for land improvement and water resources, had been able, under Brezhnev, to plan, spend, take on staff, and ruin the environment with impunity. Its most grotesque achievement was the shrivelling of the Aral Sea, once the world's third-largest inland sea. One-third of its water was siphoned off for irrigation projects, leaving fishing ports stranded fifty miles from water, and the desert sand, newly exposed, impregnated with poisonous chemicals used on the ubiquitous cotton crops. The people of these villages lost their livelihoods, and were condemned to breathe the 65 million tonnes of poison dust whipped up into the air each year by the wind, and to drink water contaminated by pesticides and defoliants. Infant mortality, in parts of the area, reached 100 for every 1000 babies born.

Minvodkhoz was a good example of what Gorbachev had in mind when he talked of 'wretched planners'. Public opinion had helped him to clip their wings on one issue. But what about their other projects? And what about the rest of the *18 million* bureaucrats who ran the country, costing the state 40 billion roubles a year, yet impervious to criticism and seemingly oblivious to Gorbachev's reforms? Public opinion would not bring them to heel.

By the time Gorbachev took his first holiday as Soviet leader, in the summer of 1986, he was beginning to realise that his reforms to date were little more than tinkering. Looking back four years later, he explained: 'At first we had the desire to achieve a new level of productivity and growth of national income, and to remove all the accumulated problems, merely by speeding up scientific and technological progress. It did not work. And that was despite the fact that in the twelfth Five-year Plan (1986–90) investment in the machine-building complex was raised by 70 per cent. It did not get going. They started using the old approaches in the projects. To stop pouring money into old ways, we set up independent expert groups, and they gave their assessments of the projects. And still it did not work. Take quality: how could we force [factories] in our monopoly situation to produce better-quality goods? We set up the system of state control, *Gospriyomka*. You see, we were trying things out all the time. And you know, we became convinced nothing would work unless we changed the economic relations themselves.'[45]

But to do that would require a step into the unknown. When Gorbachev reappeared, tanned and refreshed from his holiday, he went to Krasnodar, making speeches and bantering with people in the streets. For the first time a new word entered his vocabulary: 'democratisation'. *Perestroika* was about to move into a new, more radical and unpredictable phase.

# CHAPTER TWO

# *Principles Betrayed*

DAY-TRIPPERS on boat excursions from the Crimean resort of Yalta like to guess which dacha, half-hidden in the fragrant pine woods overlooking the Black Sea, belongs to Mikhail Gorbachev. Tour guides can usually help out: it is a mile or so out of Yalta, near the village of Oreanda, just past the white Livadia palace, where the Tsars had their summer residence, and where Stalin, Churchill and Roosevelt signed the Yalta agreement of 1945.

During his holiday there in the summer of 1986, Gorbachev was concerned by the lack of success of his foreign policies. He had made a series of wide-ranging proposals and unilateral gestures, including a moratorium on Soviet nuclear testing, a detailed timetable for the destruction of all nuclear weapons by the year 2000, and the announcement that six regiments of Soviet soldiers would withdraw from Afghanistan. But they had generally been greeted with scepticism by Western govenments – and Gorbachev understood why. As his foreign policy aide, Anatoly Chernyayev, puts it: 'We would have a good idea, but nobody in the world would believe us, because Brezhnev also used to use these pretty words. Gorbachev still remembers the response he got to the idea of the moratorium: he put forward a globally important idea, and people said it was some kind of utopianism, that he wanted to trick the West.' He had to find a way of restoring the currency of his diplomatic gestures.

The new foreign minister, Eduard Shevardnadze, had set about replacing his deputy ministers and also the Soviet ambassadors in almost every important country. He also installed a new publicity team, headed by spokesman Gennady Gerasimov, whose quips and one-liners were soon to encapsulate Soviet policy for millions of Western television audiences. America was instantly won over by the performance of Vitaly Churkin, a Soviet diplomat, at a Congressional hearing on the Chernobyl disaster. During an hour of televised interrogation he deftly parried questions and counterattacked, with all the polish of a White House spokesman, and rather more wit. The Americans were both impressed and concerned by this new breed of Soviet diplomat. For years they had had things their own way. Dull and indigestible official communiqués and mumbling diplomats in baggy suits had been no match for the sophisticated American PR business. Suddenly the Russians had woken up.

In May 1986, Shevardnadze and Gorbachev held a foreign policy conference for Soviet diplomats – a kind of 'teach-in' on the new methods. Yuli Vorontsov, who was appointed first deputy foreign minister that month, recalls that Gorbachev urged all the diplomats to 'use our own brains, to suggest our own ideas on various international problems, not to stick to old positions just because they happened to be our positions, and so on.' Gorbachev almost taunted them, demanding to know why the Soviet Union had 'absolutely no Asian policy'. Vorontsov paraphrases him: 'Use your brains, there should be some other directions in our policy for the Middle East too – why are you sticking to policies 10 or 15 years old?' It was a novelty for the diplomats to feel they were being asked to contribute to Politburo decision-making.

At the same time, the internal structure of the foreign ministry was shaken up, and new departments opened – for arms reduction, and for 'humanitarian and cultural contacts', that is, human rights matters.

Out of all this there had to come new policies too. Their main aim was to reduce the intolerable strain placed on the budget by massive defence spending, subsidies for communist regimes abroad, and the unwinnable war in Afghanistan. But morality played its part too. In the middle of 1986 Gorbachev, his views clearly influenced by the awesome tragedy of Chernobyl, started talking about 'new thinking' in foreign policy. The essence of this – though not yet articulated quite so clearly – was that in the modern world, with the threat of nuclear annihilation hanging over mankind, it no longer made sense to talk about foreign policy in terms of 'class interests'; there were 'common human interests' – above all, the preservation of the human race -- which overrode any class considerations. This new thinking genuinely began to determine Gorbachev's foreign policies from now on, contributing to the withdrawal from Afghanistan, the cooling of support for national liberation movements and eventually to the tolerance of the anti-communist revolutions in eastern Europe. But in 1986 the West had absolutely no proof of any such change in Soviet thinking. Gorbachev himself had scarcely begun to talk of it.

On holiday at his Oreanda dacha that August, Gorbachev had an idea – a gamble that might break down the suspicion, and break the arms control deadlock. He had requested briefing papers from the foreign ministry, which went first to Chernyayev, his aide. Chernyayev recalls a very hot day when they were both sitting in shorts on the terrace in front of the dacha, looking out at the Black Sea. Gorbachev suddenly said: 'You know what, Tolya, let's do it like this. I'll dictate to you, and you go off and write it up. I'll offer a meeting with Reagan at the end of September or early October. I'll write to Reagan, and we'll meet either in London or Reykjavik, whichever he prefers.' Chernyayev was startled – why Reykjavik? and why at such short notice? 'Because it's exactly half-way! And because we must have a breakthrough!'

And so the Reykjavik summit came about, the summit which almost led to the elimination of all Soviet and American nuclear weapons. It was an extraordinary meeting, which Gorbachev described in a virtuoso performance at a news conference just one hour after the summit had ended in failure. His decision to tell the whole story to the press was in itself extraordinary, for he had not had time to analyse the events: he just sat down in front of the world's television cameras and spoke his first impressions aloud. No one could doubt his sincerity; this was no calculated propaganda spiel. It was more like a jilted bride breaking down and pouring out her emotions to close friends. Gorbachev just wanted to talk and talk: 'Let's sit right through the night,' he said to the journalists.

Gorbachev said he had come with three major proposals to break the deadlock in the arms negotiations. The first was to cut both sides' strategic weaponry by half, in just five years. The 50 per cent cut would apply equally to land, sea and air-based missiles. Gorbachev added an extra concession, agreeing not to include American forward-based and medium-range missiles in the count. The Americans accepted the proposal. A historic agreement was reached, the first ever to cut, and not just limit the growth of, nuclear weapons. They moved on to Gorbachev's next proposal – to eliminate *all* medium-range missiles in Europe, forgetting previous talk about interim agreements and so forth, and adding the bait that Moscow was now willing not to count British and French missiles. Reagan was reluctant to remove all US missiles, even though Gorbachev had now agreed to the president's own original proposal of a zero option. So Gorbachev made an additional proposal: the USSR would keep 100 medium-range missiles in Asia, and the USA 100 on US territory. Reagan said yes. Another historic agreement was achieved. Finally Gorbachev made his last offer: sweeping aside all Western criticism that the Kremlin was not willing to accept effective verification of arms agreements, he said he would accept 'any form of verification' without qualification. What could Reagan do but say yes again?

Then came the crunch. Gorbachev demanded one concession from the Americans: that they renounce plans for a space defence system, Reagan's coveted Strategic Defence Initiative (SDI). To continue with it, Gorbachev argued, would be an attempt to gain military superiority at a time when the two sides were giving up such pretensions. Even here, Gorbachev did not demand a complete and immediate halt to work on SDI. All he proposed was that the Americans promise not to *deploy* any space system for ten years (while the other arms cuts were being carried out), although laboratory research could continue. Gorbachev felt he was doing Reagan a favour: 'We know the President's attachment to SDI. Our agreement to the continuation of laboratory research would give him the chance to carry through his idea to the end and establish just what SDI could do.' But Reagan preferred to rip up the three agreements already achieved during that short Reykjavik summit than to limit his SDI. Gorbachev pleaded with him: 'We are missing a historic chance. Our positions have never been so close.' It was then that he proposed that in the five years following the 50 per cent reduction, strategic arms should be eliminated altogether. Still they could not agree on SDI, and therefore the whole edifice crumbled. Gorbachev and Reagan parted, scarcely able to look each other in the face.[1]

Yet from Gorbachev's point of view the gamble had paid off. He had amply demonstrated his 'new thinking' to the world while the Americans had come, in Gorbachev's words, with 'old, mothballed ideas'. And the initiative did break the deadlock. A year later Gorbachev travelled to Washington to sign a treaty eliminating medium-range nuclear missiles in Europe.

IT WAS not just the Reykjavik initiative that Gorbachev dreamt up on his sun-drenched veranda near Yalta. He returned from holiday with equally visionary plans for domestic politics, summed up in the word 'democratisation', which he first used in Krasnodar in September. What exactly he meant by the word was not made clear until January 1987, but in the meantime Gorbachev set about improving the moral climate in the country.

Several glaring abuses made any talk of democracy absurd – as Reagan had reminded him yet again at Reykjavik. Emigration or simple travel from the country was almost impossible, and thousands of Jewish 'refuseniks' were awaiting visas to join their families in Israel or other countries. Hundreds of political prisoners were locked in Soviet jails. Despite the claim that the people were mature enough to be told the truth, the state spent millions of roubles jamming foreign radio stations. All these things presupposed a society that was nannied, unable to think for itself. It had to be changed. But Gorbachev was now toying with ideas which were bound to encounter opposition. The KGB, in the person of Viktor Chebrikov, was in no way disposed to release society from its chains. As Boris Yeltsin put it, Chebrikov suffered from the psychology of the lifelong KGB man: 'he saw Western subversion and spies everywhere, he didn't want to let anyone go abroad and he wanted to treat everyone as a potential defector.'[2]

Apart from general humanitarian considerations, Gorbachev had an additional motive. He was winning over the intelligentsia with his *glasnost* reforms, but they were still resentful at being treated like juveniles. Gorbachev's prestige in the academic world particularly suffered on account of the treatment of the best-known dissident of them all, Andrei Sakharov. The nuclear physicist turned human rights campaigner was regarded by most intellectuals as the country's conscience. He had been living in internal exile in the closed city of Gorky since January 1980, after he had criticised the Soviet invasion of Afghanistan. Gorbachev was a candidate member of the Politburo at the time, but according to a close associate, he had disapproved of the treatment of Sakharov from the start.

One of the most consistent campaigners for Sakharov's release within the Soviet establishment was Academician Yevgeny Velikhov, himself a nuclear physicist. He raised the question unsuccessfully under Andropov, and then again even more vigorously under Gorbachev, who had made him his chief scientific adviser. Velikhov found, somewhat to his surprise, that the new foreign minister supported him. Shevardnadze asked him: 'Why aren't the scientists insisting harder?' Towards the end of 1986 Gorbachev brought up the issue of releasing Sakharov and other political prisoners several times at Politburo meetings. Each time he was overruled. A colleague says scarcely anyone supported him. Then in December another famous dissident, Anatoly Marchenko, died in the camps, and Gorbachev's resolve strengthened. He could not afford to let Sakharov die in exile. He took a bold decision. Going behind the Politburo's back, he had a telephone installed in Sakharov's flat, and rang him to invite him back to Moscow to take part in public life again. Sakharov responded not by thanking Gorbachev but by reminding him that Marchenko had been 'killed in prison' and demanding that all prisoners of conscience be freed. Gorbachev was evasive, saying he could not agree with Sakharov's figures or that all those he termed prisoners of conscience were necessarily innocent. The conversation ended abruptly and coolly. What Sakharov did not, and could not, know was that by freeing him Gorbachev was already sticking his neck out. The sight of Sakharov arriving off the train in Moscow on 23 December to be besieged by pressmen and well-wishers was a great humiliation to half the members of the Politburo.

Gorbachev pushed ahead with other liberalising moves, not always with total success. On 1 January 1987 new regulations came into force to simplify and speed up the processing of applications to leave the country. But this KGB concession was coupled with a condition which worsened the situation: now only invitations from close relations abroad would be considered valid reasons for travelling. Nonetheless, 500 Soviet Jews were given exit visas in January 1987, the highest monthly total for years.

On 21 January Russians suddenly found they could tune in to the broadcasts of the BBC's Russian Service without hindrance. Jamming had been lifted, although the authorities continued for some time to block other foreign broadcasters in Russian.

The developing concept of democratisation met outright opposition from some members of the leadership. In December 1986, Gorbachev finally resolved to get rid of Dinmukhamed Kunayev, the 74-year-old leader of Kazakhstan and a member of the Politburo since 1971. Kunayev resisted to the end, and was removed unceremoniously. On 16 December Razumovsky, the party's personnel manager, went to Alma Ata, the Kazakh capital. He called a plenum of the republic's central committee and, in a mere 17 minutes, told them that Kunayev was resigning, introduced his replacement, and asked them to vote for the change, which they obediently did. But for once Gorbachev had lost his surefootedness. This was not just a cavalier way to treat a republican Party organisation (especially one so riddled with corruption that most of its members were either relatives or close friends of the Party leader). Worse, Gorbachev had chosen an ethnic Russian, with no connection whatsoever with Kazakhstan, to lead the republic. It is true that only about 38 per cent of the inhabitants of Kazakhstan were Kazakhs (there were more Russians[3]), but the native population's feelings were deeply injured by the insensitive handling of the change. The new leader, Gennady Kolbin, was chosen because of his reputation as a tough man, who would clean up the corruption, as he had previously done as second secretary in the republic of Georgia. According to Kolbin, it was Kunayev himself who suggested to Gorbachev that, if he had to go, he should be replaced by a non-Kazakh (rather than by one of Kunayev's rivals, such as Nursultan Nazarbayev, then the Kazakh prime minister, whom Gorbachev was considering for the job).

The result was Gorbachev's first ethnic crisis – and the authorities dealt with it ruthlessly. As soon as word of the coup got out, up to 5000 young Kazakh protesters gathered in Brezhnev Square, in front of the Party headquarters. At the time, it was reported that 'nationalist extremists' had rampaged through the streets of Alma Ata, burning cars and shops in protest. In fact, the generally peaceful demonstration was put down in a massive show of force.[4] When the protests began Razumovsky asked Kunayev to go out and help calm the people. Kunayev jabbed his finger at his rival, Nazarbayev, and said: 'This is your doing – you solve it.' And to Razumovsky he said: 'You've just fired me. I have no more responsibilities.' Then he went home.

It was Gorbachev's first brush with a problem which would confuse him again and again in the coming years – the nationalities question. A month later he criticised the oversimplification of national issues in the Soviet Union and said academic writings on the subject were often more like after-dinner toasts than serious scientific studies. But his own apparent inability to get inside the skin of other nationalities was to be his Achilles heel. References to being in 'Russia' during a visit to Kiev (capital of the Ukraine), and to being in Latvia (several times while making a speech in Estonia) were characteristic slips of the tongue.

WITH OR without Kunayev, 'democratisation' was hard work. Throughout the autumn of 1986 the leadership prepared for a central committee plenum, which was originally intended to deal only with the question of 'cadres': how to ensure that the right people (younger and capable of showing initiative) got into the right jobs, running industry, agriculture and the administration. The conclusion the Politburo came to was that managers should be elected by their workforces. Workers' self-management, it was hoped, would give people an interest in their work, make them feel responsible, and shake them out of their apathy. Without that, the economy would go on floundering and all the reforms would sink into the sand.

But Gorbachev's mind was running ahead to more radical ideas, extending beyond shop-floor democracy. Here he had a battle on his hands. The plenum was postponed three times, as his plans became more ambitious and the resistance to them grew proportionately. Alexander Yakovlev recalls: 'We wanted to solve the cadres question because it was they [managers in enterprises, and Party and state bureaucrats] who were acting as a brake on economic development and *perestroika*. But during the preparation we came to the conclusion that it had to be much wider, and include political reform – that is, democracy.' Yakovlev says the radicals, such as himself and Gorbachev, were already thinking in terms of genuinely democratic competitive elections, 'but they [the conservatives] crossed it all out'.

It was therefore a compromise package that was hammered out and put to the plenum, which eventually took place in January 1987. But it was momentous enough. In his speech Gorbachev proposed democratisation in three main areas:

● *Shop-floor democracy* Workers should be allowed to elect their own managers, team-leaders, and so on. The plenum accepted the idea.

● *The Soviet electoral system* Here, Gorbachev had a complicated proposal, patently a compromise. The existing sham election system for local soviets (councils) and for regional and republican parliaments, in which one carefully vetted candidate stood for each place available (and naturally won), needed 'perfecting'. In its place Gorbachev proposed that several candidates should be discussed at electors' meetings and pre-election conferences, and that the elections be held in larger constituencies, with several deputies being elected from each. It was not at all clear that this meant there would be more candidates on the ballot papers than places available, merely that the public would have the chance to *discuss* a number of candidacies before the election. The resolution passed by the plenum broadly accepted that 'the voter should have the chance to express his attitude to a greater number of candidates and effectively take part in the election process at all its stages.'

● *Democracy within the Communist Party* This was Gorbachev's most daring proposal. First secretaries of Party committees, right up to republic level (that is, including leaders like Kunayev), should be elected by secret ballot from a choice of candidates. The plenum, largely composed of officials who would have to face just such an election, did not like the idea at all. They passed a resolution which merely supported the idea of 'broadening inner-party democracy' in some unspecified way.

Gorbachev's January speech contained several other controversial propositions. In a direct challenge to the Communist Party's assumed 'right' to place its own members in every position of responsibility, he suggested that more non-Party people should be appointed to 'leading posts'. He also made several proposals intended to curb the tyranny of the Party-controlled legal system. One was the promise of a law which would give citizens the right to appeal against unlawful actions against them by officials. Another was a call for measures to 'raise the role and authority of Soviet courts' and to ensure 'strict compliance with the principle of independence of judges'. There was even a promise – all the more intriguing in the light of the recent release of Sakharov and a few other well-known dissidents – of new laws 'to broaden the guarantees of citizens' rights and freedoms.'[5]

Finally, Gorbachev proposed holding a national Party conference some time in the following year. It would be the nineteenth conference in the Party's history, but the first since 1941, and no one was quite sure what it would have the right to do. It was clear that it would be a major event, perhaps on a par with the five-yearly congresses. The Party rules stipulated that the congress was the main policy-setting forum, and that conferences could be held if necessary between congresses 'to discuss urgent questions of Party policy'. It seemed that Gorbachev already felt that the last congress, just one year before, in February 1986, had not allowed him to do enough, either to change the membership of the central committee or to push through new policies; he might use the Nineteenth Party Conference to change the Party rules, revamp the central committee, and take his democratisation proposals even further. Gorbachev failed to persuade the central committee that such a conference was necessary. Only at the next plenum, in June, did he get the committee's approval. The date they agreed on was June 1988. The intervening year was to be a battle for the soul of the Party.

THE January 1987 plenum was a turning-point. After almost two years of searching, *perestroika* now had a sense of direction – and a growing number of enemies. Gorbachev pushed his ideas in a series of speeches around the country, encouraging local organisations to start implementing his controversial plans 'experimentally', so that they became facts regardless of the central committee's views. Less than a month after the January plenum's lukewarm response to Gorbachev's proposal on elections for Party officials, for example, *Pravda* reported that the first secretary of a district in Siberia had been elected by secret ballot, from a choice of two candidates.[6] The next day Gorbachev, speaking in Latvia, praised this 'marvellous' example.[7] Similar party elections soon followed in bigger places.

The old system of electing local councils or soviets began to be held up to ridicule. *Izvestiya* printed a letter from a war veteran which described in detail the charade of 'elections' in which there was only one candidate, and an unmarked ballot paper counted as a vote in his favour. 'It is very important to ensure truly secret balloting. After all, what has been happening up to now? You get your ballot paper and everyone's eyes are upon you. You take a pencil out of your pocket and everyone knows what you intend to do. Young Pioneers [the children's organisation], and sometimes even guards, stand by the booth. If you enter the booth it is obvious that you are going to vote against the candidate. So people don't do this and go straight to the ballot box. The same thing happens at trade union and Party elections. No sooner have you found a corner than someone is looking over your shoulder. All this is bound to change considerably if we start nominating two or three candidates instead of one. Then you won't be able to place the ballot paper in the ballot box without even looking at it; you'll have to choose someone, and consequently cross someone off, to vote "against". This must be common practice.'

It had taken only a nudge from Gorbachev to spark off a public craving for real elections. By March *Pravda* was using the word 'democracy' – debased by decades of misuse from Stalin onwards – as a synonym for 'multi-candidate elections'.[8] The Estonian Party leader joked that in elections 'people have forgotten how to use their pencils!' While touring Latvia, Gorbachev suggested that the Baltic republic would be a good place to try out the new election principles. 'What do you think?' he asked his audience, which broke into enthusiastic applause. 'Hold on, now,' Gorbachev laughed, 'let's not rush into things!' But it was exactly the reaction he wanted. At the end of March *Pravda* announced that the new system of enlarged constituencies, with more candidates than available seats, would be tried out 'experimentally' in local elections in various parts of the country.

Shop-floor democracy also got off the ground. Television documentaries described how the new managing director of the RAF minibus factory in Latvia became one of the first to be democratically elected by his workers. Gorbachev also referred to this as a good example of how to force the pace of change. 'There is no need to wait for every single law to come out.The political line is clear,' he said.

The January plenum seemed to set the mood for further changes. The Soviet justice minister, Boris Kravtsov, announced that the laws which had traditionally been used against dissidents (Article 70 of the Russian Federation criminal code, on anti-Soviet propaganda and agitation, and Article 190–1 on slander of the Soviet state) might be radically altered 'in accordance with the decisions of the January plenum', although these laws had not been specifically mentioned at the plenum at all. In February, 140 political prisoners, convicted under these very laws, were freed from camps, prisons and places of exile, and it was revealed that another 140 cases were under review. An attempt was made to extract appeals for clemency or statements of recantation from the prisoners, but in the end even those who refused to comply were released.

There could be no more graphic illustration of the changes than the sight of Gorbachev and Sakharov together at an international peace forum in Moscow in mid-February, symbolising the beginning of a new era of pluralism in which even former dissidents would have a part to play.

February also brought new advances in *glasnost*. A letter in *Pravda* demanded to know 'how democratic' the decision-making process inside the Politburo was. Another reader complained that at the age of forty he had never heard of a factory director who was not a Party member. *Pravda* wrote in praise of Vladimir Vysotsky, a non-conformist balladier who, despite his enormous nationwide popularity, was virtually an official outcast until his death in 1980. *Ogonyok* broke fresh ground with a report of police brutality. In the northern republic of Karelia, it said, Soviet policemen had beaten a man unconscious to extract false confessions, cracked another's skull with an iron ball, and choked a third by clamping a gas-mask on his face. The Karelian interior minister had been dismissed and two policemen sent to jail. At last, Brezhnev himself (as opposed to his 'years of stagnation') came under direct attack. The liberal commentator Alexander Bovin wrote in a magazine that Brezhnev had 'allowed people to turn him into a monument to himself'. At the same time Brezhnev's son-in-law, Yuri Churbanov, who as first deputy interior minister had been closely involved with the 'cotton mafia' in Uzbekistan, was arrested and charged with corruption and bribe-taking.

The journal *Novy mir* announced that it planned to publish Pasternak's *Doctor Zhivago*, a book whose symbolic importance transcended its literary merits: it had been banned by Khrushchev, so its publication meant that Gorbachev's thaw was going even further than his. Other classics of Russian literature hitherto unknown to Russians – the best works of Andrei Platonov, for example, who had died in 1951 – finally became available, generally on the say-so of Alexander Yakovlev. It was Yakovlev, too, who engineered the publication of several controversial works by living writers. 'Sometimes,' he admits, 'I would have to persuade authors to drop a paragraph or two to make it easier. Usually, since they felt they could trust me, they agreed.'

Official radicalism was one thing, however, and outright opposition another. This became clear when some of the recently freed dissidents, many of whom had been imprisoned in the first place for their *samizdat* (underground publishing) activities, returned to their 'professions'. Sergei Grigoryants started up the most famous unofficial journal, cheekily titled *Glasnost*. A religious activist, Alexander Ogorodnikov, published a *Bulletin of the Christian Community*, and Lev Timofeyev a bi-monthly journal of opinion, *Referendum*. These tiny, ineffectual attempts to challenge the monopoly of the state media were scarcely tolerated. The dissidents' offices were periodically raided, documents and equipment were confiscated, and the journals could be distributed only secretly. But at least their editors were not in labour camps – though Grigoryants, who particularly irritated the authorities, was occasionally arrested.

The economy also benefited from the new atmosphere. The legislation permitting individual private enterprise, passed in November 1986, was not due to come into force until 1 May 1987, but already it was being superseded by more liberal moves. A set of decrees issued in February provided for the creation of small co-operative businesses in three areas: catering, services and consumer goods manufacture.[9] Unlike the 'individual labour activities', co-operatives were not restricted to members of one family: any individuals (though 'mainly citizens not employed in the state sector') could simply get together and set up their businesses. It was small-scale private enterprise by another name. By late November 1987 there were 700 registered co-ops in Moscow alone. Leonid Abalkin, director of the Institute of Economics, predicted that they would account for between 10 and 12 per cent of national income in 10 years.

Moscow's first co-op was being planned even before the decrees came out. In January 1987 *Literaturnaya gazeta* reported that a nineteenth-century house on Kropotkinskaya Street formerly owned by Prince Trubetskoi was being turned into a co-operative restaurant.

The five members of the co-operative obtained a bank loan with which to renovate the interior and buy equipment. They did a superb job. Walking into the restaurant, with its three cosy rooms and log fire, velvet curtains and tasteful decor, was like stepping out of the Soviet Union into another country or another time. Most of all, it reminded one of the twenties in Russia, when Lenin's New Economic Policy (NEP) allowed a thriving private economy to emerge from the ruins of 'war communism'. The head of the restaurant co-operative, Andrei Fyodorov, was a typical 'Nepman'. In a smart suit, he moved from table to table with a deferential air, asking after his customers' well-being. Although not in theory the venture's owner, he was undoubtedly the brains and the moving spirit behind it. He had the right to hire and fire staff. Prices were very high – mainly because Fyodorov was obliged by law to buy all his produce at the peasant markets – but nonetheless there was usually a queue at the door. Whatever the cost, an evening being serenaded by gypsy violinists in candlelight at Kropotkinskaya, 36 was worth it, just to escape from the Soviet Union, with its couldn't-care-less state-run eating-places.

The big money earned by some co-operatives caused considerable jealousy and resentment, while the whiff of decadence and the suspicion that most of the new Nepmen were crooked speculators, who did no more than buy up scarce goods from the state shops and re-sell them at exorbitant prices, injured not only the man-in-the-street's sense of social justice but also the man-in-the-Kremlin's dogmatic pride in communism. Fyodorov, who later became a leading figure in the co-operative movement, would have a battle on his hands as the guardians of socialist principle closed in. New high taxes and restrictions on co-ops' activities were the least of their worries. Fire-bombings and vandalism, carried out at night by paid thugs, were much worse.

VARLAM Aravidze has something of Hitler in his appearance, something of Mussolini, something of Stalin's police chief, Beria. But everything else about him is Stalin himself. He promises to save a church from desecration, and later has it blown up. His secret police wear medieval armour. Relations of 'enemies of the people' hand in parcels for them and are told they have been 'exiled without right of correspondence'; it means they have been executed. Aravidze cultivates the friendship of an artist, then has him arrested and sent to the camps, where he dies. He has been denounced as a 'member of a secret organisation' which plotted to dig a tunnel from Bombay to London and poison the people. The artist's wife and daughter hopelessly search among logs in a timber-yard for a sign of life: they have heard that the prisoners sometimes scratch their names on the logs. The logs are ground into sawdust. The victims' relatives have faith in

Aravidze: if only he knew, he would realise the mistake; when he gets to the truth, he will release them . . .

Years later, the artist's daughter finds herself in court for repeatedly digging up Aravidze's body. The dictator's son, Abel, says she is insane, and a medieval court has her confined to a mental hospital. She leaves the courtroom still vowing to dig up Aravidze: 'Burying him means forgiving him, closing our eyes to all his crimes. Aravidze is not dead so long as you go on defending him!' Abel defends his father: 'He never did anything wrong: those were complicated times; we were surrounded by enemies; we had much to accomplish.' Abel's son – the dictator's grandson – demands that Aravidze's body be exhumed: 'Are you not sick of all this endless lying?' The son shoots himself, and Abel finally digs up Aravidze's body and flings it on to a hillside, where it can be seen. The artist's daughter ends her days making icing-sugar churches.

Such is the plot of the Georgian film, *Repentance*. Outwardly, it is dreamlike, a phantasmagorical allegory. But down to the last detail it is the grotesque history of the Soviet Union. Soviet citizens emerged from cinemas in 1987 literally shaken by what they saw. For the film not only showed them the nightmare of totalitarianism. It also reminded them that for the past twenty years they had been living a lie, and that the truth could not be buried and forgotten: Stalin would go on living until he was exhumed.

*Repentance* was made in 1984, during Chernenko's reign, by Tengis Abuladze. It could not have been done, he says, without the help of the then Georgian Party leader, Eduard Shevardnadze. But even Shevardnadze's help was not sufficient to enable the film to be shown immediately. It joined hundreds of others lying on the shelf until the Film-Makers' Union set up its 'conflict commission' in 1986. When the Union chief, Elem Klimov, watched *Repentance* that autumn, he realised it was a special case, and told the other members of the commission not to do anything by themselves: he would take care of it. 'I understood,' he said, 'that it wasn't just a talented film, but that if it was shown it would be the first serious sign that political change had begun in our country. It could only be decided on the "top floor".' Klimov took the matter to Alexander Yakovlev, who explained that it would be hard to get such a film released 'because it would raise the themes of Stalinism, repression, the past.' Yakovlev, who at that stage was a central committee secretary but not yet on the Politburo, had to resort to subterfuge. 'Abuladze was sitting here in my office,' he recalls. 'We decided to release just 500 copies of the film – to be shown to the "chosen few", as it were. Then everyone would forget about them. It was a compromise, a limited run, to show in a few towns. That's what we did. I said to Abuladze: "Keep quiet about our agreement, pretend it had nothing to do with you." He's a good man, very intelligent . . . In the end we printed 7000 copies! It's a great film."

Klimov was right. When the film went on general release, at around the time of the January 1987 plenum, it caused a sensation, and marked a turning-point: *glasnost* was now being turned away from current difficulties to the roots of the Soviet Union's crisis, its past.

Just seven months earlier Gorbachev had told a private gathering of writers that the time had not yet come for Soviet history to be rewritten: 'If we started busying ourselves with the past we would waste all our energy. We would set people against each other. We need to move forward. We will see to the past eventually: we'll put everything in its place. But at the moment we must direct all our energy forwards.'[10] Now, with the January plenum behind him, he was ready to take on the past. 'The truth must be complete,' he told top journalists and writers at a meeting in the Kremlin on 13 February. 'We must not forget names, and it is all the more immoral to forget or pass over in silence large periods in the life of the people. History must be seen for what it is.'

Until now the Soviet people had lived in a world where dozens of the country's leaders – including most of Lenin's closest comrades, anyone who had fallen foul of Stalin, Khrushchev and a host of others – became 'non-persons' soon after they died or were ousted from power. School history books were devoid of leaders: the years of Soviet power were presented as a succession of Communist Party congresses which miraculously took decisions and changed course several times in the name of a faceless entity known as *narod* – the People. Soon the country would be celebrating the seventieth anniversary of the October Revolution. The press was bound to be full of historical articles leading up to this event. Gorbachev wanted to ensure that the past was neither idealised nor blackened from beginning to end: 'We had both sides, the joyful and the bitter . . . There were mistakes, grave ones, but the country went forward. Take the years of industrialisation and collectivisation [under Stalin]. That was life, it was reality. It was the fate of our people, with all its contradictions – the achievements and the mistakes.'[11]

The radical press responded eagerly. Proceeding from the view that more than enough had already been written about the 'joy' and 'achievements' of Soviet history, however, they concentrated almost entirely on the darker side: the labour camps, Stalin's purges, the terror. *Moscow News* printed for the first time Lenin's famous *Testament*, dictated towards the end of his life, in which he advised his colleagues to get rid of Stalin.[12] 'Non-persons' such as Nikolai Bukharin, the moderate Bolshevik revolutionary referred to by Lenin as 'the favourite of the Party' but later executed by Stalin, and Leon Trotsky, Stalin's bitter enemy, were both fetched out of oblivion by the playwright Mikhail Shatrov, in a new work, *The Peace of Brest-Litovsk*.

A 'fat journal' (literary monthly) published Anatoly Rybakov's novel *Children of the Arbat*, with its chilling account of life in Stalin's world of denunciations and fear.[13] In a television phone-in programme, Rybakov spoke of 'illegal arrests and executions by shooting', and added: 'We lost many millions of people in the mass repressions of the 1930s.'[14] *Ogonyok* published the eloquent statistics about Stalin's murder of the Soviet high command: 'three out of five marshals, all ten army commanders, three out of five army group commanders, 50 out of 57 corps commanders, 154 out of 180 divisional commanders, and 401 out of 456 colonels.'[15] To understand the effect of such statements on the Soviet public, it is enough to recall that the most damning criticism of Stalin contained in the standard Soviet school history book was that he had created a 'cult of [his own] personality' and 'seriously violated the Leninist norms and principles of Party and state life.'

The point of all this was not really in the figures or the detail of Stalin's crimes. Gorbachev's call for the reassessment of history had a much deeper purpose. He had come to understand that the roots of his country's problems did not lie in the Brezhnevite years of stagnation but in Stalinism (even if at this stage he still declined to use the word). As a child of the thirties he had been brought up under Stalin; as a young adult he heard Stalin's crimes denounced by Khrushchev, and then watched the gradual process of 're-Stalinisation' under Brezhnev.

Only Stalin's crimes – and not even their full extent – had ever been exposed. His *system* remained intact. It was Stalinism in this broader sense that Gorbachev was now determined to dismantle. He called for the blank spaces to be filled in because without a truthful picture of Soviet history there could be no accurate analysis of the present situation. It was not the ghost of Stalin that had to be exorcised, but living Stalinism, in all its incarnations:

● *The political system* The state was ruled by a single party, itself run on the basis of democratic centralism, whereby decisions taken at the top were final and binding on all lower organisations. The Party was assigned a leading role in society, giving it the right to control all other institutions, such as the courts, the press, cultural organisations and trade unions.

● *The economy* The communist ideal of 'common ownership of the means of production' came to mean state ownership. The market economy was replaced by rigid central planning, which developed its own huge bureaucracy and concentrated on heavy industry.

● *The legal system* Strict police control was established over individuals' activities, and dissent was punishable by imprisonment, confinement to mental hospital, or death. Courts, like everything else, were controlled by the Party. The borders of the country were effectively closed.

● *Ideology* The state fostered the belief that humans could be moulded by propaganda and ideology into a new ideal form of humankind, based on collectivism rather than individualism. The rightness of all policies, laws, tactics and so on was measured against the pervasive and unchallengeable official ideology, based on a selective reading of Marx and Lenin.

● *Nationalities* The Soviet Union was a centralised, Russified state. Stalin left his mark even before he became supreme leader: as nationalities commissar under Lenin, he established the basic national frontiers within the Soviet state. Later he incorporated the three Baltic republics of Lithuania, Latvia and Estonia, plus Western Ukraine (taken from Poland) and Moldavia (taken from Romania). After the War he deported whole nations from their homelands for alleged collaboration with the Germans; these included Crimean Tatars, Meskhetian Turks and ethnic Germans.

● *Information*, including information from abroad, was tightly controlled and censored.

● *Foreign affairs* Stalin and his successors perceived the Soviet Union as being surrounded by enemies. This led to isolation, an arms build-up, and the cultivation of an 'enemy image' of the West.

None of these features of Stalinism was changed by Khrushchev and Brezhnev; they remained essentially unaltered up to the day Gorbachev took power. Their most crippling effect was on the Soviet mind. An 80-year-old Russian told me how he had observed the morals of the nation going downhill ever since the Revolution. It was not always the case, he said, that people scowled at you or looked at you as if you were eccentric if you held a door open for them. He put it down to the atheism of the state: 'People are told there is nothing more to life than the present moment – they have no God to fear, and no higher concept of goodness.' To prove the point that such attitudes were not inborn, but born of the system, he noted that even in the 'civilised' Baltic republics, things were being dragged down to the general Soviet level after 40 years of Soviet rule.

If the ethics of collectivism eroded individual goodness, the economics and politics of Stalinism made things worse, by creating shortages and privileges which forced honest people to stoop to petty corruption. It is common for Soviet citizens to give gifts of some sort to ensure that shop assistants keep back a scarce commodity for them, and almost all Russians bribe doctors to obtain better service: those whose own line of work does not allow them to offer some service in return give a box of chocolates or money, while teachers can offer free tuition to the doctor's grandchild, and a plumber can fix his leaky taps for nothing. The doctor, in turn, provides a scarce medicine to the visa official in order to get permission to travel abroad, and the visa official gives the medicine to the professor who promises to get his son into university. Individuals in Soviet society are competitors for any kind of goods that are in short supply, i.e., almost everything. For shortages affect not only food and consumer goods: permission to travel abroad is also a commodity to be bargained over: and services – plumbing, dentistry, and so on – may be of high or low quality depending on the 'reward' being offered.

In the Soviet Union it comes as a shock when one encounters a sales assistant who is willing to spend time with one, showing products, offering advice, or just smiling and chatting. For a salesperson brought up in this system sees no benefit in being nice: customers are a nuisance. An Aeroflot salesgirl once shouted at me for the best part of half an hour because I could not tell her the reference number of some tickets which she was keeping in a drawer for me. She refused to find the number from her computer, and shouted: 'It's because of people like you that *our* lives are so difficult!' Had I been her gynaecologist, or her son's English teacher, her attitude would, of course, have been quite different.

The individual working in the economy was made to feel a mere cog in a huge machine driven from the top. The Soviet worker was not expected to show initiative or enterprise: that was the job of planners in Moscow, who could supposedly see better what the country needed and how it should be achieved. So no worker wanted to take a decision without referring up to have it approved: he was both afraid of the consequences of making the wrong decision and also aware that any idea not approved at the top stood little chance of being adopted. Worse, real business enterprise was often punishable by law. In the early seventies a collective farm chairman in Kazakhstan, Ivan Khudenko, was punished for doing exactly what Gorbachev was later to demand of Soviet managers. He asked the authorities what results they wanted, by when, and how much money he was being allocated. Then he told them to leave him to get on with things. By reducing his workforce to a minimum, paying them well, and quadrupling productivity, he produced seven times as much high-quality produce as the state required. He thus earned the hatred of all his neighbours, who were producing so much less on the same soil, and of the Party, whose bureaucratic system he demonstrated to be useless. He was found guilty of 'violating financial discipline' and sent to the camps, where he died.

The system produced indifference, laxity, drunkenness, irresponsibility, and refusal to take decisions. The sociologist Tatyana Zaslavskaya describes how the command economy is directly responsible for the Soviet Union's food shortages: 'When people are subject to total command and do not see the fruits of their labour, they only do the things they are ordered to do – but they do them badly, shoddily, always trying to deceive. The peasants sow seeds neatly at the edge of the field because a committee might come and check, but in the middle they don't care how it is done. When the crops grow they are harvested with the help of people from the cities, but nobody cares about storing them, so they are left to rot in the rain. The lorries to transport the grain are not properly maintained, so it gets scattered all over the roads. Our country produces huge quantities of mineral fertilisers. A consignment is transported to a railway station and dumped there. The collective farms are told to take it away, but they don't bother, so the fertiliser sits in the rain and turns brick-hard. Finally the secretary of the local Party committee says, "If you don't take it away, you'll be punished." So some peasants go and collect it, and a few years later huge piles of fertiliser are discovered dumped in a ditch not far from the railway station. They never even bothered to take them to the fields – they just moved them, to make the Party secretary happy.'

It was attitudes like that which led to the tragedy of Chernobyl. The next few years would witness more disasters which were either due to or exacerbated by the same psychological legacy of Stalinism. The deaths of 25000 in the earthquake that struck the Armenian towns of Leninakan and Spitak in December 1988 were the bitter harvest of decades of dehumanising communist rule. Of course, thousands would have died anyway in such a powerful quake, but even the official Soviet inquiry established that far fewer would have perished had not building regulations been ignored in this seismically active zone. To save money and time, perhaps to fulfil construction plans ahead of schedule and thus increase bonuses, houses were built to withstand earthquakes of lower intensity than the danger level indicated on seismic maps of the region. Moreover, even the maps were drawn up with artificially lowered safety margins by experts caught up in the local corruption ring. During the construction work itself, cement intended for the concrete panels of which the multi-storey apartment blocks were built was stolen for private needs and replaced with sand. I observed the panels turning to dust as cranes lifted them during the rescue operation in Leninakan. In the Brezhnevite economy (Stalinism minus the discipline), substandard and half-finished buildings were passed by the inspectors because otherwise they, and their colleagues, would lose bonuses. Loftier notions of responsibility and professionalism were degraded.

For a planner sitting at a desk in Moscow, far-flung parts of the Soviet Union were mere names on a map. At the stroke of a pen he could build a nuclear power station in Lithuania, or develop shale-mines in Estonia, or decree that factory A should be built 5000 miles from its suppliers, B, and customers, C. Little problems like that could easily be overcome, for he also had the power to build railways wherever he liked, and to send freight trains empty in one direction and half-full in the other. This may sound like a travesty, but it is how the system worked. As for the ecological damage that might be done by such projects – the concept rarely entered a Soviet planner's head.

'Success' was measured only in terms of gross output (the succinct Russian word for 'gross figures' – *val*– became almost a swear-word under Gorbachev). The logic of the system was: if we produced x million tonnes of steel this year, then next year we must produce x+5% million tonnes – regardless of whether that would help to produce goods that people required.

The bureaucratic mentality turned the world upside down. A Soviet publishing house where I once worked used to produce thousands of tonnes of tedious, loss-making propaganda, but a senior editor – the very model of unthinking punctiliousness – once explained to me why they used single quotation marks rather than double ones: 'It saves ink!'

In the Ukrainian city of Lvov the local Party chief, who declared himself to be a strong supporter of *perestroika*, once told me they had 'solved' the problem of providing the whole region with tomatoes and cucumbers by building two gigantic hothouse complexes. So many of the 'certainties' of Soviet life were summed up in his words: the conviction that only the state could provide tomatoes and cucumbers successfully; the notion that two huge complexes was a better idea than scores of small ones, regardless of problems of transportation and storage which it might cause; his self-satisfaction (I could find no tomatoes or cucumbers in the shops of Lvov when I was there); and his ignorance of how other countries provided vegetables, in other words those who really *had* solved the problem.

Stalinism turned Soviet society into a moral swamp, the awfulness of which will probably only be fully appreciated when the country begins to recover from it. Eventually Russians will follow the East Europeans who, after their revolutions of 1989, were able to compare themselves directly with Westerners, and began to open up their own archives. They were ashamed to learn how low they had sunk: how many of them had collaborated with the secret police; how many had joined a Communist Party they despised to further their careers or earn a trip abroad; how even their churches had compromised themselves; how they all, in the end, shared responsibility for allowing it to happen.

In the Soviet leadership, only Alexander Yakovlev had sufficient understanding of the West to be able to put the Soviet experience in context. Gorbachev had more information available than most, but even he was too shielded from both Western and Soviet reality to appreciate the situation fully. He did not attribute the defects to socialism as such, but saw them as 'distortions' of the Leninist ideal. Much ink has been spent in the years of *perestroika* discussing where, when and how things 'went wrong' – with Stalin, Lenin, or with the very notion of socialism. Gorbachev's view was unambiguous: if the Soviet Union could get back to the path outlined by Lenin (particularly in his later writings), then socialism would be saved.

The film *Repentance* cast doubt on the entire enterprise. In its last scene an old woman is seen walking up a cobbled road. She asks whether the road leads to a church, or temple. A woman tells her it does not. 'What's the point of that!' retorts the old woman. 'What's the good of a road if it doesn't lead to a temple?'

GORBACHEV set himself two arduous tasks during his 1987 summer holiday. One was to finish writing his speech for the seventieth anniversary of the Revolution in November. He had started it in April, and continually redrafted it, for he intended it to be a milestone – a fundamental revision of Soviet history which would rehabilitate 'forgotten' leaders, such as Khrushchev and Bukharin. It was also a learning process for him: he was influenced, for example, by reading the biography of Bukharin by the American Sovietologist, Stephen Cohen, which his aide, Ivan Frolov, sent him in the summer.

His second task was to write a book for Western and Soviet readers about the meaning of *perestroika* and 'new thinking'. He completed the book, and it was published in October. But it was not easy, for he found himself constantly distracted.

Ever since the January plenum there had been a growing backlash against *perestroika*. Gorbachev's opponents saw in his talk of democratisation a betrayal of the principles of what they called socialism. Prior to the plenum, the reforms had worried those whose livelihoods would suffer from them (mainly *apparatchiki* and crooks). They now also concerned those ideological purists who saw Marxism–Leninism under attack. 'It is from the January plenum that you can date the conscious resistance to *perestroika*,' says Alexander Yakovlev. 'Until then the Party and state *apparat* thought: well, we've got new leaders, let them talk, we'll carry on as before. The January plenum let them see we meant business. It was hard for them to say they were *against* democracy, of course, but after the plenum they started writing in the press about "deviations from socialism", "attacks on the Party" and so on.' Gorbachev tried to look on the bright side: it was, he said, 'a characteristic of truly revolutionary changes' that 'some are inspired, some thrown into confusion, and others find the changes simply unacceptable'.[16]

While the radical press continued to explore 'forbidden' themes, papers such as *Sovetskaya Rossiya* and *Pravda* began to publish articles of a much more conservative tenor. As the historian Roy Medvedev later recalled, 'In August, September and early October the entire intelligentsia was worried by what was happening. Had our Party begun to pursue a completely different policy?'

It was now that Yegor Ligachev, the Party's number two (and acting chief during Gorbachev's absence), began to reveal that he did not go along with all of Gorbachev's reforms. He appeared to be not at all convinced, for example, that a wholesale reappraisal of the past was necessary. In August Ligachev went to the town of Elektrostal, near Moscow, and told an audience of teachers that the Stalin period had been 'a time of new heights in arts and literature', and that the main thing about the Brezhnev period was the successes in the economy and in achieving military parity with the USA. He condemned attempts to present Soviet history as 'a chain of mistakes' and to use Stalin's oppression to 'hide the achievements of the people, who created a mighty socialist power.'

In September Ligachev held a meeting with editors, at which he demanded the resignation of Yegor Yakovlev, the editor of *Moscow News*, for publishing a short obituary of Viktor Nekrasov (a Soviet novelist who had won the Stalin Prize, but was now a 'non-person' merely because he had settled in Paris).[17] Yakovlev at once wrote to Gorbachev, complaining that he could not work in such conditions, and that Ligachev was flouting Party decisions.

Even more disturbing for Gorbachev was a letter he received in the middle of September from Boris Yeltsin, the Moscow Party chief. It contained an unheard-of request: he wanted to resign from the Politburo and from his post as Moscow Party chief. More than half of his letter was a denunciation of Ligachev's style of work as second secretary. It was because of Ligachev's 'persecution' and the Politburo's lack of support, Yeltsin wrote, that he felt obliged to step down. He asked Gorbachev to release him from his duties without referring the matter to a plenum of the central committee, which normally approved personnel changes at this level. Gorbachev must have been shocked by the letter, even though he was aware that Yeltsin was having – and causing – problems. But he showed no sense of urgency in dealing with Yeltsin's highly unusual request. On his return from holiday, Gorbachev telephoned him, but the two give varying accounts of what they agreed. According to Yeltsin, Gorbachev said, 'Let's meet later', and Yeltsin took this to mean he would be called in at any moment. 'After all,' he wrote in his memoirs, 'it is not every day of the week that a member of the Politburo resigns, with a request not to refer it to a plenum.'[18] According to Gorbachev, however, they agreed that it was not the right time to discuss the matter, and that they would meet and talk things over after the Revolution celebrations in early November.[19] One way or another, a fortnight passed with no word from Gorbachev, and Yeltsin decided to take things into his own hands. As subsequent events would show, the general secretary's tardiness was a disastrous mistake.

69

BORIS Nikolayevich Yeltsin was born in 1931, the son of poor peasants in the plains to the east of the Ural mountains. Even as a boy, according to his memoirs, he had a knack of getting into scrapes and adventures: he lost two fingers after breaking into an ammunition store, stealing a grenade and hitting it with a hammer. There was already a hint of rebelliousness at school: he ruined an end-of-term celebration by standing up and denouncing his class-teacher as unfit to teach because she 'crippled children mentally and psychologically'. His favourite word to describe himself is 'awkward'.

His career, however, was fairly standard: he studied civil engineering, worked his way up from foreman to head of the Sverdlovsk housebuilding organisation, and then moved into Party work, at first in charge of construction, but rising by 1976 to head the Sverdlovsk regional Party. It was a responsible job, in charge of a heavily industrialised region with a high concentration of defence enterprises. His behaviour was unusual for a Party boss. People in Sverdlovsk still fondly remember his regular factory visits and habit of riding on the trams with 'ordinary' people. But during the Brezhnev years he kept his unorthodox political views, if he had them, well hidden. Otherwise Ligachev and the KGB, which keeps detailed files on all Party functionaries, would never have brought him to Moscow in 1985. The only doubts they had, according to Politburo member Vladimir Dolgikh, concerned his health, and reports they had received about his tendency to become emotional'.

His radicalism flourished quickly after he became Moscow Party chief in December of that year. At the Twenty-seventh Party Congress just two months later, in his first major speech, he made two proposals which became Party policy only much later: first, he called for a shake-up of the entire structure of the central committee and demanded that its departments should stop duplicating ministries, and secondly, he proposed that all special privileges for leaders should be abolished.

His views soon became known in Moscow, and his popularity soared as Muscovites saw him making real changes. He sacked the corrupt mayor, Vladimir Promyslov, whose favourite occupation, Yeltsin said in a well-leaked question-and-answer session with Party propagandists, was 'travelling to Moscow's twinned cities, where the anti-alcohol laws didn't apply'. At the same meeting he attacked *apparatchiki* who used their official black Volgas to ferry their wives and children around town, and called for the replacement of all corrupt Party officials at every level with people of 'crystal purity'. He appointed twenty-three new district Party secretaries (out of thirty-three) and launched an all-out attack on the 'mafia' which controlled the city's Party cells, trade network, building organisations and police. By April 1986 he was able to report that 800 managers of retail and wholesale trade organisations had been arrested on corruption charges. But, Yeltsin recalls, 'we were never able to get our hands on the really big operators in the "black economy"..., and neither could we touch the top end of the mafia, with its links to politicians.'

Not surprisingly, all this activity caused resentment in certain quarters. But most of the population began to adulate Yeltsin. He worked at a furious pace, taking only about four hours' sleep each night. He visited scores of factories, sometimes travelling to them on trains and buses with the early shift workers, to experience their difficulties for himself. He would drop in at shops and personally expose and humiliate managers who were hoarding supplies or selling them through the back door instead of to the masses queuing at the counter. In an attempt to improve food supplies he arranged for scores of *yarmarki* or fairs to be set up around the city. The secret was in the method of delivery: huge lorries would arrive at these fairs from collective farms all over the country, bringing their produce direct, rather than condemning it to rot or be pilfered at Moscow's notoriously corrupt distribution depots. It was the kind of visible reform that Yeltsin considered essential to convince the public that *perestroika* was more than just a slogan. Another popular move was his decision to allow one of Moscow's prettiest streets, the Arbat, which had recently been pedestrianised, to be used as a place for unofficial entertainment. Soon there were buskers, pavement artists and kebab-vendors on the Arbat – all much too decadent for Yegor Ligachev. He went there to see things for himself and then complained at a Politburo meeting that there 'was no order' and that the Moscow Party committee must 'take measures'. Vladimir Dolgikh recalls that there was a furious row at that meeting, with Yeltsin defending the new regime on the Arbat and most of his colleagues arguing that 'the people who live there are virtually held hostage: it brings them nothing but inconvenience.'

The two men scarcely agreed about anything. Not only did Ligachev often cut across what Yeltsin was trying to do in Moscow, but ideologically the two were far apart. They had regular quarrels over the perquisites and privileges enjoyed by Party officials, which Ligachev saw as a justified reward for the work they did. Yeltsin was once reprimanded for admitting to foreign diplomats that there were political prisoners in the Soviet Union. In the summer of 1987 Moscow city council, with Yeltsin's encouragement, issued a directive which permitted demonstrations to be held in Moscow, provided the organisers gave notice of the venue and likely number of participants. At a Politburo meeting on 10 September, during Gorbachev's absence, Ligachev attacked Yeltsin for this and set up a commission of inquiry into his handling of affairs in Moscow. This was the final straw which prompted Yeltsin to write his letter of resignation to Gorbachev.

Gorbachev's delay in responding may have reflected the fact that his patience had also run out. He too had begun to clash frequently with the maverick Moscow boss. He regarded Yeltsin's constant criticisms at Politburo meetings as unconstructive. And his personal attacks on Ligachev were embarrassing. Gorbachev could not afford to side with Yeltsin against Ligachev, who controlled the Party apparatus and represented a significant swathe of opinion which Gorbachev could not just wish away.

Yeltsin describes a Politburo meeting earlier in the summer at which Gorbachev's patience with him had snapped. They were discussing an early draft of the speech Gorbachev was to make on the seventieth anniversary of the October Revolution. Most of the members made insignificant comments, but Yeltsin had come with a list of twenty serious criticisms. 'Something unexpected then happened,' writes Yeltsin. 'Unable to restrain himself, Gorbachev broke off the session and stormed out of the room. For about thirty minutes the entire membership of the Politburo and the secretaries sat there in silence, neither knowing what to do nor how to react. When he reappeared, he started a tirade that had nothing to do with the substance of my comments but was aimed at me personally. Evidently he was letting fly with all the thoughts, complaints and resentments that had been building up inside him over recent months. What is more, his choice of words was highly critical, almost hysterical. I wanted to leave the room in order to avoid listening to so many remarks that were close to being insults.'[20]

THE central committee plenum of 21 October 1987 was intended to review the course of Soviet history. It ended up changing it.

Just before 10 a.m. 450 full and candidate members of the committee took their seats in the plenums hall of the Kremlin. Gorbachev delivered a report in which he informed them of the main points of the Revolution anniversary speech which he was to give before a big audience of Soviet and foreign guests on 2 November. A comparison between what Gorbachev told that closed plenum and his public speech two weeks later tells us much about the confines within which he still had to operate. The public speech was seen as a certain step forward, in that Gorbachev analysed, albeit briefly, the roles played in Soviet history by Bukharin, Trotsky, Khrushchev and others, and condemned Stalin's crimes as 'enormous and unforgivable'. Yet many intellectuals were disappointed by his insistence that there was no alternative to Stalin's crash programme of industrialisation and collectivisation of agriculture, by his rejection of the more moderate policies proposed in the 1920s by Bukharin, and by his cop-out on the extent of Stalin's terror – which cost, he said, merely 'many thousands' of lives.

In his closed report to the October plenum, by contrast, Gorbachev had been much more forthright. He gave figures to illustrate the extent of the terror: 10 of the 13 Bolshevik revolutionaries who survived till 1937 were purged; so were 1108 of the 1966 delegates to the 1934 Party Congress, and 70 per cent of the central committee which they elected. He talked of 'thousands of red commanders, the flower of the army on the eve of Hitler's aggression' who were also killed in the terror. (In the November speech he did not even mention the army purges.) Moreover, he argued that all the 'triumphs' of the time – 'in building socialism, in the Second World War and in the post-war reconstruction' – were achieved *despite* Stalin, not because of him. This was real revisionism – just what many felt was lacking in the later speech. But at one point Gorbachev seemed to sense his central committee audience's growing unease at this damning account of Stalinism, and added: 'Comrades, please bear in mind that not everything I have stated here will go into the jubilee speech in detailed form. It will only include general, overall assessments of the complex periods in our history . . .' It was not just that many in the central committee would be loath to approve a speech which was so frank about the crimes and failures of the 70 years they were celebrating; Gorbachev was also sensitive to the feelings of many ordinary Russians who lived through those years, honestly believing they were working to build socialism. How could he tell them, on the country's anniversary, that their lives had been in vain?

After covering the main points to be included in his anniversary speech, Gorbachev moved on to the present day. Not expecting his words to be published, he delivered one of his strongest-ever condemnations of his conservative opponents, many of them sitting in the plenum hall.[21] He said *perestroika* was entering a new stage which would be 'the critical period in all our work'. Referring to the growing resistance to the democratisation plans introduced in January, he almost jeered at his critics: 'Of course, none of them say they are against *perestroika*. No, no, they are only against the "costs", and worried lest our ideological foundations be shaken by the growing activity of the masses. That's where the threat to socialism stems from, it turns out – from the growing political and social activity of the masses! No, that doesn't threaten socialism, it threatens the penpushers, the bureaucrats, those who have usurped what belonged to the people and have forgotten the interests of the people.' He said that the costs of standing still were much worse than any that might arise in the process of renewal, and continued: 'We must learn to identify, expose and neutralise the overt opponents of *perestroika*, those who are holding things up, sticking spokes in the wheels and gloating over the difficulties and failures, those who are trying to push us back into the worst years of the past.'

You could hardly have had a clearer statement of Gorbachev's radicalism, yet within the hour he was forced to become a centrist.

When Gorbachev finished his report, Ligachev, who was chairing the meeting, asked for any comments. Yeltsin started moving towards the rostrum, and Ligachev hastily tried to bring the proceedings to a close. Gorbachev intervened: 'Comrade Yeltsin has a statement to make.' Ligachev had to give his arch-rival the floor.

Yeltsin's speech was nervous and muddled: he had only prepared a few notes, not being sure whether he would screw up the courage to speak at all. He made it clear at once that he had nothing to say about Gorbachev's speech, which he 'fully endorsed', but wanted to get a number of problems off his chest. First, he said that despite a call at the last plenum, in June, for a change in the work of the Secretariat, nothing had changed in Ligachev's style of work. 'Bullying reprimands and dressings down' were intolerable. He claimed that constant promises that *perestroika* would yield results in two to three years disoriented people, because in the past two to three years little had changed. Until the January 1987 plenum, people had been enthusiastic about *perestroika*; but since the summer their faith had begun to ebb. He said that the Kremlin issued so many decrees and documents that local authorities had begun to ignore them. Then Yeltsin moved on to more dangerous ground. Speaking (as Gorbachev had just done) about the lessons of the past 70 years, he declared that the defeats of those years were 'due to the fact that there was a lack of decision-making by consensus; that cliques were formed; that the power of the Party was put into a single pair of hands; that he – one man – was totally immune from all criticism.'

Just in case anyone in the audience had not understood his allegory, Yeltsin spelt it out: 'I am very worried that there is still not a good atmosphere in the Politburo, and that recently there has been a certain increase in what I can only call adulation of the general secretary by certain full members of the Politburo. I regard this as intolerable, particularly now, when we are introducing democratic, principled forms of relations to one another, truly comradely relations. It is intolerable. To criticise to someone's face – yes, that is necessary – but not to go in for adulation, which can gradually become the norm again, can become a "cult of personality". We cannot permit this. It must not be allowed.'

This insinuation that Gorbachev was a Stalin in the making was earth-shattering enough, but Yeltsin had one more bomb to drop. 'And finally . . .' He paused. 'I am clearly out of place as a member of the Politburo. For various reasons. Evidently there is my lack of experience, as well as other factors. Perhaps it is simply the lack of support from some quarters, especially from comrade Ligachev, which has led me to believe that I must put before you the question of my release from the duties and obligations of a candidate member of the Politburo. I have already handed in my request to be allowed to resign.'

There was uproar in the hall. Not even the other members of the Politburo expected it, because Gorbachev had not told them about Yeltsin's letter to him. As for the ordinary members of the central committee, who had not witnessed Yeltsin's conflicts at Politburo meetings, they must have been thoroughly confused, for Yeltsin failed to explain either his references to 'dressings down' or his comments about Ligachev.

Yeltsin had broken all the rules. He had not only chosen a festive event at which to offer his resignation, but he had gone well beyond the bounds of permitted criticism. No member of the central committee had ever heard anything like it, and when Gorbachev opened the floor to debate, twenty-five of them went to the rostrum to condemn Yeltsin – and support Ligachev. The accusations became more and more bitter as the day wore on. The session turned into an analysis of Yeltsin's character: he was accused of immaturity, defeatism, pettiness, ambition and vanity. His work in Moscow was mocked: one speaker, referring to the new *yarmarki*, said he had built 'stupid little pavilions' all over the place which stood empty and got on people's nerves. The Ukrainian leader, Shcherbitsky, said he presumed Yeltsin got his information only from *Moscow News*. A Moscow construction worker made perhaps the nastiest comment: 'How we respect you, Boris Nikolayevich! We got rid of Khrushchev twice as fast. But now we're so democratic, we keep trying to *persuade* you . . .'

Gorbachev, summing up, tried to save the day by praising the 'unity' of the central committee and insisting: 'We are on the right path, comrades, we are on the right path!' But it must have been one of the worst days of his life, because he saw that the central committee did not just leap at Yeltsin's throat, but at his own policies too – the construction worker's snide comments about Khrushchev and democracy were scarcely in the spirit of Gorbachev's speech that day.

The plenum passed a resolution declaring Yeltsin's intervention to have been 'politically mistaken'. The question of his resignation was postponed until after the Revolution festivities. On that the plenum ended, and the leadership went to desperate lengths to prevent the truth about what had happened from leaking out.

But rumours of the bust-up, many of them wildly wrong, grew so strong that they threatened to eclipse all interest in the approaching anniversary. On 31 October Anatoly Lukyanov, a central committee secretary, held a news conference at which he admitted that Yeltsin had offered to resign, but he gave few details. The Western press wires were buzzing with the news all night, but at home the cover-up continued: TASS sent a message to all Soviet news organisations 'categorically' forbidding them to carry Lukyanov's statement about the October plenum.

That the conservatives had scored a major victory and cornered the radicals became clear on 3 November, when Yakovlev gave a news conference to explain the importance of Gorbachev's jubilee speech the previous day. Asked about the Yeltsin affair, he clammed up and even lied: what happened at the plenum, he said, was 'nothing special, a normal internal Party affair', Yeltsin had not complained about a 'personality cult' or about the pace of *perestroika*. Asked whether it was not millions that died in Stalin's purges, rather than the 'thousands' referred to in Gorbachev's speech, Yakovlev said that the figures bandied around in the West were 'on the conscience of those who think them up.' Was it not time to publish Khrushchev's secret 1956 report about Stalin's crimes, someone asked. Yakovlev replied cynically: 'What difference does it make to you? It has been published in the West!' Finally, asked why TASS had banned publication inside the country of Lukyanov's statement about Yeltsin, Yakovlev replied: 'You shouldn't be reading TASS's internal memos.'[22] Western reporters were horrified. Many left the hall shaking their heads: 'If this is "Mr Glasnost", God help them!'

Yakovlev's defensiveness helps to explain why Gorbachev was so angry with Yeltsin. In his report to the October plenum, just before Yeltsin spoke, Gorbachev had criticised only his conservative opponents. From now on he had to criticise the right and left in equal measure. Yeltsin had handed the right a victory by forcing Gorbachev to take up a more centrist position, at least publicly. Within the leadership, Yakovlev was now left alone to fight the liberal cause. It meant that in the run-up to the Nineteenth Party Conference the following June the radicals, who would otherwise have been arguing in much the same vein as Yeltsin, had to distance themselves from him and take a more moderate line. New words were coined – 'ultra-leftist', 'pseudo-revolutionary' and 'political adventurism' – which now had to be trotted out whenever the old curses – 'conservatism' and 'dogmatism' – were used. Eventually, Gorbachev would persuade the Party to reorganise the Secretariat and *apparat*, and give up its privileges, just as Yeltsin had demanded. It might have happened sooner, however, had not Yeltsin provoked the conservatives with his behaviour at the October plenum.

As soon as the anniversary celebrations were over, Yeltsin was thrown to the wolves. On 9 November he was taken to hospital with severe headaches and chest pains. Two days later Gorbachev rang him and insisted that he attend a full meeting of the Moscow Party committee, even though doctors had forbidden him to get up. 'I shall never be able to understand that,' says Yeltsin. 'In the whole of my life I have never heard of anyone, whether a worker or a manager, being dragged out of a hospital bed to be dismissed.' Yeltsin says he was pumped full of sedatives and dragged – 'my head spinning, my legs crumpling under me, scarcely able to speak because my tongue wouldn't obey, and understanding practically nothing that was happening around me' – first to a Politburo meeting, and then to the session of the Moscow committee.

The session was like an old-fashioned Stalinist show trial. When Mikhail Poltoranin, then editor of *Moskovskaya pravda*, went into the hall, he saw that the first three rows of seats were empty. Then those who were to speak came in, apparently from a briefing with Gorbachev and Ligachev, and filled up these rows. Gorbachev opened the meeting by refuting all of Yeltsin's claims about the lack of success of *perestroika*, and accusing him of placing his personal ambitions above the interests of the Party. The other speakers, mostly Yeltsin's subordinates with various grievances, moved in for the kill. His October speech had been a 'calculated stab in the Party's back'. He was variously described as a 'Jesus Christ', martyred for his 'terribly revolutionary commitment to social renewal and democracy', a 'Napoleon', an 'ultra-leftist' and 'super-radical'. Not content with one round of sackings in the Moscow Party, he had embarked on a second. At city Party meetings only pre-planned speeches were allowed. Yeltsin, said one speaker, 'very quickly became the kind of boss he himself had railed against at the Party Congress. That is the gulf between words and deeds. He started to believe in his own infallibility and shut himself off from the Party activists. There were 250 district Party committee meetings over this period, and Yeltsin attended only two of them. Someone might say that he visited dozens of factories and enterprises – yes, he did, but they were just excursions for him. He would march through the shopfloor, making a great show of himself.'

'You forgot, Boris Nikolayevich,' said a district secretary, 'that you have to think about people. There isn't a person in the country who does not love Moscow. But you, Boris Nikolayevich, I'm afraid, don't love Moscow, or Muscovites.'

'Working for Boris Nikolayevich was torture,' said another.[23]

Poltoranin saw how Yeltsin listened to these attacks with his head in his hands. 'His lips were purple – he was all blue and he had difficulty holding his head up.'

Yeltsin dragged himself to the rostrum to reply, supporting himself on the backs of chairs. He made a brief, incoherent speech in which he confessed his 'guilt'. The only accusation which he challenged was that he did not love Moscow. He then stumbled back to his seat on the stage to hear the verdict. Instead of accepting his offer of resignation, the committee voted unanimously to fire him 'for gross shortcomings in the leadership of the Moscow city Party organisation'.

According to Poltoranin, Ligachev, who had watched his opponent's downfall with malicious pleasure, was one of the first to leave the platform. Then the others filed out, leaving only Gorbachev and

Yeltsin. Gorbachev made to leave, then turned and saw that Yeltsin was sprawled over the table. He went back, lifted him up by the elbow, and led him out through the door. Gorbachev helped Yeltsin back to his old office, where they sat together for a while. Then an ambulance came and took Yeltsin back to hospital.

WINTER started hesitantly in 1987. Leaden skies alternated with pale sunshine. Heavy falls of snow turned to slush during the day and froze overnight. Politics, too, were thrown into a bewildering state of limbo. After the events of the autumn, no one knew for sure what the rules were. Small groups of students took to the streets with petitions, some calling for Yeltsin's reinstatement, some merely demanding that his speech at the October plenum be published, so that people knew the truth. The organisers were called before their Party committees and reprimanded. Political meetings were held at workplaces all over the capital to explain why Muscovites had lost their hero.

A liberal historian cancelled two public appearances rather than face questions about the Yeltsin affair. A decision about whether to release a controversial new film about Afghanistan was postponed. An exhibition of works by Vadim Sidur, an avant-garde sculptor, was suddenly closed after a telephone call from the cultural section of Moscow city council, which claimed that the exhibition was not 'in the interests of the state'. *Pravda* published a strongly-worded attack by three writers on a new film about the problems of Soviet youth. The main problem with young people, they indicated, was their love of rock music 'which like a narcotic is capable of crippling the defence-less minds of adolescents'.

In December, winter set in for real. An exuberant Ligachev, now at the peak of his power, went to Paris to tell French communists that in the entire history of the Soviet Union 'not a single year was lost'. In an interview with *Le Monde*, he spoke almost boastfully about his role as deputy leader. On his return to Moscow he took over the running of the country while Gorbachev spent a week in Washington, signing the medium-range missiles treaty. The historian Roy Medvedev says the conservative upsurge was particularly palpable that week. He claims that firm plans to rehabilitate Bukharin were postponed. At the same time, dissidents from all over the country held a human rights conference in Moscow, but when they turned up at the banqueting hall they had hired for the opening session, miles out in the snow-swept suburbs, they found a heavy padlock on the door and a sign saying it was closed for cleaning.

YEGOR Kuzmich Ligachev (or Yuri Kuzmich, as his colleagues call him) is a true Siberian, ruddy-faced, stocky and tough. Born in 1920 in a village near Novosibirsk, he trained as an aircraft engineer in

Moscow and then returned to Novosibirsk where he soon gave up engineering in favour of Party work. Though a firm believer in the principles of Stalinist socialism, he was well aware of Stalin's crimes: his fiancée's father was shot in 1937, accused of being 'an agent of Japanese, British, French and German intelligence'. At the height of the Khrushchev 'Thaw', he was chosen as Party secretary of the district in Novosibirsk where the Siberian Division of the Academy of Sciences was set up, and was in close contact with the liberal-minded academic community. After four years in the apparatus in Moscow, he was sent by Brezhnev in 1965 to head the Party organisation in Tomsk, also in Siberia. Here he remained for the entire 18 years of Brezhnev's rule, his career stagnating, although he is regarded as having been a fairly successful provincial boss. By the time Andropov brought him back to Moscow, he was as sick as Gorbachev of the corruption, inefficiency and – above all – the indiscipline of the Brezhnev period.

Ligachev is a true Party man, somewhat in the Andropov mould; puritanical, teetotal, and so committed to hard work that he decreed that all Party meetings in Tomsk should be held on Saturdays. He even banned smoking in public places and at the Party headquarters in Tomsk, forcing the *apparatchiki* to smoke secretly in the toilets, like schoolboys. It is hard to imagine him taking bribes. He sincerely – not to say dogmatically – believes in the Party's mission, and in an idealised image of 'the working class'. To this day he speaks only in Marxist clichés. In 1989 he insisted, against his colleagues' wishes, on publishing a collection of his speeches, and included one from 1959 in which he praised the decision of twelve scientists to tutor 107 building workers, free of charge, three times a week, for six months, to help them prepare for university entrance. 'It seems to us that this is an example of correct interrelations between the intelligentsia and the working class,' he added.[24] That, one imagines, is Ligachev's idea of communism.

Such views were not out of place in the first years of *perestroika*, when Ligachev and Gorbachev had a close working partnership and saw eye to eye on most things. Ligachev's difficulties began when Gorbachev started trying to make the economy and government work better by removing the Party's right to interfere in them. Ligachev, by contrast, firmly believed in the Party's *duty* to make things work. Back in 1949, when he led the young communists' organisation in Novosibirsk, he issued a series of instructions to farmers in which he informed them: 'manure from socialised cattle, as well as manure from collective farmers' personally-owned cattle is used as fertiliser.'[25] He was soon removed from his post as young communist chief for *vozhdizm* – an overbearing, presumptuous style of leadership.[26] But he remained just as patronising 40 years later. Even when paying lip-service to the need to get rid of 'command-administrative methods', as the management style of the Brezhnev era was dubbed, Ligachev tended to use precisely those methods to achieve that end.

Vladimir Dolgikh, who watched him at close quarters in the Politburo and Secretariat, says: 'I believe he was too interfering and ran the central committee the way he had run a regional Party committee. The central committee is a different thing. He should have been less concerned with specific issues, more with strategy.'

Ligachev resisted the market economy, private enterprise and democratisation because he saw that they loosened the Party's – or his own – direct control over things. Similarly, he believed the duty of the press was to promote Party policies, not to cast doubt on them. He objected strongly to blanket criticism of Soviet history: as far as he was concerned, socialism was being built at every stage. Speeches by Ligachev and Gorbachev at a central committee plenum in February 1988 showed how different their views on this were. Ligachev expressed outrage at suggestions that 'we have built the wrong kind of socialism', whereas Gorbachev spoke of the need to 'decisively renounce the dogmatic, bureaucratic and voluntaristic legacy, for it has nothing in common either with Marxism–Leninism or with genuine socialism.'[27]

His former aide, Valery Legostayev, recalls Ligachev being infuriated by a newspaper article which described the Soviet people as a nation of slaves. Ligachev picked up the telephone to complain to Gorbachev about it. At the end of their long conversation Ligachev put down the phone, paced round the room, and said to Legostayev: 'I can't agree with that. Were I to agree with that, I'd have to cross out my whole life.' Like his rival, Yeltsin, Ligachev is emotional, and finds it hard to hide either his feelings or his opinions. 'He wears his heart on his sleeve,' says a colleague.

Ligachev himself now admits that he used to reproach Gorbachev for having 'insufficiently stable and consistent views' on the market, private property, and the revision of history. 'I began to perceive a gulf between his words and his deeds,' he says. 'When we discussed how the media were blackening our past, he would agree with me – but that was just talk, and nothing was done about it. I also believe his position on private property is wrong. He thinks it should be allowed in the services sector. He says, "What are you worrying about, Yegor Kuzmich? Our academicians tell me that even ten or fifteen years after we start privatisation, it will only embrace seven per cent of the total." I said to him: "Mikhail Sergeyevich, that is a delusion. I tasted private property in my childhood [under the New Economic Policy of the twenties] and I know: they will not be content with seven per cent. Big business and private capital will hog everything."'

Ligachev drew his authority from two quite separate conservative tendencies: the Party-state apparatus, which was scared of losing its power, positions and privileges; and the ideological purists, who sincerely believed in old-style communism. But there was more to him than that. He also came from an age-old tradition of Slavophilism, which denied the possibility of progress by importing Western ideas and values, and looked instead to a 'purer' Russian heritage. The split between Slavophiles and Westernisers had dominated Russian nineteenth-century intellectual life. In the Soviet Union there was a similar division within the Communist Party itself: Alexander Yakovlev, for example, had been sent to Canada as punishment for his criticism of Russian nationalism, which enjoyed the support of Mikhail Suslov, Brezhnev's ideology chief. Gorbachev's reforms involved a decisive opening-up to the West in every way, including a much greater receptiveness to Western ideas and culture. The Slavophiles' opposition to this trend was expressed most vividly by a group of writers who enjoyed Ligachev's support: Valentin Rasputin, Yuri Bondarev, and others. The main vehicles for their views were the thick literary journals *Nash sovremennik* ('Our Contemporary') and *Molodaya gvardiya* ('Young Guard'), while the 'progressive' journals such as *Novy mir* ('New World'), *Znamya* ('Banner'), *Druzhba narodov* ('Peoples' Friendship') and *Oktyabr* ('October') were mainly Westernising. Rasputin, whose views appear to echo Ligachev's (though he is not a Party member), came to prominence with stories lamenting the destruction of Siberian village life in the name of progress; he was one of the most vocal campaigners against the Siberian rivers diversion scheme. But when he ventured beyond such themes he began to sound plain reactionary: he berated the radical late-night television show *Vzglyad* ('Viewpoint') for defending homosexuals and interviewing prostitutes, and claimed there was proof that rock music 'causes dangerous changes to the haemoglobin in the blood'. Likewise, Ligachev, in his speech to teachers at Elektrostal, exhorted them to counter the 'craze for primitive music' by inculcating love of 'the best works of the fatherland's composers, and folk music'.

THE conservatives found fresh evidence for their fears that *perestroika* was undermining the foundations of the Soviet state in events that began to unfold in the Caucasus in February 1988. Emboldened by Gorbachev's calls to reassess the past, the elected council of Nagorny Karabakh voted to take the region, with its 80 per cent Armenian population, out of the control of the republic of Azerbaijan – where Stalin, as nationalities commissar, had placed it in 1923 – and to incorporate it into Armenia, from which it was separated by a narrow strip of Azerbaijani land. There had always been a seething racial and religious enmity between the Turkic, Muslim Azeris and the Christian Armenians, which had merely been suppressed in the pre-Gorbachev police state. The Armenians of Karabakh felt their cultural, educational and linguistic rights were violated, and that the area – an 'autonomous region' administered from the Azerbaijani capital, Baku – was underfunded and poorly developed. Although the region had been populated by Armenians for centuries, the Azeris claimed that it contained some of their holiest shrines.

At the end of February the Armenian capital, Yerevan, witnessed the biggest protest demonstrations in Soviet history. Hundreds of thousands of people – perhaps up to a million – thronged the square in front of the opera house to support their kinsmen's call for reunification. They assumed that their demand was fully in line with the policies of *perestroika* – there were almost as many portraits of Gorbachev and Lenin as banners for unity. But that was not how it was seen in the Kremlin. Armenia instantly became out of bounds to Western journalists, who even found their telephone calls to well-informed Moscow dissidents were cut off as soon as Yerevan was mentioned.

Politburo envoys were dispatched to Nagorny Karabakh and Armenia, and Gorbachev and Yakovlev received two Armenian writers in Moscow. Gorbachev from the outset excluded the possibility of redrawing any national frontiers within the Soviet Union. But he seemed sympathetic. He promised a 'just solution', and set up a special commission, reversing a central committee decision of just one week earlier. He even apologised for a TASS report which had outraged Armenians by calling the demonstrators – who were entirely peaceful and included most of the population of Yerevan and many more bussed in from other areas – 'extremists'. He said a central committee plenum would be held to overhaul the entire nationalities policy, apparently leaving the door open for change. But Gorbachev understood that these developments had wider implications, and were playing into the conservatives' hands. He told the Armenians they were stabbing *perestroika* in the back. According to Arkady Volsky, who was later appointed as Moscow's troubleshooter in Nagorny Karabakh, Ligachev took a hard line, opposing even the more moderate options being floated, such as putting the region under direct Moscow rule, or raising its status from 'autonomous region' to full republic.

The two writers returned to Yerevan and reported their talks with Gorbachev. The crowds in the square agreed to halt their demonstrations, giving the Kremlin until 26 March to find the promised 'just solution'. But suddenly things went out of control. Crowds of Azeris rampaged through the city of Sumgait, on the Caspian Sea, murdering at least thirty-two people, mostly Armenians, raping and mutilating many more, and pillaging apartments. Sickening stories of the atrocities quickly reached Armenia. Passions became inflamed, and refugees started pouring across the border between Azerbaijan and

Armenia, in both directions. Even more ominously, the authorities in the two republics began to align themselves with their quarrelling peoples, bringing the threat of inter-republican feuding for the first time.

The conservatives in Moscow began preparing their move – not against Armenia, but against *perestroika* itself.

ON 13 March the newspaper *Sovetskaya Rossiya* printed a full-page article entitled, 'I cannot betray my principles', described as a letter from a Leningrad chemistry lecturer, Nina Andreyeva. In it, she defended Stalin's achievements, 'which put our country among the great powers', and inveighed against those who sowed 'ideological confusion' by writing of 'our spiritual slavery', 'the predominance of boors in power' and 'the communists who have allegedly dehumanised the country's life since 1917'. She said that the latest historical works by the radical playwright Mikhail Shatrov 'distorted the country's history of socialism'. The notion that Stalin had Trotsky murdered was, she said, an unsubstantiated accusation. Echoing Ligachev (and directly contradicting Gorbachev), she derided those who said that 'current relations between states belonging to two different socio-economic systems are devoid of class content'. The class struggle was by no means outmoded – indeed, the central question in Soviet society was: which class was in charge of *perestroika*? Her answer was that it was in the hands of 'left-wing liberal intellectuals' (a fair description of Yakovlev) whose idea of socialism put individual values before 'proletarian collectivism' and who 'allege that we have constructed the wrong kind of socialism and that today, for the first time in history "there has emerged an alliance between the political leadership and the progressive intelligentsia".' In answer to this, Nina Andreyeva demanded that 'the leading role of the Party and of the working class in building socialism and *perestroika* be recognised. At one point in the letter, her anti-intellectual stance bordered on anti-Semitism. She said that the desire of Jews to emigrate amounted to treason, and she resurrected Stalin's anti-Jewish term, 'cosmopolitanism', as allegedly an attribute of the left-wing liberal ideology whose downfall she demanded. She also condemned recently created informal organisations (political clubs), with their calls for 'pluralism which is by no means socialist', and their talk of setting up a 'parliamentary regime', 'free trade unions; and 'autonomous publishing houses'. Finally, she quoted from Gorbachev's most recent speech: 'Under no pretext, comrades, should we betray our principles.' It was a neat quote, for the principles he had in mind were the antithesis of hers.

Had these been the ravings of a mere chemistry teacher, they would have been of little consequence. But this was no ordinary letter.

Printed in a publication owned jointly by the Party's central committee and the Russian Federation government, and specially advertised
on the front page, it had semi-official status. It was later described as a
'manifesto of anti-*perestroika* forces' and its appearance as a plot which
almost derailed Gorbachev's reforms.

Valentin Chikin, the paper's editor, had not always appeared to be a
conservative. Under Andropov, when he was deputy editor, he had
written a series of articles under the heading 'Reading Lenin anew', in
which he had used historical analogies to drive home contemporary
messages more candidly than Andropov himself could in public
speeches. Half-way through Chernenko's rule, when the old man,
aged 73, was ill, Chikin broke the official silence with an almost impu-
dent allusion to the illness of Lenin's mother, when she was 73: 'At
that age,' he wrote, 'any ailment can be worrying.'

But as Gorbachev began to break with the cautious Andropovian
reforms of his first year, so Chikin found a more natural ally in Yegor
Ligachev, whom he visited regularly at the Secretariat. In the gloomy
months following Boris Yeltsin's dismissal, *Sovetskaya Rossiya*
became staunchly conservative, opposing the liberal press's infatua-
tion with Stalin's crimes, and even attacking harmless proposals to
rename streets. In February the newspaper received Nina
Andreyeva's long letter, which perfectly summed up Chikin's own
reservations about the way *perestroika* was going.

Chikin and Ligachev had a long private meeting at this time, at
which they may have discussed the letter – though this cannot be
proved. It certainly seems unlikely that Chikin would have proceeded
as he then did without Ligachev's consent, for his actions were as
covert and calculated as in any conspiracy. The following story
of this remarkable event has been pieced together from first-hand
accounts given by journalists, Nina Andreyeva herself, and members
of the Politburo.

The letter had arrived unsolicited at the paper's culture department. It was given to the science editor, Vladimir Denisov, who knew
Ligachev well, having previously worked as *Sovetskaya Rossiya*'s correspondent in Tomsk while Ligachev was Party chief there. When the
propaganda editor, Vladimir Dolmatov, asked Chikin why ideological
material was being handled in the science department, he was told 'it
just happens that way'. The paper rang Nina Andreyeva to ask her to
make some changes to her article, and on 9 March Denisov arrived in
Leningrad to help her make the final revisions. Andreyeva says he
merely shortened her new version, without adding or distorting
anything.

On Saturday 12 March the editorial board held its usual midday
conference. The page-proofs of the next day's paper were pinned up on
the wall, and each article was discussed. At the end of the conference

Chikin surprised his staff by suggesting a last-minute change: 'There is a proposal by one of our colleagues to replace page three with the letter from Nina Andreyeva. I would like you all to read it and give your opinions.' Since it was a Saturday and most people were anxious to get home (Sunday was a day off as the paper does not appear on Mondays), not everyone bothered to read the piece. Chikin also left the building, having taken the decision to publish without waiting for any objections from his staff.

The paper's managing editor, Vladimir Pankov, was furious that an entire new page had been type-set and proof-read without his knowledge. He was shocked when he read it. 'I understood that it was a torpedo which would explode and wreck *perestroika*,' he recalls. 'It was a signal for attack, that was clear to me.' Dolmatov, the propaganda editor, who felt the same way, believes the page had already been read and approved in the central committee, for when he rushed off to suggest to Chikin's assistant that they should at least print a note saying that the editorial board did not share Nina Andreyeva's views, he was told: 'How can we say we don't agree with her if Ligachev himself has said it's a splendid article?'

The article appeared in the issue of 13 March. Ivan Laptev, then editor of *Izvestiya*, remembers the shockwaves it sent out. 'Every day at 9.15 we have an editorial conference. I went there that morning after reading the letter and said, "Friends, I believe an open attack has been launched against *perestroika*. We all have to make our choice: how do we respond as journalists and citizens?" Our entire board backed *perestroika*.' Journalists on every other paper were asking themselves similar questions.

The next day, Monday, Gorbachev left on a state visit to Yugoslavia, and Yakovlev left for Mongolia. That morning Chikin arrived a few minutes late for his editorial conference and announced to his staff that he had just had a call from Ligachev, praising the article. An hour or so later, Ligachev summoned the editors of the main newspapers to the Kremlin. Laptev recalls that there were about a dozen people present. Ligachev spoke first about other matters, and then said: 'I read an excellent article yesterday in *Sovetskaya Rossiya*, a wonderful example of Party political writing. I hope you have all read it. I would ask you, comrade editors, to be guided by the ideas of this article in your work.' He said that this was not only his opinion.

TASS, whose director had also attended the meeting with Ligachev, at once issued a recommendation to provincial newspapers to reprint the Nina Andreyeva article. Many of them did so. Liberal intellectuals felt that *glasnost* was at an end. For three weeks no newspaper dared to print a reply. A journalist named Lyudmila Saraskina wrote one, and *Moscow News* was about to publish it. At the last minute the editor was rung by the head of the Novosti news agency, the paper's proprietor, and told that there was a ban on all comment regarding Nina Andreyeva. Even Laptev's journalists on *Izvestiya*, who had taken such a firm stand before Ligachev's recommendation, were cowed into silence.

Gorbachev returned to Moscow on the 18th and Yakovlev the next day. Both had been shown the article while away, and understood its significance. Gorbachev, according to his aide, Georgy Shakhnazarov, talked about it several times while in Yugoslavia, and 'saw it as a gauntlet that had been thrown to us'. Yakovlev, who read it in Mongolia, says he knew at once who was behind it: 'I didn't have to guess – it was obvious.' They knew they had to act decisively. Yakovlev recalls: 'It was precisely because the press fell silent and took fright that I realised we had to react. At that time it was still possible to smother *glasnost*.'

Even more worryingly, Ligachev used the absence of Gorbachev and Yakovlev to try to upgrade his own official status. His name appeared more than once ahead of those of his Politburo colleagues, violating the strict rule that only the general secretary is listed out of alphabetical order.[28]

The Politburo met on 24 March. After dealing with other business, mainly the events in Nagorny Karabakh, Gorbachev asked who had read the Nina Andreyeva article. Ligachev said he had, and suggested that it was a natural reaction to attempts to 'blacken our history'. He hotly denied that he had had anything to do with the article's appearance, though he maintained that it was acceptable for such articles to be published 'to provoke discussion'. Gorbachev, Yakovlev and Ryzhkov argued that an official rebuff had to be issued, for if the leadership's position was not made clear people would not know where they stood. Several members of the Politburo were against making an issue of it. But Gorbachev saw it as a matter of principle: you had to be either for or against Nina Andreyeva. The meeting ended inconclusively, and continued for the whole of the following day as well.

Evidently Ligachev managed to convince Gorbachev that he had not been involved with the article prior to its publication. Ligachev says that a few days after the Politburo *post mortem* Gorbachev telephoned him and said: 'I am satisfied, Yegor, that you had nothing to do with the publication of the article.' That was not the point, of course: Ligachev's offence was his recommendation of the article as a guideline, *after* publication – a fact which Gorbachev could easily establish. It is not clear whether the Politburo issued a formal rebuke to Ligachev for his role in the affair, but he was certainly taken to task over it. The Politburo decided that in future, although Ligachev would remain 'second secretary', in charge of the Party apparatus, Yakovlev should take sole charge of the press. Yakovlev was asked to oversee the drafting of a full-page rebuttal of the Nina Andreyeva article, to be published in *Pravda*.

*Sovetskaya Rossiya*, meanwhile, was preparing its own selection of readers' replies to Nina Andreyeva, almost all of them in favour of the article. Chikin was discussing the planned page with his department heads when his direct Kremlin telephone rang. According to Vladimir Pankov, Chikin's face grew pale. He put his hand over the mouthpiece and motioned his colleagues out of his office. Forty minutes later he called them in again and told them that the call had been from Gorbachev, who had said: 'I can't understand. We thought you were for *perestroika*. We are beginning to get the idea that your paper has an incorrect understanding of it!' They would have to drop the follow-up page, Chikin said, for *Pravda* was planning a very different kind of response. 'He was a completely crushed man,' says Pankov.

TASS was also informed of the 'new' Politburo line, and sent a revised instruction to newspapers on 29 March (incidentally, while Ligachev was out of Moscow, visiting the town of Vologda). This time it said that papers should reprint the Nina Andreyeva article only 'in agreement with the local Party authorities', thus indicating that it no longer had top-level approval as a 'guideline'.[29]

On 5 April, *Pravda* printed its hard-hitting rebuff – unsigned, to underline its authority. It described the Nina Andreyeva letter as an attempt to revise Party decisions on the sly, and refuted each one of her arguments, point by point.

Ligachev's carefully timed attempt to sabotage the reforms and rally his troops before the Party Conference in June had failed. The crisis was defused. After three weeks in suspension, *glasnost* picked up speed again – just in time to ensure that preparations for the Conference went ahead in a blaze of radical journalism.

# CHAPTER THREE

# *Revolution from above*

THE Nina Andreyeva affair made one thing clear: Gorbachev could not rely (as he had tried to since the January 1987 central committee plenum) on the Party leadership or even on the press to help him shake off the past and democratise Soviet life. He needed to encourage ordinary people to put so much pressure on the conservatives that they would no longer be able to resist. Between April 1988 and the end of the year, Gorbachev skilfully enlisted popular support for broader democratisation, and used it to push through momentous reforms, with incalculable consequences. It was a high-risk policy, which could easily get out of hand.

It has often seemed as if Gorbachev was feeling his way, with no clear goal. His policies – particularly his shifts to ever more radical forms of democracy – looked like concessions forced upon him by events.

But interviews with his closest advisers suggest that this was not quite so. According to them, Gorbachev was aware even in the autumn of 1986, when he first started speaking of democratisation, that logically this must lead to the end of the one-party system; and from early 1988 he started working out a plan for step-by-step progress towards full, multi-party democracy. Only the timing and precise detail of that plan, according to these sources, was influenced by outside events. They say that Gorbachev encountered opposition within the Politburo at every stage; this forced him to adopt the tactics which led outsiders to believe he was only improvising.

This view helps to explain many of Gorbachev's early public statements on the multi-party system, and also many of the strange hybrid forms of democracy which paved the way to the abolition in early 1990 of the Communist Party's constitutional right to rule.

Speaking in Khabarovsk back in the summer of 1986, Gorbachev had let slip a phrase which was omitted from the published text of his speech: *glasnost* and self-criticism were necessary, he argued, because 'we don't have any opposition parties, comrades'.[1] He sounded almost wistful, as if he understood that mere openness was no real substitute for democracy. This was followed by the start of the 'democratisation' process, and the first moves introduced in January 1987, which Alexander Yakovlev says would have gone further had it not been for the conservatives' opposition.

In early 1988 the 'inner circle' – Gorbachev, Yakovlev and Gorbachev's radical aides, Ivan Frolov and Georgy Shakhnazarov – worked out their strategy for the ultimate introduction of multi-party democracy, with a view to putting the idea to the Nineteenth Party Conference in the summer. They agreed that it must be done carefully, in stages, with the Party in control of the process (and the conservatives in the Party under their control) until the very end, in order to avoid anarchy. There is no suggestion that any of them ever wanted the communists to lose power, of course, but they wanted the Party to win legitimacy democratically, and to rule with the consent of the people rather than by imposition. They were well aware that to undermine the Party's all-pervading hold on society *before* democratic structures were set up to replace it could bring chaos, not least in the economy, where the Party's parallel structure oiled the wheels of the centrally-planned system.

They did not discuss democracy in terms of the abolition of Article Six of the Soviet Constitution, which defined the country as a one-party state – partly because it would have been absurd to put such a proposition to the Party at that time, but mainly because they planned to rewrite the entire Constitution once the Party had accepted new principles of democracy, and the new Constitution would naturally not include such an article.

Such was the opposition from the majority of the Politburo and central committee, however, that Gorbachev did not even dare to mention his ultimate goal to them. Vladimir Dolgikh says that he himself put it to his Politburo colleagues in the summer of 1988 that they ought to take a stand for or against a multi-party system, since the matter was already being raised in the press. He reports that Gorbachev looked around the table and said: 'I think we are all agreed on this – that there should be one party, the Communist Party.' Gorbachev was not actually lying: at this stage he believed that the Party must remain firmly in the saddle, preparing the way for democracy.

His aide, Georgy Shakhnazarov, explains: 'Everybody understood that a system of free elections would gradually and necessarily lead to a multi-party system, but we never discussed this issue at that time. As often happens in revolutionary situations, there are things which seem banal today but which you couldn't even mention then. Anyone who at that time had said openly that we were progressing towards cancelling the leading role of the Party and introducing a multi-party system, and that the Party might lose power, would have been swept aside.'

Gorbachev had to move slowly. The most radical plan for which he could obtain approval was that which was included in a discussion document – *Theses of the Central Committee* – which was published towards the end of May 1988, a month before the Conference began. The *Theses* described the reforms to date as 'only a prelude to the . . . profound and all-round democratisation of the Party and society'. But they were vague about what this meant. The general principles – which marked the minimum Gorbachev hoped to get approved by the Conference – included: extending sessions of parliament to make it less of a rubber-stamp body, limiting office bearers to a maximum of two five-year terms, and reforming the election system to allow free nomination of candidates.

The *Theses* called for a dramatic shift of power from Party committees to elected councils or soviets: the Party was to exercise its influence not by duplicating the work of the soviets but by the presence of Party members in the soviets (just as parties in Western democracies govern by having their members elected to councils and parliaments). The document resurrected the idea (rejected by the January 1987 plenum) of competitive elections for all Party posts. It also suggested there should be a change in the Party rules to allow the partial replacement of the central committee between the five-yearly congresses. Gorbachev had noted earlier that previous Party conferences had elected new members to the central committee, and he hoped to do the same at this one: the committee was not merely overwhelmingly Brezhnevite, but some 15 per cent of its members were 'dead souls', having been sacked from the posts (as regional secretaries or ministers) which entitled them to their seats. Many of Gorbachev's important recent appointees, on the other hand, were not on the central committee. (In the end he was unable to push this plan through.)

While the document lamented how ancient the leadership had grown (the lack of 'natural rejuvenation of personnel'), it seemed to suggest that a more regular turnover should be achieved by limiting Party officials to two terms in office, rather than by imposing an age-limit – an idea which was widely canvassed by pro-Gorbachev writers around this time. If, as seems likely, Gorbachev also favoured this approach, he probably dropped it at the insistence of Ligachev, who was 67 and had insisted even two years earlier that leaders should be allowed to continue if they were working effectively: 'we should be looking at the real results of their work, not at the calendar.'

The point of the *Theses* was not to set down firm principles, however, but to provide a platform for discussion. The challenge was taken up with glee by a press feeling re-liberated after the Nina

Andreyeva débâcle. Writers turned their attention from traditional *glasnost* fare such as Stalin and corruption to make bold suggestions for political reform. The proposals ranged from referendums on changes in the Party leadership to equal opportunities for non-Party people, from publication of proceedings at central committee plenums to the creation of a presidential system. Radicals objected to loopholes in the *Theses'* proposals which would allow the two-term rule to be waived in exceptional cases, and demanded constitutional guarantees against the re-emergence of terror and one-man rule. The poet Yevgeni Yevtushenko coined the phrase 'non-Party party', to encompass the millions of non-communists who must also be represented in government.

NO ONE knew exactly what the rights or functions of a Party conference were. The last one had been held in 1941, under Stalin, and provided few guidelines. The Party rules were also sufficiently vague as to allow virtually anything. The one thing that was clear was that Gorbachev felt that events had moved on so far since the last Party congress, in February 1986, that he needed an equally large and representative gathering of grass-roots representatives to approve the next stage in his plans. The election of 5000 delegates to the conference was supposed to start in April, but did not get properly under way until late May – the delay being partly due to the Nina Andreyeva affair and partly to Gorbachev's worries that the 'wrong' kind of delegates would be chosen. In April he called provincial Party bosses to Moscow, apparently to instruct them as to the kind of delegates they should arrange to have elected. On 7 May *Pravda* warned that there must be 'no mistakes' in choosing delegates, who would have to give 'a firm rebuff to the conservatives'. It looked like a call to radicals to manipulate the elections – and at the same time a stern warning to those in the *apparat* who might try to manipulate things their way.

Since the *apparat* was still firmly in the hands of Ligachev, it was not surprising that many of Gorbachev's most obvious supporters failed to be elected, some despite his explicit backing. The situation in Moscow seemed to be typical. At a meeting of the capital's Party organisation 319 delegates were chosen – from a list of 319 candidates. It was at the nomination stage that the deals and compromises were struck between left and right. The radical historian, Yuri Afanasyev was probably the most outspoken writer on Stalinism, and was regarded as a key figure of *perestroika*, yet a district committee of the Moscow Party elected a fourth-year girl student described as a 'recognised youth leader and commissar of a construction detachment' instead of him. The leadership of the Moscow city committee, however, ruled that Afanasyev should be nominated as well, in view of his reputation for 'scholarly works and trenchant journalistic

91

articles'. That was one victory for the reformists. Vitaly Korotich, editor of *Ogonyok*, also failed in Moscow, but he too was lucky – he was elected by a Party organisation in his native Ukraine.

Other radicals were less fortunate. At the Moscow selection meeting the capital's Party chief, Lev Zaikov, named twelve 'passionate supporters of *perestroika*' – all household names – who had failed to be nominated. In the course of the meeting, after close questioning from the hall, only four of them (the economist Leonid Abalkin, film-maker Elem Klimov, and editors Grigory Baklanov and Yegor Yakovlev) were added to the list, and duly elected as delegates. Those who failed included Gorbachev's adviser on social questions, Tatyana Zaslavskaya, three radical economists, Nikolai Shmelyov, Andrei Nuikin and Gavriil Popov, and the playwright who had so upset Nina Andreyeva, Mikhail Shatrov. It must have been a great disappointment to Gorbachev that fewer than half of his 'test cases' were chosen – the more so as he gave his personal endorsement to one of them, the playwright Alexander Gelman, in the course of the meeting. Gelman had recently warned of dire consequences if *perestroika* failed: 'healthy forces', disillusioned once too often, would leave the Communist Party, and the reactionary rump would be overthrown by the discontented masses. Conservatives at the Moscow selection meeting declared that Gelman had spoken out 'against the Party and its leading role' and therefore was unsuitable as a delegate. Gorbachev, sitting on the platform, spread his hands in amazement at this, and defended Gelman as a 'serious, modest and profoundly talented' man. But still he was blackballed.[2]

Stories of skulduggery came in from all over the country. *Izvestiya* printed comments from readers indignant at the *apparat*'s manipulation of the elections: 'Bah! The same old faces!' 'The bureau of the regional committee picked forty-eight names from seventy nominations – exactly the number required. Here's your 48 – vote for them! What kind of election is that?' 'I expected that some of the delegates would be distinguished from us, mere mortals, not just by the shine of their medals but also by the shine of their thoughts!' 'The *apparat* was best prepared for the election. It started drawing up lists of candidates and carried out "consultations", also within the *apparat*. Rank-and-file communists were largely excluded from this work.'[3]

This was just what Gorbachev had feared: that the massive Party bureaucracy, scared both by his reforms and by the rank-and-file's support for them, would stuff the Conference with its own representatives, so that they could vote down any further encroachments on their power and privileges. On 1 June Gorbachev took the unprecedented step of publicly endorsing what amounted to a popular insurrection against conservative Party leaders in the far-eastern island of Sakhalin. Speaking at a news conference during a visit to Moscow by

President Reagan, Gorbachev referred to a 'debate' which had led to the 'strengthening' of the Sakhalin leadership as proof that *perestroika* had reached the province's 700 000 people.[4] Few Westerners understood what he was talking about, but Soviet newspaper readers knew exactly. That day's *Sovetskaya Rossiya* reported that Pyotr Tretyakov, the provincial Party boss, had consistently abused his positon by allocating new housing to his friends and relatives. Under his rule, life for ordinary people had grown steadily worse, while Party and local government functionaries enjoyed the services of a special hospital, hotel, dairy and shops. Their holiday home was notorious – 'situated in a nature reservation and fenced off from mere mortals'. In mid-May it transpired that Tretyakov and his cronies had arranged for their own selection as delegates to the Party Conference. The citizens of the provincial capital, Yuzhno-Sakhalinsk, poured on to the streets to protest. They declared that they had no confidence in the Party leadership and elected a group of eight representatives who acted, in effect, as an alternative government, negotiating with the Party leaders. After what the newspaper described as a 'tumultuous week', they brought about both an end to the privileges and the resignation of Tretyakov.[5]

It was this that Gorbachev praised as 'measures and decisions necessary for the process of democratisation on Sakhalin to gather speed'. His explicit support for civil disobedience to break the conservatives went much further than his previous vague calls for people to throw off their lethargy and commit themselves to *perestroika*. Within days there were demonstrations in other parts of the country. In Omsk more than 8000 people held what *Pravda* called 'the first town meeting in living memory not staged from above'. The reason was the same: a 'narrow circle of leaders' had carefully chosen candidates who names 'were a complete surprise even to the secretaries of [those candidates'] primary organisations'.[6] A few days later 5000 people gathered in Yaroslavl, where the Party chieftains had gone so far as to choose as a delegate their *former* first secretary, Fyodor Loshchenkov, who had been sacked for what *Izvestiya* called 'his "contribution" to stagnation'.[7] As a result of their protest, Loshchenkov was quietly dropped from the Yaroslavl delegation.

Gorbachev had invited public pressure, but sometimes he got more than he bargained for. Three days before the Conference began, the whiff of revolution came to Moscow itself as demonstrators gathered on Pushkin Square – not with complaints about how the Communist Party had elected its delegates, but with much more wide-ranging political demands. There were fewer protesters than in Omsk or Yaroslavl, but more than the capital had seen for many decades.

It was a sweltering, blue-skied Saturday afternoon, and the air was full of fluff drifting down from the poplar trees. Bare-chested workers on mobile cranes were erecting huge official posters and banners in honour of the Conference. Shortly before three o'clock, two small knots of people started to form on the square outside the *Izvestiya* newspaper offices on Gorky Street, not far from the statue of Alexander Pushkin, Russia's national poet and bard of liberty. The two groups represented different forms of opposition to the Communist Party. One, the more militant, consisted of activists from the Democratic Union, a group which had set itself up in May as an opposition party, calling for the establishment of a Western-style multi-party democracy and economic system. The other knot included members of various left-wing political clubs of a generally Euro-communist persuasion, equally disillusioned with the achievements of the Soviet Communist Party but dedicated to true 'workers' democracy' rather than the restoration of capitalism. The latter group had come here to proclaim the launch of a 'popular front', calling for a more radical kind of *perestroika* than that on offer from Gorbachev.

At first each group attracted only a few dozen active supporters. The popular front were better organised; they put up a makeshift platform around the wall above an entrance to the metro station, unfurled banners and portraits of Lenin and Gorbachev, and took out loudspeakers to address the public. Attracted by the unusual sight, people began to gather. Soon almost 2000 people were on the square. They were not alone: scores of police had also turned up, and their little squat buses, with curtained windows, were parked around the square, ready to carry off troublemakers.

But for all the appearance of being well-prepared the police were overwhelmed and confused by this unwonted event, and things soon turned nasty. The popular front, loudly proclaiming their aims under banners reading 'No to Stalinism' and 'All power to the soviets', were left relatively unmolested. But the Democratic Unionists, chanting 'Down with the KGB' and distributing leaflets calling for a multi-party system, bore the brunt of the authorities' as yet rudimentary crowd-control tactics.

The chants and slogans grew louder and bolder. So did the metallic snarl of the police loudhailers, calling uselessly for the crowd to disperse. Then scuffles broke out, and members of the Democratic Union were hustled off to the waiting buses, to roars of 'Fascists!' and 'Executioners!' from the crowd. Even innocent passers-by were now involved, joining in the political discussions and arguing with the Moscow police chief, who was observing the scene from a corner of the square: 'We just want to hear what these people have got to say,' one man argued. 'Why won't you let us?' The police chief muttered something about anti-Soviet slogans. As a bus moved off, an arrested youth pushed his head out of the window and held his fist in the air, shouting 'Freedom!' The square resounded with cheers and applause.

Suddenly, this was no longer an insignificant gathering of a few political activists: the people of Moscow were gulping the air of democracy and getting light-headed with it. Old sepia photographs of Petrograd on the eve of the 1917 Revolution kept flashing through my mind. For the first time since Gorbachev proclaimed revolution from above, it seemed to have caught on in the streets of Moscow. For a few hours under a blistering June sun, the people, not the police, were in charge of Pushkin Square. A month later the Supreme Soviet would approve draconian decrees to limit the right to demonstrate and to provide special interior ministry forces with new combat uniforms and anti-riot gear.[8]

WHEN Gorbachev had given the keynote speech at the Twenty-seventh Party Congress in February 1986, he was interrupted with applause 132 times. By contrast, his four-hour address on the opening day of the Nineteenth Party Conference on 28 June 1988 received but twenty-one rounds of applause – and no standing ovation at the end. Partly this reflected the more sober, less adulatory style of politics which had set in by then. But above all it confirmed that the cream of the Party, on whom Gorbachev was relying to carry out his 'revolution', were decidedly unenthusiastic about it. They showed where their sympathies lay by giving Ligachev thirteen rounds of applause in the course of a mere 20 minutes.[9]

Just what did the audience like in Gorbachev's speech? Their first applause – an hour and a half into it – was more or less invited, when Gorbachev thanked those who had worked and fought in Afghanistan 'on behalf of the Party and people'. Thereafter the delegates saved their applause almost exclusively for Gorbachev's most cautious or conservative statements – indeed, for precisely those words that looked as if they could have been inserted by Ligachev. They clapped when he declared that democracy must not imply irresponsibility and lack of discipline, and that sometimes democratic rights were used for undemocratic purposes; when he mouthed the platitude that there was no alternative to friendship between the different Soviet nationalities; when he said people should feel proud of their 'socialist Fatherland'; and – especially – when he insisted that *perestroika* would fail without the 'guiding activity of the Party', and that there was no question of abandoning socialism.

By contrast, they listened to the major portion of Gorbachev's speech in apparently stunned silence. Their reaction was hardly surprising, for the historic reform package he unfolded was designed to overturn the entire political system, and would lead inexorably – as many of the delegates doubtless realised – to the erosion of Communist Party rule in the Soviet Union. The reform went far beyond anything mentioned in the *Theses*, and even the central committee members had not been informed of all its details. It envisaged deep changes to the Party itself, to the organs of state power, and to the election system.

The plan gave concrete form to the idea of separating the functions of the Party and the state, so that the Party would exercise only 'political leadership' and not interfere with the right of parliament to make laws, the government to run the country, and economic managers to manage the economy. To this end, Gorbachev proposed restructuring the Party apparatus to eliminate those economic departments which had hitherto duplicated the departments of government, and to slash the size of the Party bureaucracy.

The old Supreme Soviet, which had met for two or three days a year to rubber-stamp decisions taken by the Politburo or central committee, was to be replaced by a new working parliament, which would meet for up to eight months in the year. This body, also to be known as the Supreme Soviet, would have 400–450 members, chosen from a new 'super-parliament', the Congress of People's Deputies.[10] Two-thirds of the Congress's 2250 members would be elected directly by citizens, the other third by 'public organisations' such as the Party itself, trade unions, women's and youth organisations and so on. Gorbachev said he envisaged the parliament as a body devoid of 'long speeches and over-organisation': its sessions 'should be lively and demanding, compare proposals, discuss amendments, additions and objections.' If decisions were not always unanimous, said Gorbachev, evidently feeling he had to explain the rudiments of parliamentary life, 'that is a normal phenomenon in the democratic process.' As for the members of parliament, they would be elected under a system which guaranteed 'the right of unlimited nomination of candidates, broad and free discussion of them, and strict observance of a democratic election procedure.'

The idea of a two-tier parliament, consisting of a Supreme Soviet indirectly elected from a larger Congress of People's Deputies, had been opposed in the run-up to the Conference by some of the group which drafted the reforms.[11] Gorbachev's progressive aide, Georgy Shakhnazarov, urged him to institute an ordinary, directly elected parliament. But Gorbachev (who, Shakhnazarov says, likes to borrow Western ideas but root them in Soviet traditions) was swayed particularly by the arguments of his old university friend Anatoly Lukyanov, by then a central committee secretary, who had written a doctoral thesis about the Congress of Soviets – the original Soviet parliament, created by Lenin and abolished by Stalin in 1936. Gorbachev preferred to go back to something similar to Lenin's congress than to borrow fully the idea of a Western parliament.

The new head of state would be the Chairman of the Supreme Soviet – a quasi-presidential post which included all the functions previously carried out by the Party leader, including overall control of law-making, social and economic programmes, foreign policy, defence and security, chairmanship of the Defence Council, and the right to nominate the prime minister. The creation of this post was crucial to the transfer of power from the Party to elected and publicly accountable officials, thus bringing the political system closer to something recognisably based on the rule of law – albeit with built-in advantages at this stage for the Communist Party (through direct representation for the Party and other communist-dominated bodies). Assuming, as Gorbachev did, that he himself would become the new head of state, it was also a way of reducing the chance of his being removed from power by plotters within the Party (as Krushchev had been in 1964); a 'president' elected in the new way could be removed only by parliament.

There were several elements in the plan which struck many liberals as undemocratic. One was the provision of guaranteed seats in parliament for Party-backed 'public' organisations. This clumsy arrangement, which had no parallel anywhere in the world, was almost certainly introduced at the insistence of the conservatives, although it may also have fitted in with Gorbachev's own view that the Party must make sure that it remained in control of the democratisation process at this stage.

Another controversial proposal concerned the lower levels of the state structure, where elected councils or soviets were to become real organs of local administration, freed from the overbearing domination of Party departments. Gorbachev puzzled many delegates by saying that 'as a rule', the first secretary of a district or regional Party organisation would be 'recommended' for the post of chairman of the district or regional soviet. This proposal obviously contradicted the concept of *separating* Party and state bodies; indeed, it looked like a manoeuvre to preserve Party domination. The economist, Leonid Abalkin, struck the first dissonant note of the Conference by criticising the idea, and other radical delegates followed suit.

But in fact, it was one of Gorbachev's wiliest moves against the conservatives. As Gorbachev explained to Shakhnazarov (who had also privately criticised the proposal), he too wanted proper separation of Party and soviet posts – but the only way he would be able to persuade hardline first secretaries, who were terrified of being left powerless, to agree to the policy was by suggesting that *they* would have the chance to run the soviets.

So on the third day, when Gorbachev took the floor again to explain his idea, which he said had not been understood properly, he justified it in two quite different ways. His first argument – that making the local Party boss chairman of the soviet would both enhance the authority of the soviet and at the same time reaffirm the Party's leading role – was intended to mollify the conservatives. His second argument, however carefully he phrased it, showed that he actually saw the idea as a weapon against those very conservatives. Party leaders, he explained, would not automatically become chairmen of the soviets; they would first have to be elected by the people. In other words, the top Party bosses at every level and in every region would have to undergo a public vote of confidence. If they failed that test, they would 'have to draw the appropriate conclusions from this'. Gorbachev understood that if even now the public was outraged enough to demand the dismissal of old-style leaders like the Party boss in Sakhalin, then when proper democratic local elections were held, the voters would help him to sweep out corrupt and conservative Party chiefs everywhere. Since a large number of Conference delegates were regional and district first secretaries, the idea predictably earned a cool reception. Ligachev, who spoke on the fourth and last day, significantly failed to come to Gorbachev's help in winning delegates over to this, the most controversial part of the reform package.

The proceedings of the Conference were not shown in full on television, but extracts from the main speeches were broadcast. Some of them had viewers' jaws dropping in astonishment – the moment, for instance, when a Siberian Party secretary demanded the sacking of 'stagnation period' leaders, and then, asked by Gorbachev whom he had in mind, named Politburo members Gromyko and Solomentsev, *Pravda* editor Viktor Afanasyev, and foreign affairs expert Georgy Arbatov. People had never heard such things being said in public before.

But that was nothing compared to the showdown on the final day – between, of course, Yeltsin and Ligachev. Yeltsin had managed to get himself elected at the last minute as one of thirteen delegates from the Party organisation in Karelia, but the leadership had no intention of letting him speak. Gorbachev had made it quite clear after the events of October 1987 that as far as he was concerned Yeltsin's political career was finished.

After the morning break Gorbachev announced that there would be time for only eight to twelve more speakers before lunch,[12] and that in the evening session they would discuss and vote on six resolutions, before winding up the Conference. Yeltsin, who was sitting at the very back of the balcony, sent two notes to the presidium, asking for the floor, but received no reply. He decided, as he puts it in his memoirs, 'to take the rostrum by storm'. He left his seat, went downstairs, and strode up the central aisle of the Palace of Congresses holding his red Conference card high above his head. As he approached the platform the speaker on the rostrum broke off, and a hush fell on the hall. Yeltsin climbed the three steps to the platform and confronted Gorbachev directly, demanding to be allowed to speak. Gorbachev, completely taken aback, motioned Yeltsin to sit down in the front row. There were several minutes of confused whispering between Polit-buro members on the platform, while various aides kept toing-and-froing between them and Yeltsin, trying to coax him to leave the hall. They persuaded him that if he went out, a member of the presidium would come to talk to him. The Tajik delegate at the rostrum contin-ued with his speech, but no one was listening. Yeltsin started walking up the aisle to the exit. Some delegates and journalists whispered to him that he must not leave the hall: he would never be let back in. Yeltsin decided not to risk it. He turned round, walked all the way back down the aisle, and sat in the front row again, staring at Gorbachev. Two speakers later, shortly before two o'clock, Yeltsin was given the floor.

It was a hard-hitting speech, and much more persuasive than his intervention at the October plenum. Most of it contained constructive policy suggestions: genuine elections for all Party and state office-bearers; no exceptions to the two-term rule; an age-limit of sixty-five (which, incidentally would require Ligachev to step down at once). He claimed that the Party leadership (in particular Mikhail Solomentsev, head of the Control Commission) was preventing prosecution of the leaders of certain republics, whom he called 'millionaire bribe-takers'. He called for dismissal from the Politburo of those members who shared the 'guilt' for bringing the country to its present state. He sug-gested that each time a new Party leader came to power, he should be able to bring in a new team to the Politburo and *apparat*, so that he would not be trapped by having to work with an old administration. *Perestroika*, he said, had not solved any real problems so far, and in order to restore people's faith in it, just one or two 'specific tasks for the good of the people' must be set, to be solved in the next two or three years, rather than dissipating efforts in all directions. Moving on to the question of openness, he declared that the public should have full information about their leaders – including their biographies, salaries and views (all treated until now as secret). As for the Party's accounts, he said that even members of the central committee knew nothing about how its 'hundreds of millions of roubles' were spent – only the *apparat* knew. 'I can only observe,' he went on, 'that, apart from rational and necessary expenditure, the Party also spends its money on building luxurious houses, dachas and sanatoriums on such a scale that one is ashamed when the representatives of other parties [i.e. from the socialist countries] visit them.' Warming to his pet subject – privilege – he declared that if there were shortages in socialist society they should be felt 'in equal degree by everyone without exception'. Yeltsin's careful evocation of socialist principle to support his cause drew applause even from conservative delegates. He rammed his point home, demanding an end to all privileges for the élite (denoted by the prefix *spets-* in Russian) 'because we do not have *spetskommunisty* (special communists)'. Finally, he proposed that the central committee apparatus should be cut drastically – to one-tenth of its size.

His proposals were radical, but the delegates listened respectfully – until he came to his final point: a request for his own 'political rehabilitation'. The hall broke into slow-handclapping to prevent him from continuing, and Yeltsin made to leave the rostrum, but Gorbachev intervened: 'Let us remove the secrecy from the Yeltsin affair . . . Go ahead, Boris Nikolayevich.'

Yeltsin recalled that his speech to the October 1987 plenum had been declared to be 'politically erroneous', yet almost all the issues he had raised in it had since been brought up in the press, and even in Gorbachev's speech to the present Party Conference. 'I consider,' he went on, 'that the only error in my speech was that I delivered it at the wrong time, immediately before the seventieth anniversary of the October Revolution.' He asked the delegates to remove the stigma from him by rehabilitating him.

Again, he won applause from the delegates, who – like most Soviet audiences – appreciated an emotional speech even if they disagreed with its content.

A lunch-break was announced, during which a counter-attack of sorts was arranged. It was led by Ligachev, whose speech thrilled his audience of *apparatchiki* but made him a laughing-stock among the Yeltsin-loving public. (Recordings of Yeltsin's and Ligachev's speeches were shown on television that evening.) He denied that the Party apparatus enjoyed any privileges other than that of 'being in the forefront, fighting for Party policies and serving the people with their faith and truth.' Their average wages put them in twenty-sixth place in the country, he said (missing the point that it was their special access to scarce goods that counted, not wages). In the course of a fierce attack on the press, he said the liberals' favourite newspaper, *Moscow News*, which had printed figures about privileges, was not worthy of being called a newspaper. He made childish comparisons between how well he had worked as Party leader in Tomsk and how badly Yeltsin had allegedly worked in Sverdlovsk – which scarcely fitted with his confession that it was he who had recommended Yeltsin for work in the central committee on the strength of his achievements in Sverdlovsk. He rudely referred to Yeltsin throughout by his first name only and the familiar pronoun, *ty*: 'You, Boris, have not drawn the correct political conclusions . . . You and I differ not only on tactics, but also on strategy . . . You, Boris, worked as secretary of [Sverdlovsk] for nine years and imposed rationing on it, firmly and for a long time . . .'

The Russian public quickly distilled the essence of Ligachev's speech: '*Ty, Boris, ne prav!*' – 'Boris, you are wrong!' This was then neatly parodied, and the phrase 'Yegor, you are wrong' became the motto of the anti-Ligachev campaign. It appeared on banners, walls and leaflets, and was shouted, to much hilarity, from loudhailers at protest rallies for many months.

It looked as if the Nineteenth Party Conference, like the October plenum, had degenerated from a major event into a slanging-match and assault on Boris Yeltsin's character. Ligachev was followed by other speakers, apparently pre-selected, who rubbed more mud in Yeltsin's face. One of them went so far as to blame Yeltsin for the suicide of one of his former subordinates, who had thrown himself out of a window, 'after an undeserved dressing-down for the poor food supplies in his district'. It was an hour or so before the session got back to the agenda – examining the Conference resolutions – and things dragged on for so long that a promise to broadcast Gorbachev's closing speech live was dropped, evidently just forgotten in the chaos.

But the chaos may have helped Gorbachev to commit delegates – virtually by sleight of hand, in the last minutes of the Conference – to a strict, and speedy, timetable for the implementation of the reforms. Ivan Laptev, then editor of *Izvestiya*, believes Gorbachev's 'conjuror's trick' was the most important event of the four-day Conference: 'We are used to being presented with excellent speeches, but have no mechanism to make sure that proposals get implemented with any sense of urgency.' Gorbachev clearly realised there was a danger that the Conference could end, having adopted most of his sweeping reforms, and that the delegates would then go home and try to forget about them. He had already warned them that the decisions taken at the Conference must not suffer the same fate as those of the January 1987 plenum, which the conservatives had sabotaged. Yet, until this point, no one had mentioned any timescale for the latest reforms. They could have stretched out over years.

Suddenly, at the end of his closing speech, Gorbachev reached into his jacket pocket and pulled out a slip of paper, on which he had scribbled one more resolution. 'Nobody knew about it beforehand,' says Laptev.

The official minutes of the Conference have Gorbachev saying at this point: 'On the instructions of the presidium let me propose the draft of one more resolution.' In fact, the presidium appears to have had nothing to do with it; Gorbachev actually said, as he fumbled in his pocket, 'I promised a resolution . . . let me find it now . . . it's a, so to speak, er, this document was drawn up very quickly, so it may be criticised, but I think it's essentially correct: "On certain urgent measures for the practical implementation of the reform of the country's political system".' Laptev says Gorbachev looked nervous: 'You could see that he felt some doubts about whether he could pull it off.'

When Gorbachev read the text of his document, it took everyone aback. It said that the necessary amendments to the Constitution should be passed at the next session of parliament [in the autumn], that a general election should be held – on the new principles – the following spring, and that the new-style parliament should be functioning by April 1989. Local and republican elections to new democratic parliaments should follow in the autumn of 1989. The Party apparatus, meanwhile, should be reorganised and cut in size by the end of the current year.

Again, the official record cheats: it pretends that Ligachev then put the resolution to the vote. In fact, Gorbachev concluded, 'That's what I've said . . . [confirming that *he* wrote the text] Are there any objections? Allow me to put it to the vote.'[13]

The delegates raised their hands unanimously in favour. Ten seconds later, before they could even digest what Gorbachev had read out, they were all standing to sing the 'Internationale', and the Nineteenth Party Conference was over. Laptev heard some Party workers asking each other afterwards: 'What have we done?'

Many of them, it would turn out, had signed their own political death-warrants; for Gorbachev brooked no delay. From now on, having gained his Party's approval to give up much of its power, he pushed through the necessary legislation with the steady hand of an undertaker hammering nails into a coffin.

GORBACHEV's revolution from above was accompanied by a steadily rising tide of independent political activity. A new word had gained currency during the latter half of 1987: *neformaly*, or 'informal' [i.e. unofficial], organisations. The concept covered a multitude of associations, from political discussion clubs to ecological, cultural, conservationist or sports groups, their only common feature being their independence of the Communist Party. They were the first cells of a developing civil society – a society in which the Party would no longer control every sphere of life, including all other organisations. The *neformaly* had developed spontaneously in the new atmosphere of *glasnost*, and in many directions. Some of the earliest were small groups of enthusiasts who got together to restore ancient buildings, especially churches, or other neglected historical sites. In Leningrad a group known as *Spasenie* ('Salvation') campaigned to save the Hotel Angleterre, where the poet Yesenin had committed suicide, from demolition. In Moscow various groups could be seen at weekends carefully sorting through rubble in churches, rebuilding walls and restoring frescoes.

One of the oldest groups, *Pamyat* ('Memory'), took its campaign for the protection of Russia's cultural heritage to ugly extremes, espousing nationalistic and anti-Semitic slogans and blaming the destruction of Russia's environment and architecture on a conspiracy of Zionists and freemasons. The organisation grew rapidly, setting up groups all over Russia and holding rallies, addressed by black-shirted leaders, in factories and parks. The apartment of one of its leaders, Dmitry Vasilyev, smelt of incense, like an Orthodox church, and was decorated with his own photographs of churches and the movement's logo – a bell and the words 'Patriotic Association, Memory'. The organisation became a menace to all Western-oriented, liberal or Jewish organisations. While Vasilyev made speeches citing the 'Protocols of the Elders of Zion' (an anti-Semitic forgery), Pamyat thugs smashed up art exhibitions and co-operative restaurants, and created an atmosphere which probably contributed to the increasing rate of Jewish emigration.

Hundreds of small political groups sprang up, representing the entire spectrum of thought, though mainly sympathetic to Gorbachev and urging a more radical version of *perestroika*. Some, like Club Perestroika, which held twice-weekly seminars with guest speakers at one of Moscow's economic institutes, aimed primarily to encourage free discussion. Others, like the Club for Social Initiatives, were embryonic political parties. One of its leaders, Boris Kagarlitsky, had been expelled from the Communist Party and imprisoned under Brezhnev for his Euro-communist tendencies. As his club became known, he would receive Western journalists at his place of work – a tiny cubby-hole beside the lift shaft of a block of flats, where he was employed as an attendant. He spent most of his time there writing political pamphlets or on the telephone to fellow activists in other cubby-holes around Moscow. It was a scene repeated all over the country, and all over Eastern Europe, where future government ministers held body and soul together by working as janitors, stokers and porters.

A major milestone in the growth of the *neformaly* was a conference held in August 1987 by about 600 representatives of some fifty left-wing groups from all over the country, including the Club for Social Initiatives. They formed a new umbrella group, the Federation of Socialist Clubs, which broadly supported *perestroika*. Unlike the old generation of dissidents who had recently emerged from the camps, these groups tended to look not to the West for inspiration but to a 'third way' of humane socialism, with workers' self-management and 'socialist ownership', rather than unfettered capitalism. Significantly, they were provided a hall in Moscow by the city Party committee, then led by Boris Yeltsin, and the Novosti press agency helped to publicise their activities. Several of the clubs involved were to become active in the campaign to rehabilitate Yeltsin.

It is clear from Gorbachev's speeches that he approved of the emergence of such clubs. But it became less easy for him to justify them to his Politburo colleagues when overtly anti-communist groups began to organise themselves, including, in May 1988, the Democratic Union, the first to call itself an opposition party, rather than an 'informal organisation'. Its members held regular unsanctioned demonstrations, which were invariably broken up by police, but aroused increasing curiosity among the public.

Another example of successful grass-roots activity was a movement known as Memorial, which campaigned for a monument and research centre in memory of the millions of victims of Stalinism. It stood out from the thousands of other informal organisations because it was supported by dozens of well-known scientific and cultural figures, including Andrei Sakharov, dissident historian Roy Medvedev, writers Yevgeny Yevtushenko, Andrei Voznesensky and Anatoly Rybakov, and many others. On the first day of the Nineteenth Party Conference, the film-maker Elem Klimov and historian Yuri Afanasyev carried a petition containing 40 000 signatures into the Palace of Congresses; and in his closing speech Gorbachev supported the idea of building a memorial in Moscow to the 'victims of lawlessness'. In October 1988 Memorial's leaders held a preparatory conference in the Cinema House in Moscow. In November it organised a 'Week of Conscience' in the house of culture of the Moscow Electric Light Factory, at which survivors of the camps displayed mementoes of the Terror in a hall dominated by a huge wall-map of the Gulag Archipelago, the network of labour camps that covered the country. Finally, in January 1989, Memorial was officially founded at a national conference in Moscow. It became a powerful pressure group, not only collecting money for a monument, museum and archive, but steadily uncovering new mass graves from the Stalin years. At Kuropaty in Belorussia, for example, where at least 30 000 people were killed but not a single document existed to prove the crime, Memorial began a successful search – both for the graves and the documents.

ON the fringes of the Soviet Union, in the non-Russian republics, the informal associations took on a nationalist slant, since whatever their original concerns – conservation, the past, the environment, culture or local politics – they were bound sooner or later to touch upon the greater issue of the republics' relations with Moscow. This was especially so in the three Baltic republics, Estonia, Latvia and Lithuania, which had been part of the Soviet Union only since the Second World War. Here, some of the first *neformaly* were Green groups, concerned by the pollution of their air and rivers and the Baltic Sea.

In the summer of 1988 I attended a rally in a small Latvian town, Sigulda, organised by the Club for the Protection of the Environment. At first, speakers criticised the factories which had poisoned the fish in the local river. There were jars of murky river water on display to prove the point. But it soon became clear that the endangered species the demonstrators were most concerned about were the Latvian people themselves, who barely make up half of the republic's population, thanks to massive Russian immigration since the War. The banned red-white-red flag of pre-war Latvia was showing, and the most passionate speeches condemned Stalin's mass deportations of Latvians and demanded that Lettish be made the republic's official language. Two petitions circulated – one demanding the return of the national flag, the other protesting against plans for a nuclear power station in the republic. It was a highly respectable gathering: one of the strongest speeches was made by the town magistrate. But there was a nervous, tense atmosphere all afternoon, which I first attributed to fears that the meeting might be broken up by police. Then I realised it was due to the fact that these thousand good burghers of Sigulda were all suppressing their innermost desire: not to clean up the river, nor to get their flag back or extract an apology for the deportations, but to regain the statehood they had enjoyed between the wars – in a word, to get rid of the Russians and their alien, Soviet, government. What appeared to me as tension was in fact a powerful invisible bond which every Latvian present felt. When they broke into an old Lettish folk song, they were making a political statement about the colonial status of Latvia.

In scenes like that throughout the summer months of 1988, national self-awareness suddenly flowered in all three Baltic republics. Their situations were superficially different. Ethnic Lithuanians comprised 80 per cent of their republic's 3.6 million inhabitants; Estonians 60 per cent of Estonia's 1.5 million; and Letts only just under half of Latvia's 2.6 million (while they accounted for only one-third of the population of the capital, Riga). Lithuanians are Roman Catholic, and their capital, Vilnius, looks like a Polish town, while Letts and Estonians are Protestant, and their capitals, Riga and Tallinn, are more Germanic in appearance. But the visitor instantly recognises that all three belong to central Europe, with its coffee shops, cream cakes and ladies wearing hats and twin-sets, not to Russia, with its vodka, bread and peasant women's kerchiefs.

Their common fate brought them closer. All three nations had been part of the Tsarist empire, and gained independence when Lenin signed peace treaties with them in 1920. They enjoyed parliamentary democracies, though with increasingly authoritarian governments, until 1939, when Hitler and Stalin carved up eastern Europe between them. Under the terms of secret protocols to the Molotov–Ribbentrop Pact (whose existence Moscow denied until 1989), the three Baltic republics were assigned to the Soviet sphere of influence, and the Red Army was able to invade them in the summer of 1940. Rigged elections were held and pro-Soviet parliaments elected which voted for incorporation into the USSR. After that, Sovietisation was swift. In a matter of months the 'bourgeois' system was abolished and replaced by Soviet systems of government, education, culture and economy. During the night of 14–15 June 1941, some 130 000 Balts – farmers, intellectuals, priests and anyone suspected of even the remotest connection with the old regime – were deported to Siberian labour camps. Shortly thereafter the Baltic states found themselves under Nazi occupation, and when the Red Army drove the Germans out again in 1944 the Soviet authorities resumed their pre-war policies with redoubled enthusiasm. In 1948–9 wholesale collectivisation of agriculture led to another huge wave of deportations. The brutal policies scarred the national consciousness for ever. The three tiny nations looked with envy to Finland, which had shared their history until the War, but managed to escape Stalin's grasp afterwards, becoming a prosperous, developed, non-aligned capitalist country – precisely the kind of state most people in the Baltic republics wanted.

Moscow used the republics, with their sophisticated and industrious people and ready-made infrastructure, as a site for badly planned economic projects. This had a catastophic effect on the area's environment, culture, languages and demographic situation. Natural resources were ruthlessly exploited, with no heed to environmental damage. Factories were built, and Russian migrant workers brought in to man them. Few of them bothered to learn the local language; most were unskilled workers with no interest in culture, whether Baltic or Russian. The Balts began to feel swamped.

It was the Estonians who led the Baltic revival at first. As early as September 1987 four economists put forward the first comprehensive plans for economic self-sufficiency and autonomy from Moscow. The aim, according to one of them, Tiit Made, was to realise 'Lenin's idea of the Soviet federation', whereby Moscow would control only defence and foreign policy, while all economic decision-making would be in the hands of the republics. Under the existing system, no less than 91 per cent of Estonian industrial production was determined by Moscow, through all-Union ministries. Under the four economists' plan, the entire economy would be transferred to republican control: the Estonian Council of Ministers would run its own budget and finances, eventually introducing its own convertible currency, with which it would trade freely both with other Soviet republics and with the West. Estonia's model would be Denmark or Holland: it would be an exporter of foodstuffs, textiles and chemicals; and the economy, freed from central planning and the Party-dominated bureaucracy imposed by Moscow, would be run on free-market – or 'market socialist' – lines. The economists expected the West's share in Estonia's trade gradually to increase, but presumed the continuation of the Soviet Union as Estonia's major trade partner (supplying oil, gas, steel and so on). The point was that the other Soviet republics should become equal partners in trade rather than colonial outposts ruled by diktat from Moscow. The plan became known by its Estonian initials – IME – standing for 'Self-Accounting Estonia'. *Ime* is also Estonian for 'miracle'.

In the spring of 1988 the strands of Estonian national sentiment – economic, anti-Russian, ecological – began to coalesce into a political movement. In April the so-called 'creative unions' (that is, the unions of writers, artists and composers) held a joint conference in Tallinn at which they worked out the first comprehensive blueprint for Estonian sovereignty. Their plan won support from virtually the entire Estonian population – and put the non-Estonians on guard, causing a rift in the republic. It became the foundation stone for the establishment of the Soviet Union's first 'popular front' – a grass-roots movement, combining radical Party members and non-Party liberals, dedicated to thorough reform of the political and economic system, to the eradication of all traces of Stalinism, and to the establishment of a new, decentralised system of federal government in the Soviet Union. All these goals coincided, as general concepts, with Gorbachev's, but the details went well beyond his present plans – and, more worryingly, were driven not by a dedication to Soviet rule but by national ambitions.

The Estonian Communist Party was caught on the hop. It opposed virtually every plank of the Popular Front's programme. But in a clear sign that Gorbachev saw the developments on the whole as positive, he recalled the Estonian-born ambassador to Nicaragua, Vaino Väljas, and installed him as Party leader in Tallinn, replacing the Brezhnevite Karl Vaino. Väljas's first move was to decree that discussions in the central committee should be held in Estonian, not Russian.

A remarkable situation came about, described by an Estonian official as 'dual power'. The local Communist Party was forced to make one concession after another, gradually giving up firmly held positions in favour of demands put forward by the Popular Front. The Party, it seemed, could no longer rule without the Front's approval.

Exactly the same thing happened in the other Baltic republics. In October Gorbachev replaced both Latvia's and Lithuania's communist leaders with more radical figures just before the founding congresses of the popular fronts there. Arvidas Juozaitis, a founding member of *Sajudis* ('Movement'), as the Lithuanian popular front was known, says its first congress, in October 1988, was a 'real revolution', broadcast live to the nation. 'It was a psychological high point,' says Juozaitis. 'After that, everyone understood that Lithuania was moving towards independence.' Everyone, except Gorbachev. He sent warm greetings to *Sajudis*, describing it as a 'positive force which can serve *perestroika* and strengthen the Soviet Union'. He appears to have had little understanding of what was really going on in the Baltic republics.

By contrast, he understood all too well the consequences of the ethnic feuding between Armenia and Azerbaijan over Nagorny Karabakh, which had grown steadily more bitter since it flared up in February 1988. By the summer, billions of roubles of production had been lost due to a general strike in the disputed territory itself, constant stoppages in Armenia, and the knock-on effect on industries all over the Soviet Union. Gorbachev's apparent sympathy for the Armenian cause at the outset soon evaporated, probably as he came to understand the awesome consequences for the country's unity if the Armenians were to set a precedent for the redrawing of internal frontiers: there were several other small nations unhappy with their present territories or status. Soviet Germans, Meskhetian Turks and Crimean Tatars had all been deported en masse from their homelands after the War, and all were now clamouring to be allowed to return. Yet to satisfy them would mean carving out a new homeland from someone else's territory. Abkhazians wanted autonomy from Georgia. Uzbeks and Tajiks made claims to each other's territory. Indeed, this Pandora's Box was so full that Gorbachev decided not even to open it.

He was receiving conflicting advice from his colleagues, but appears to have heeded Ligachev, who emphatically ruled out the redrawing of national frontiers in May, when he was despatched to Baku to oversee the sacking of the old Azerbaijani Party leader. On the same day, Alexander Yakovlev was in Yerevan to install a new Armenian Party boss. He gave a different message, from which the Armenians drew some comfort.

The changing of local leaders made little difference, because power, especially in Armenia, had all but slipped out of the Party's hands anyway. The Karabakh Committee, a group of respected Armenian leaders who had led the campaign for the reintegration of Nagorny Karabakh, was banned in March, but continued to operate, virtually supplanting the Communist Party in many enterprises. Its equivalent in Nagorny Karabakh itself, the 'Krunk' committee, was officially admitted by July to be more powerful and influential than the Party, the Komsomol or any other organisation.[14]

It was under the immense pressure of these popular organisations that the Armenian Supreme Soviet sparked a constitutional crisis by voting in June to accept Nagorny Karabakh's request to join Armenia. The Azerbaijani parliament naturally denounced the move, and it was left to the presidium of the Supreme Soviet in Moscow – the country's top legislative body – to sort out the dispute.

Here, something extraordinary happened. At the presidium's

special session on 18 July, large portions of which were later televised, Gorbachev revealed a side of his character which few had seen before. Viewers were astounded to see him lecturing, hectoring and interruping senior colleagues. He would invite experts to give their advice, then confound them by having more facts and figures at his fingertips than they did, and publicly humiliated them if he disagreed. Most disturbingly, Gorbachev sided unashamedly with the Azerbaijanis, reserving his whiplash entirely for the Armenians. It was clear that Gorbachev had gone into the meeting with his mind made up that Nagorny Karabakh must remain in Azerbaijan, and then simply bulldozed his way, with angry, impatient and often illogical interventions, to the desired conclusion – the 'unanimous' adoption of a resolution ruling out change.[15]

His authoritarian, almost boorish performance – particularly his nastiness towards respected Armenian intellectuals – dismayed many of his supporters. In just two-and-a-half hours, the time it took to broadcast the edited highlights from the presidium, he forfeited much of his hard-won support among the intelligentsia. It was a public relations disaster – the talk of the institutes and artistic clubs the next day. Many of his admirers shook their heads and said: 'I didn't like the look of that.' Once again, Gorbachev had fallen foul of a local ethnic problem.

GORBACHEV could scarcely afford to lose the support of the intelligentsia, for they were the mainstay of *perestroika*.

Stalin had tried his best to wipe out the intelligentsia. Following his perverted 'proletarian' logic, film-makers at the time sometimes portrayed, alongside muscular dam-builders and steel smelters, a puny, bespectacled figure of fun – the *intelligent* (pronounced with a hard 'g' and the emphasis on the final syllable). The post-revolutionary emigration of the aristocracy, the civil war, Stalin's Terror and another wave of emigration after the War, left the country bereft of its best thinkers. There was no place for doubters like Pasternak's Doctor Zhivago in Stalin's, Khrushchev's or Brezhnev's Russia. The prejudice against brains had a long and deep effect.

To this day 'workers' have a double standard. On the one hand the intolerance which 'proletarian ideology' had encouraged remains strong. On the other, workers almost expect the intelligentsia to do their thinking for them. I remember hearing an Armenian worker speaking on television about the working class's attitude to the conflict with Azerbaijan: 'Our intelligentsia explained the situation to us,' he said, 'and things calmed down a bit.' Little has changed since the nineteenth century, when Vissarion Belinsky, the 'father of the Russian intelligentsia', wrote that the Russian public saw writers as 'their only leaders, protectors and saviours'.

The term 'intelligentsia' itself requires some explanation, for it is purely Russian. It certainly does not just mean 'intellectuals' in the British sense, and it is not merely a question of having a university education. I once asked some leading intellectuals to give their definitions.

Vitaly Korotich, editor of the magazine *Ogonyok*, said an *intelligent* was 'someone capable of thinking independently'. Nikolai Shmelyov, one of the most independent of Soviet economists, said it was a person of culture, who thinks first of others – 'what used to be known as a "decent chap".'

Yegor Yakovlev, editor of the radical newspaper, *Moscow News*, said it was a moral and social term, and that the recognition of the intellectual today showed that Soviet society had moved along the path from conformity of thought to pluralism, from intolerance to mutual understanding. 'The first criterion that marks out an *intelligent* is his determination to make the world around him a better place.'

The term has been almost synonymous with 'liberal' or 'progressive' ever since the 1850s, when it was coined. Under the repressive rule of Tsar Nicholas I, intellectuals who could find no application in society for their talents came to be known as 'superfluous people.' Under Brezhnev, the historian Natan Eidelman said, a new class of superfluous people, or 'internal émigrés' appeared. Andrei Sakharov was one of them.

Eidelman defined the intelligentsia as the active section of society, which sets the tone for the consciousness of the nation. 'Even Khrushchev, who relied on the intelligentsia, had a strong anti-intelligentsia complex,' said Eidelman. While previous leaders all underestimated its role, 'Gorbachev and the other leaders of the Party are actively involving the intelligentsia.'

It was journalists, writers, essayists and poets who more than any others pushed *perestroika* forward. The congresses of the Baltic popular front movements were full of men wearing beards and corduroy trousers, and smoking pipes – the modern equivalent of Stalin's wire-framed glasses. The flourishing political clubs were largely the domain of the intelligentsia. In the Party leadership too, brainpower began to replace lathe-turning experience as the main qualification. Gorbachev, with his law degree from Moscow University and later diploma in agronomy, was the best educated leader the Soviet Union had had since Lenin.

AS Gorbachev's popularity began to wane, however, most intellectuals looked to Alexander Yakovlev as their best hope within the Party leadership. Bald and owlish, he looked and spoke like an *intelligent*, although he was the son of peasants. He was born in 1923, in the province of Yaroslavl, north of Moscow, and was seriously wounded at the front during the War. He graduated from the Yaroslavl teachers training college in 1946 and then went in for full-time Party work. In the late fifties, during which he spent some months as an exchange student at New York's Columbia University, he wrote a doctorate at the Party's Academy of Social Sciences.

His outward charm and modesty conceal a tough political infighter. After Stalin's death he was brought into the central committee apparatus, where he climbed to become deputy head, and for four years acting head, of the propaganda department. Yakovlev clashed regularly with his overlords in the central committee Secretariat. One of his first acts of defiance was in 1966, when the writer Andrei Sinyavsky and the translator Yuli Daniel became the first dissidents to be put on trial in the Brezhnev period. Yakovlev was asked by Mikhail Suslov, the chief ideologist, to take care of the 'propaganda side' of the trial. Yakovlev refused – tactfully saying it was the culture department's job, not his. The Brezhnev leadership, he recalls, 'treated me with the utmost distrust', and left him in limbo, refusing to appoint him head of the department he was running.

It was then that he first came into contact with Gorbachev, at that time Party first secretary in Stavropol. Yakovlev recommended Gorbachev, among others, for the vacant post of propaganda department chief, but Gorbachev was against the idea – rightly, Yakovlev now realises, 'because in this totalitarian system where one set of ideas exists, whoever is in charge of ideology gets crushed whenever there is a change of power.'

In the early seventies his distaste for the kind of Russian nationalism and neo-Slavophilism sponsored by Suslov landed him in more trouble. In a 10 000-word article entitled 'Against Anti-Historicism', he called on authors to stop idealising the 'stagnating daily life' of the Russian village. As a punishment, he was sent to run the Soviet embassy in Canada in 1973. He remained there until Gorbachev met him again on his visit to Canada in 1983, and within a month brought him back to Moscow to head the prestigious Institute of World Economy and International Relations. His influence as the principal architect of *glasnost* has already been described.

Yakovlev was clearly influenced by his exposure to Western ideas and achievements at Columbia University and in Canada. This did not prevent him from being a stern critic of American foreign policy, however, especially during the Reagan presidency. His influence on Gorbachev's foreign policy has been great: it was principally Yakovlev who provided the theory of 'new thinking', while Eduard Shevardnadze, the foreign minister, turned it into reality. In 1985 he described international politics as 'multi-polar', meaning that new centres of power, such as Western Europe and Japan, were dislodging the two superpowers from their previous dominating positions. This

111

was reflected in Gorbachev's decision to appoint Shevardnadze in place of Andrei Gromyko, who had become preoccupied with the US–Soviet relationship. Yakovlev's views on the development of capitalism and socialism were significant. His concept was subtler than that of the convergence of the two systems: individual countries, whether capitalist or socialist, could learn from each other and extract anything useful from either system. When Gorbachev started talking about a 'common European home', it was precisely this that he had in mind: a home not divided into two antagonistic political and military blocs, but consisting of numerous individual, non-aligned states, co-existing and collaborating regardless of their varied internal systems. The people of Eastern Europe, who were allowed to overthrow their communist rulers in 1989, have much to thank Yakovlev for.

THE new ideology of Soviet foreign policy – multi-polar and putting universal human values (especially the preservation of mankind from the nuclear threat) before class interests and support for 'proletarian' liberation movements – was explained to 1000 diplomats at a major conference in the foreign ministry in July 1988.

Less than a month later, in a speech in the city of Gorky, Yegor Ligachev publicly challenged the new ideology. He insisted that 'international relations are of a class nature' and claimed that to say otherwise would 'sow confusion in the minds of our people and our friends abroad.' Worse, he invoked Lenin on the subject of Party unity – 'Following a decision by competent bodies, all we Party members act as one person' – in order to give his words the appearance of being agreed policy. 'I do not think we can go on endlessly returning to things on which we have already reached agreement and which have become directives of the Party,' he added.

In the same speech, also supposedly speaking in the name of the Party, Ligachev attacked the market economy too. The Western model, based on private property and the labour market with its 'ruthless laws and chronic unemployment', was, he said, 'fundamentally unacceptable for the socialist system'.[16]

These statements were very damaging. With Gorbachev on holiday, Alexander Yakovlev had to put the record straight on both matters.[17] But his words did not have the weight of Ligachev's. Ligachev was still deputy leader. His position as the Party's number two, in charge of the central committee Secretariat, was undiminished despite the Nina Andreyeva setback, and the Party Conference had demonstrated his popularity with the *apparat*. He continued to use his authority during Gorbachev's absence to cool the climate of freedom and public involvement that Gorbachev had carefully nurtured before and during the Party Conference. In August people in Moscow watched the newly formed riot squads going into action against peaceful demonstrators, read press attacks on liberal causes, and were incensed by restrictions that were imposed on subscriptions to the most popular and radical newspapers. A phrase I heard regularly in Moscow that month was: 'The frosts have come back.'

During his holiday Gorbachev devised an ingenious way to deprive Ligachev of his influence. On 24 August he sent a memorandum to the Politburo from his holiday retreat in which he outlined his views on how the Party apparatus should be restructured.[18] In effect, he simply destroyed Ligachev's power base. Instead of twenty well-staffed central committee departments, subordinate to Ligachev's Secretariat, Gorbachev proposed that there should be only nine, and that the staff of the central committee should be drastically cut from its current size of 1940 officials and 1275 secretarial and technical staff. He also spoke of setting up new 'commissions' on the main policy areas, without elaborating.

The point was not primarily to undermine Ligachev, of course. The restructuring – which the Party Conference had agreed to in principle – was meant to deal a blow to the Party's ability to interfere in the economy by abolishing all the industrial departments which had duplicated and supervised government ministries. Gorbachev said that only three industrial departments would remain to deal with the economy, defence industries and agriculture. These must restrict themselves to fundamental questions and 'in no case indulge in tutelage or petty interference in the practical work of state organs.' As a sweetener Gorbachev recommended that there should be a pay increase for those functionaries who remained, and a later instruction ensured that those being made redundant would keep their previous salaries and privileges in their new jobs.[19] The Politburo accepted Gorbachev's outline on 8 September, and gave him a free hand to make further 'concrete proposals' – meaning, in particular, the naming of a new 'cabinet'.

Ligachev's breach of Party discipline was obviously still rankling with Gorbachev when he made a trip to Siberia the following week. As he emerged from the Lenin Museum in the town of Shushenskoye he seized on a question put to him by a television reporter to launch into a defence of the 'priority of universal human values' over class interests – even though the reporter's question had been about something quite different.

His five-day Siberian tour brought him face to face with a level of public discontent he had not encountered before. In the city of Krasnoyarsk his traditional pavement chats with 'the working people' turned into an embarrassing display of public anger, widely shown on television. He was met with a barrage of complaints – about empty shops, the lack of heating, warm clothes, children's shoes and meat, pollution, profiteering co-operatives, leaky roofs – while the bosses had none of these problems. When he was shown round a 'typical' shop, voices could be heard in the background saying that it was all a show, that the shop was better stocked than ever before.

He could do nothing but accept the criticisms, and in turn fling many of them at his hosts in the local leadership, who squirmed with embarrassment in front of the television cameras. Gorbachev saw it as another opportunity to impress upon people that it was up to them to make use of the opportunities afforded them by *perestroika*. He censured them for appealing to him as if he was some great tsar who could sort out their petty problems: 'You should give your leaders a good shake-up!' he said. That brought another torrent of complaints: 'It's useless! Just look at the brand-new houses here, Mikhail Sergeyevich, it's impossible to live in them. Within a month there are huge cracks in the floor, and the doors don't shut. It's dreadful, leaks everywhere – when it rains you get water all over the flat – and that's not the end of the story . . .'[20]

Gorbachev was shaken by the experience. He saw that people had simply lost faith in *perestroika* – though they were prepared to use the new freedoms to challenge and contradict him as never before. He decided to act quickly to halt the demoralisation. In a speech to newsmen on his return to Moscow, he praised the new activity of ordinary people, but admitted that this alone was not enough to bring about the necessary changes, and observed cryptically that 'old and new methods' would have to co-exist in this transitional period: 'We can see that some problems cannot be solved now unless you intervene in the old way, as before. What can you do? That's real life!'

What he meant, though none of his audience guessed it, was that he was about to execute a carefully planned coup against his opponents in the leadership – using good old-fashioned dictatorial methods.

At two perfunctory and unscheduled meetings – a central committee plenum lasting one hour on 30 September, and a session of the Supreme Soviet lasting 45 minutes the following day – he abolished the Secretariat, demoted Ligachev, removed five senior politicians of the Old Guard, including President Andrei Gromyko, and installed himself as head of state.

Gorbachev had kept his cards well hidden while planning all this. At his meeting with journalists, just a week before, he had referred to two forthcoming plenums which would implement the decisions of the Nineteenth Party Conference on agriculture and ethnic relations, but said not a word about the one he was about to spring on his colleagues – even though it was concerned with the very cornerstone of the Party Conference's reform package. He called the meetings at such short notice that the foreign minister, Eduard Shevardnadze, suddenly had to cancel engagements in New York to return for them.

It is believed that Ligachev was on holiday in the week before the plenum, and played no part in its planning.

There was no discussion at either meeting, just brief nomination speeches, Gromyko's resignation speech (in which he pledged his continuing support for *perestroika*), and unanimous votes, by show of hands, to pass every motion put by Gorbachev. Apart from Gromyko, those who were removed from power were: Mikhail Solomentsev, Politburo member and head of the Party Control Committee, whom Yeltsin had accused at the Party Conference of protecting bribe-takers; Vladimir Dolgikh, candidate member of the Politburo in charge of heavy industry; Pyotr Demichev, an old Brezhnevite Politburo member whom Gorbachev had earlier removed from positions of real influence by appointing him to the ceremonial post of deputy head of state; and Anatoly Dobrynin, the long-serving ambassador to the US, whom Gorbachev had brought back to Moscow as central committee secretary in charge of foreign affairs.

But even more important than the resignations was Gorbachev's announcement about the new central committee commissions, which he had only mentioned in passing in his earlier note to the Politburo. It became clear that the commissions, each headed by a Politburo member, were intended to replace the old Secretariat. This was a blow to Ligachev, who as number two, in charge of the Secretariat, had controlled the entire central committee apparatus with its twenty departments – which in turn continued to lord it over the ministries. The six new commissions would be served by just one department each, and would be purely concerned with drawing up policies. Most importantly, they would be directly answerable to the Politburo and Gorbachev, not to a 'second secretary'; that powerful position, the source of Ligachev's power, ceased to exist.

The allocation of portfolios struck a further blow to Ligachev. To his dismay, he was removed from ideology and put in charge of the agriculture commission. Two things made matters even worse. First, Gorbachev had indicated in his note to the Politburo that he saw the existence of an agriculture department, separate from the economy as a whole, as a temporary measure. Secondly, Ligachev was not even trusted to handle this area alone: another full Politburo member (and agricultural specialist), Viktor Nikonov, was made his deputy.

Ligachev admits that from this point he ceased to feel 'comfortable' in the leadership: 'In the first three years of *perestroika*, when I ran the Secretariat, I felt wonderful, my heart was singing every morning as I went to the office,' he says. As for the creation of commissions to replace the Secretariat, he says: 'Why did comrade Gorbachev do that? I don't know. I think it was a great mistake. I think Mikhail Sergeyevich made the wrong decision there. It was not discussed at the Politburo.'

Gorbachev felt obliged to remove Yakovlev from ideology as well as Ligachev, though Yakovlev's new job, in charge of foreign policy, was closer to ideology than Ligachev's farming portfolio. Ideology went to a new man with centrist views, Vadim Medvedev. Two other appointments were predictable: Georgy Razumovsky was put at the head of the commission for party development and personnel (overseeing appointments, as he had done before), and the uninspiring Nikolai Slyunkov retained the economics portfolio.

Why Gorbachev chose former KGB chief Viktor Chebrikov to run the sixth commission – on legal policy, overseeing the establishment of a law-based state – is a puzzle. It was seen by some as a case of putting the fox in charge of the chickens – and indeed Gorbachev would soon regret it. It may be that Gorbachev intended Anatoly Lukyanov, his old friend from law school, to be the main architect of future laws. Lukyanov was elected at the next day's Supreme Soviet session as the new deputy head of state, working directly under Gorbachev himself. If this was Gorbachev's reasoning, he underestimated the continuing desire of Party officials such as Chebrikov to interfere directly in government business, even though this was precisely what he wanted to stop by restructuring the apparatus and creating the six commissions.

An immediate effect of this major reshuffle was that one of *perestroika*'s earliest policies, the disastrous drive against alcoholism, was finally dropped. This was a victory above all for the prime minister, Nikolai Ryzhkov, who had always opposed the extreme forms which the campaign had taken. He recalls how, towards the end of 1988, he finally 'exploded' at a Politburo meeting. 'I couldn't restrain myself. I got up and demanded: "How much longer are we going to continue like this?" ' He presented his colleagues with statistics which showed just how close the zealots had come to imposing prohibition on the country. Even in the first six months of the campaign in 1985 (before additional orders were given to step it up) the number of shops selling alcohol throughout the country had been more than halved, and in one republic, Kirghizia, cut by 90 per cent. In Astrakhan province only 5 liquor stores remained out of 118, and in Gorbachev's home province of Stavropol only 49 – for 2.5 million people. Certain regions had banned the sale of alcohol altogether. Sales of sugar (and other sweet products used in home-distilling) had risen by 18 per cent, and led to rationing almost everywhere. It was calculated that the quantity of moonshine alcohol being produced practically made up for the shortfall in official sales, and the number of prosecutions for home-distilling had risen thirteenfold over two years. The exchequer had suffered a huge drop in tax revenue. Sales of alcohol substitutes – perfumes, toothpaste, glue, window-cleaner and shoe-cream – had soared, and their use had caused 44 000 cases of poisoning in 1987, 11 000 of them fatal. In two years the number of registered drug-addicts had risen from 9000 to 20 000. Ryzhkov says be concluded his outburst by threatening to give the order unilaterally to cancel the campaign, whatever his colleagues said. They agreed to permit the sale of dry wines, champagne, cognac and beer in food shops again, in order to cut the size of the queues. That was in September. But it was not until mid-October, after the sacking of Solomentsev and the demotion of Ligachev, the campaign's chief supporters, that the Politburo finally agreed to abandon the campaign.[21]

It did so on a day when Ligachev was on leave. It was a remarkable time for the new agriculture secretary to be away, for on the same day (12 October) there was a major conference on farming in the central committee, addressed by Gorbachev and attended by several other senior Politburo members. Ligachev's absence seemed to confirm his unhappiness with his new position.

THE new central committee commissions, it turned out, met very rarely, confirming the suspicion that Gorbachev's main purpose in creating them (apart from undermining Ligachev) may have been to throw the top echelons of the Party into such disarray that they could no longer work effectively. This made it hard for them to interfere in government matters, or to put up any sort of opposition to the constitutional reforms which Gorbachev now had to push through parliament. In reality, the Politburo was the only effective policy-making body left.

Gorbachev was thus able to steamroller his reforms through, at his chosen speed. Drafts of the constitutional amendments and of the new election law were ready for publication on 22 October. There was to be just five weeks' public discussion before they were put to the Supreme Soviet and passed into law. But this was to prove less easy than Gorbachev imagined, for the detail of the draft laws caused an uproar. This time it was not the conservative *apparat* that objected to the erosion of their power, but the liberals, to the constraints being placed on them.

Many radicals complained, in the press and at public rallies, that the reforms were ill-considered, reactionary and about to be rushed into law with undue haste. The main objection was to the allocation of one-third of the seats in the new 2250-member Congress of People's Deputies to communist-dominated 'public organisations'. Many also took exception to the fact that the Congress would have limited rights, its main function being to elect 542 of its own members to form a smaller standing parliament, the Supreme Soviet. This, they felt, would give the *apparat* ample opportunity to ensure that 'their' deputies were in a majority. A further clause, which provided for the rotation of one-fifth of the Supreme–Soviet's members each year, seemed to provide the Congress (which most people expected to be dominated by the conservatives) with a chance to weed out 'troublemakers'. The only fair and democratic system, the radicals protested, was one-person one-vote, with direct elections to a 'normal' parliament.

These objections, though they received considerable publicity, had no effect on the substance of the reforms. Officials claimed that less than one per cent of comments received from the public were negative. But the draft laws precipitated a massive wave of dissent in some of the republics which could not be ignored.

People in the Baltic republics and Georgia, especially, saw the laws as an attempt to rob them of sovereignty – just weeks after Gorbachev had been sending messages of encouragement to the new popular fronts, which were campaigning for greater independence. The fronts alleged that the new Congress and Supreme Soviet had such all-encompassing rights that power would be 'super-centralised' in Moscow, and their own national rights infringed even further. They argued that the new constitution swept away even the pretence of federalism in the Soviet Union in favour of a unitary state. Baltic economists said that plans already approved for regional economic autonomy would be destroyed.

The Kremlin tried to allay such fears by insisting that the amendments represented only a first step to democratisation. Stage two would deal with regional autonomy. But as far as the Balts and Georgians were concerned, this was putting the cart before the horse. By early November two-thirds of the Estonian population had signed a petition against the reforms and disillusion with Gorbachev was growing fast. There was talk, for the first time, of secession as the only solution if parliamentary means failed to prevent the reforms being adopted.

The Politburo held a crisis session, reminded people that there would soon be a special central committee plenum on the nationalities question, and despatched three Politburo members to the Baltic republics to try to calm things. But Viktor Chebrikov, arriving in Tallinn on 11 November, discovered that even the Estonian Party leader, Vaino Väljas, opposed many of the proposals and wanted at least to delay a final decision on them. The following day, 100 000 people demonstrated in Tbilisi, the Georgian capital, protesting against the constitution and demanding independence.

On 16 November the Estonian parliament caused an unprecedented constitutional crisis by passing a declaration of sovereignty and giving itself the right of veto over all Soviet laws. A set of amendments to the Estonian constitution brought it into conflict with the Soviet constitution on several counts. It recognised the right to private property. It declared that the land, air, minerals, forests, natural resources and principal means of production in the republic were the exclusive property of Estonia, rather than of the Soviet people. And it declared the banks and all-Union enterprises to be Estonian property. The right of veto contradicted Article 74 of the Soviet constitution, which stated that in the event of conflict between all-Union and republic laws, the law of the USSR should prevail.

Estonian newspapers rushed the laws into print to ensure that they would come into effect – ten days after publication – before they could be declared null and void by the Supreme Soviet, whose session was scheduled for 29 November.

The Lithuanian parliament limited itself to a symbolic gesture, replacing the Soviet state flag with its own red, green and yellow one. The newly elected Party leader, Algirdas Brazauskas, argued that the 'noble aim of full sovereignty' could not be achieved at once. But huge crowds protested in Vilnius at their government's failure to follow Estonia's lead, and the new Sajudis popular front declared that they had 'treacherously knifed the Estonians in the back'.

The Presidium of the Supreme Soviet met on 26 November to dis-cuss the crisis. At it, a furious Gorbachev assailed the suave, silver-haired Estonian president, Arnold Rüütel, much as he had dealt with the Armenians at a similar session four months earlier. The Presidium predictably declared the Estonian amendments null and void. But their efforts were not without effect. The Presidium conceded that the rights of the republics must be expanded and legal mechanisms cre-ated to guarantee them.

As a result, the draft amendments to the Soviet constitution were modified before being put to the Supreme Soviet at the end of the month. At the session, the most undisciplined in the Supreme Soviet's history, a few Baltic deputies still spoke out – and even voted against – the changes. But with the vast majority of the members of this docile parliament trained always to raise their arms to approve Party deci-sions, Gorbachev had little difficulty in pushing through his historic reform package. On 1 December 1988 the rubber-stamp parliament effectively voted itself out of existence by passing the laws to enable the election of its more democratic successor.

WITH this triumph in his pocket, Gorbachev set off at once to New York, where he made one of his most memorable speeches. In a fifty-five-minute address to the United Nations General Assembly, he spoke about the dawn of democracy at home and the results of 'new thinking' in foreign policy. The link between the domestic and foreign elements of his speech was important. For the first time since he had coined the phrase 'new thinking', Gorbachev felt able to demonstrate what it meant. It had been hard for the West to trust his foreign over-tures so long as the Soviet state maintained its totalitarian structure at home. So although he had important arms initiatives to announce, it was the domestic and ideological rationale behind the changes that Gorbachev was most intent on driving home.

He began by impressing upon his audience that, whatever Ligachev might have been saying to the contrary a few months earlier, the international class struggle no longer determined Soviet foreign policy: relations between states had to be 'de-ideologised', he said, and based on 'common human values, consensus and co-development'. With an eloquence missing from his earlier foreign policy statements he hammered home the point that he wanted to bury the Cold War, and that neither side could progress at the expense of the other. He wanted to talk only about the unity in the world, not the splits. Ideological and other differences between states should not hold them apart, but be used as a source of mutual enrichment. Gorbachev had evidently renounced Marxist dogma about the 'rules' of historical development. He neither regarded antagonism between imperialists and communists as inevitable, nor expected socialism, as the 'higher' state, to emerge victorious from the struggle.

In a crucial passage, scarcely noticed at the time because it belonged to the realm of theory while the speech contained headline-grabbing arms proposals, Gorbachev extolled freedom of choice as a universal principle. As so often, some observers misunderstood him, assuming that he was admonishing the *West* to allow freedom of choice, whereas he was actually expounding the new philosophy on which his own foreign policy was based. The proof of the pudding came less than a year later, when the Kremlin connived at, and in some cases actively encouraged, the dismantling of socialism in Eastern Europe, on the grounds that this was the free choice of the people. Had we all studied Gorbachev's speech more carefully, and believed it, the revolutions of 1989 would have come as little surprise, for he stated unequivocally that freedom of choice meant 'multiformity' within both the capitalist and socialist systems, and that this presupposed 'respect for the views and positions of others, tolerance, readiness to perceive something that is different as not necessarily bad or hostile, and the ability to learn to live side by side while remaining different and not in full agreement with each other.'

He then came to the nub of his argument – that his reforms brought the Soviet Union closer to the standards required of it under the Universal Declaration on Human Rights. He reported that democratisation now encompassed politics, economics, spiritual life and ideology. He raised a few eyebrows by claiming that there were now no political or religious prisoners in the Soviet Union, but went on to announce new legal guarantees against such persecution, as well as a whole series of new laws aimed at ensuring individual rights and paving the way to a 'law-based socialist state'. He painted a picture of a society being humanised – rethinking the death penalty, allowing citizens to emigrate or travel abroad freely, and opening up to the free exchange of information (the jamming of all foreign radio stations had been hurriedly ended just a week before).

As an earnest of his intent, he made several unilateral disarmament gestures which could not easily be dismissed as mere propaganda. Over the next two years the size of the Soviet armed forces would be reduced by 500 000 men, about one-tenth of the total. The Russians would withdraw 5000 tanks (half of the total) from East Germany, Hungary and Czechoslovakia, and another 5000 from the European part of the Soviet Union, as well as 8500 artillery systems and 800 combat aircraft. This was a major step towards redressing the imbalance between the Warsaw Pact and NATO forces in Europe. Acknowledging for the first time that Soviet forces in Europe had hitherto been configured for attack, he said that the removal of the tanks would give the remaining forces an 'unambiguously defensive structure'. Finally, he called for 1989 to be a 'decisive year' in disarmament.[22]

IT WAS a brilliant speech – an end-of-year report full of pluses for his own achievements at home and abroad. But Gorbachev had no time to savour his triumph.

That very morning of 7 December – night-time in New York – a devastating earthquake shook Armenia. First reports reaching Moscow were vague, and Gorbachev was not alerted. At 5 p.m. in Moscow, the prime minister, Nikolai Ryzhkov, received the first eye-witness account from Armenian leaders, who had just returned from the disaster zone to the capital, Yerevan. They described a scene of almost total destruction. Half of the city of Leninakan (population 250 000) had been reduced to rubble, and in the smaller town of Spitak (population 20 000) no building was left standing. Communications were disrupted, roads blocked, bridges destroyed. Half of the area's inhabitants, it seemed, must have perished or be trapped under the rubble.

Ryzhkov, who had already established a Politburo commission and dispatched the health minister, Yevgeny Chazov, to the area, decided to go himself. He urgently tried to telephone Gorbachev, but was told he was at the podium delivering his historic address to the United Nations. Ryzhkov left a message asking Gorbachev to call him back as soon as he had finished. Gliding through the streets of New York in his black limousine to a lunch with President Reagan and Vice President Bush on Governor's Island, Gorbachev returned Ryzhkov's call, and was given the tragic news. He approved Ryzhkov's decision to go to Armenia, but delayed a decision on his own return until more became known.

The rest of Gorbachev's programme in New York – relaxing in Central Park, opening a Russian exhibition and touring the Metropolitan Museum – would have been tactless in the circumstances. The next morning he flew straight back to Moscow, cancelling planned visits to Cuba and Britain. In a sense, it all added to the impression of Gorbachev as one of the world's towering figures – the international statesman one day; the concerned, Tsar-like father of his people the next.

And yet, once again, he misjudged a tense and delicate national situation. Nikolai Ryzhkov recalls: 'I believed that this tragedy should smooth over the national hatred between the Armenians and Azerbaijanis. Even wars stop when there are natural disasters or cataclysms. But unfortunately that did not happen, even during the disaster. I remember the first days when we needed earth-moving equipment. We set up a "green route" on the railways to allow equipment to get through from the Urals, but at 800 kilometres a day it still took four days for the machines to arrive. So we had to use everything that was to hand – in [the neighbouring republics of] Georgia and Azerbaijan. Georgia gave us everything, within the first 24 hours. But when Azerbaijan started sending machines – bulldozers, tractors and so on – they were met at the border by Armenians and told to go away. We had to replace the Azerbaijani train drivers with Russians to get the machines in. The gulf was so wide and deep that the earthquake did not bridge it at all. That surprised me. And however much I tried to persuade people, we could do nothing.'

Gorbachev was also taken aback when he toured the earthquake zone on 10 December. An Armenian journalist, Zori Balayan, was right by the side of Gorbachev and Raisa and says he saw tears in their eyes as they surveyed the tragic scene. Gorbachev approached a young man who was sifting through rubble to find his mother, not knowing whether she was dead or alive. But when Gorbachev tried to comfort him, the man started talking about Karabakh. Gorbachev's expression changed to one of shock and incomprehension.

In the evening, travelling back to Yerevan with Ryzhkov in a bus, Gorbachev spoke emotionally about the devastation he had seen. They saw a big crowd at a crossroads on the capital's main street, and Gorbachev asked the driver to stop the bus. He got out and started speaking to the people: 'Nikolai Ivanovich [Ryzhkov] and I have just been there and seen what a terrible catastrophe it is. Let's think about what we can do . . .' Suddenly someone interrupted him: 'That's all very well, but what about Nagorny Karabakh?' Ryzhkov recalls that Gorbachev was stunned, and snapped back: 'What are you saying? You should forget everything, you've got to help! You should be thinking about how to get the victims out – and you bring up Karabakh!'

As a human being, Gorbachev's consternation was understandable. But as a statesman he ought to have understood the Armenian mood better. Since he had so brusquely rejected the Karabakh cause in July, things had only got worse. A state of emergency had been declared in the disputed region after more violence had broken out, with Armenian houses being set alight in the main Azeri-dominated town of Shusha. Troops were deployed around government buildings in Yerevan, as mass demonstrations and strikes paralysed the republic. In November two members of the Karabakh committee were elected to parliament in a by-election: they were not allowed to be on the ballot papers, but a huge majority of voters scored out the official candidate and wrote in their names. Ethnic rioting in the Azerbaijani city of Kirovabad left six more Armenians dead. Night curfews were imposed in Baku and other Azerbaijani cities – and also in Yerevan, though there had been no violence there. During November 100 000 refugees fled their homes in the two republics; many Armenian refugees were temporarily housed in Leninakan and Spitak when the earthquake struck. No wonder the majority of Armenians saw the devastation as some inexplicable act of God, somehow linked to the attempted genocide of their nation which began with the Turkish massacre of 1915. Arkady Volsky, the central committee troubleshooter who had been sent to Nagorny Karabakh in July, had reported to the Supreme Soviet on 1 December that the area was 'on the boil'. And still Gorbachev could not understand the feelings he encountered in the middle of the earthquake.

His mercy trip to Armenia ended in disaster. Just before leaving, he gave an airport interview to Soviet television which incensed the entire Armenian nation. He spoke in sweeping terms about how the Karabakh issue was being 'exploited' by 'unscrupulous people, demagogues, adventurists, corrupt people, black-shirts' and even 'men in beards', who were 'hungry for power'.[23]

Gorbachev clearly did not understand that the 12-man Karabakh Committee, far from being unscrupulous extremists, were respected moderates, who had provided moral leadership to the Armenians for several months while the Communist Party had drifted deeper into disgrace. When the earthquake struck, they promptly directed their considerable organising abilities to the relief effort, and immediately sent busloads of helpers to the area. This was seen as 'interference', however. Before Gorbachev left Yerevan the police started rounding them up.

Ironically, when Gorbachev earlier stopped his bus to speak to the crowd, he was saved from a much bigger demonstration by a member of the Karabakh Committee, Ashot Manucharyan, who appealed to a large crowd outside the committee headquarters in the writers' union, not to inflame matters by marching to where Gorbachev was. An hour later, soldiers entered the writers' union and arrested Manucharyan and twenty-one others. Six members of the committee were given 30 days' imprisonment.

According to Zori Balayan, the *Literaturnaya gazeta* correspondent, newspapers were then forbidden by the central committee to print anything positive about the Karabakh Committee and its sympathisers: 'In all our stories about the earthquake, we had to somehow criticise Armenian "extremists".'

There could have been no better way to rally popular support for these 'extremists'. Several of them would later be elected to parliament, and, as Balayan put it, 'Gorbachev was going to have to talk to those "bearded men" as equals.'

'Bearded men' – intellectuals, rebels, raw young politicians – were the children of *perestroika*. Gorbachev had encouraged grass-roots activity to help him push through his revolution from above. With it, he had succeeded in marginalising many of his opponents, and in persuading (or fooling) the Party into signing away its monopoly on power. But the instrument he had used – a new, radicalised public opinion – could no longer be relied upon to obey him. He had unleashed a revolution from below, which would force the pace of change and take the initiative out of his hands.

# CHAPTER FOUR

# *Revolution from Below*

IN THE good old days, Soviet elections were upbeat occasions. There were red flags everywhere and uplifting music played from loudspeakers to inspire the masses as they interrupted their Sunday afternoon strolls to stop at a polling station, pick up a ballot paper and pop it straight into the ballot box. They did not even need to look at the paper: an unmarked ballot counted as a vote for the single candidate whose name appeared on it. If some voters failed to turn up, officials generally voted for them, ensuring a 99 per cent turnout and the election of 1500 carefully vetted mediocrities to a parliament with no powers. It was a pointless, elaborate farce.

By contrast, the Soviet Union's first contested general election in 70 years was both highly serious and utterly disorganised. The three-month campaign, which began on 26 December 1988, was improvised, chaotic and jubilant. The rules allowed candidates for the 1500 constituency seats in the new Congress of People's Deputies to be nominated by work collectives or at public meetings attended by at least 500 local voters. Candidates nominated in this way did not automatically find their way on to the ballot papers, however. First, they had to be approved at a registration meeting[1] presided over by the local election commissioner (usually a member of the *apparat*) and attended by supporters of the candidates and other selected members of the public. The scope for manipulation at such meetings was great.

Another 750 deputies were to be chosen from a bizarre set of public organisations, ranging from the Communist Party, the Komsomol and trade unions, to the Stamp Collectors' Union, the Friends of the Cinema, the Red Cross Society, and other organisations representing music lovers, anti-alcohol crusaders and sports fans. Only all-Union organisations were eligible, which excluded the new popular fronts in individual republics. They, and other 'informal' groups, could only support candidates standing in the ordinary constituencies.

125

Stage one – the nomination of candidates – lasted a month. Most of the voters' meetings were a mixture of official incompetence and anarchy – a salutary first lesson in democracy.

At one typical event, 600 citizens (100 more than the quorum) packed a public hall in the Krasnaya Presnya district of Moscow, while hundreds more stood in the snow outside. Most had come to support the nomination of Andrei Nuikin, a radical journalist who was backed by the Moscow Popular Front. There were two other candidates – the head of a local construction trust and a retired colonel. Shortly after the meeting got under way a man in a leather jacket leapt to the rostrum and announced that his name was Ostrovsky, that he was a journalist, and that he was nominating himself. He was greeted at first with laughter, but gradually won the audience round as he explained his programme.

The brief story of the three-and-a-half-hour meeting is that each candidate, apart from Ostrovsky, had an agent who nominated him, giving a short biography. Then each candidate gave a short speech and answered questions from the floor. Then there was a vote, which Nuikin won.

That sounds straightforward. In fact, it was chaos from beginning to end. It would have helped if the chairwoman, the head of the local council, had known the rules. Instead, she put every procedural matter, however trivial, to the vote. The meeting voted to have another chairman, who ended up sharing the job with the chairwoman, doubling the havoc. Then they had to nominate, discuss and vote on seven members of the presidium, who did little more than decorate the stage – until it was noticed that no one was taking minutes, and it was decided, by democratic vote, that the presidium should do so.

Then various individuals started jumping the gun, climbing up to the rostrum without being asked. 'Who the hell are you?' the crowd roared, while other speakers joined the fray, using two microphones at either side of the hall. The chairman tried to call the hall to order, saying: 'Comrades, I'm old and in ill health. I can't shout above this noise.'

'If you're ill, why the hell are you chairman?' came the response from the back of the hall. A neighbour reprimanded the heckler, and the two came to blows.

The chairwoman asked for Nuikin's agent to take the floor. No one responded. 'Oh, all right, then,' she said, 'I'll nominate him to get things going.'

'You can't do that, you're supposed to be neutral!' someone bawled.

A representative of the crowd outside came in and presented a list of 255 signatures in favour of Nuikin. The meeting voted in favour of including them in the final vote, but later they had another vote and changed their mind. The final decision would probably have been taken by a show of hands, but a white-haired old man claimed there were people in the hall who had not registered, so it was decided to hold a secret ballot of those holding pink cards. Some rowdies at the back of the hall continued to chant, 'We want a show of hands!' for some minutes.

Only Nuikin received more than half of the votes. This entitled him to go forward to stage two, the registration meeting, popularly regarded as the *apparat*'s means of filtering out undesirables. Nuikin was duly filtered out, failing to obtain 50 per cent of the vote at a meeting packed with his opponents. This system, which was intended to reduce large candidate lists to a more 'manageable' number to go on the ballot papers, was heavily criticised. At some registration meetings the participants and candidates themselves refused to carry out the task, arguing that it was more democratic to register all the candidates, even if they numbered twelve (as they did in one Moscow constituency), so that the electorate could make its own choice.

Despite the difficulties, most of the best-known radicals did become candidates, either in constituencies or in one of the public organisations. Most were nominated in several districts, so that they had a chance of being registered in one place even if they were weeded out in others. The editor of *Ogonyok*, Vitaly Korotich, found his nomination meeting in Moscow disrupted by thugs from the right-wing Pamyat organisation, and claimed that his registration meeting, at which he was turned down, was manipulated by the election commissioners. He was eventually registered, and elected as a deputy, in a constituency in the Ukraine.

In all, 8000 candidates were nominated at the first stage, but only 2850 of them passed the registration stage, leaving on average less than two candidates for each available seat. In more than one-quarter of constituencies there was only one candidate on the ballot paper; and in Georgia well over half of the seventy-five seats were uncontested. In many cases, local Party leaders had manipulated the procedures to ensure they had no opponents.

Polling day for the constituency deputies was 26 March, but most of the 750 seats reserved for public organisations had already been filled by then. The Communist Party itself set a bad example by fielding exactly 100 candidates for its 100 seats. The candidates were chosen by the Politburo from 312 nominees, and were all 'elected' by just 641 voters at a central committee plenum. Undemocratic though the procedure was, it did have some merit. First, the list of candidates was effectively drawn up by Gorbachev. It included several radicals and only a minority of central committee members, whereas a free vote by the central committee might have produced a majority of *apparatchiki*. Secondly, Gorbachev invited many outsiders to take part in the plenum (a manoeuvre once used by Khrushchev), thus making sure that it was a more radical body than the central committee itself, many of whose members had long ago been sacked from the posts which gave them the right to a central committee place.

The results of the voting were published – and were fairly predictable. As in all Soviet elections, where the voter does not put a cross beside his chosen candidate but scores out the name(s) of those he opposes, uncontroversial or little-known figures got in with few votes against them, since few people had any reason to object to them. The largest number of no-votes – 78 – went to Ligachev, and the second largest – 59 – to Yakovlev. Both, in other words, had the most enemies in the central committee or among the invited voters. Twelve votes were cast against Gorbachev. All 100 candidates were elected, 52 of them – mainly workers and peasants – unanimously. The voting pattern explains the real reason why the Politburo insisted on having 100 candidates for 100 places: had there been even one 'spare' candidate, the loser would have been Ligachev; had there been two losers, Yakovlev would have gone too.

Probably the most controversial election was that of the dissident Andrei Sakharov. He was nominated in many constituencies, but decided to stand for election as a deputy from the Academy of Sciences which, as a 'public organisation', had the right to twenty seats. Several scientific institutes nominated him, but the Presidium of the Academy decided not to register him as a candidate. This caused an uproar, especially in academic circles. Sakharov, after all, was considered by the intelligentsia and many others to be the conscience of the nation. A parliament without him would be worthless. Hundreds of academics demonstrated outside the Academy, demanding the resignation of the Presidium and the inclusion of Sakharov on the ballot papers – but to no avail. Finally, when it came to the election on 21 March, the scientific community had to resort to a conspiracy: a huge number of voters crossed out the entire list of twenty-three candidates, ensuring that only eight of them cleared the 50 per cent hurdle, and necessitating a second round of voting to fill the remaining twelve seats. This time, Sakharov and several other radicals who were passed over in the first round were registered as candidates and easily elected.

In the constituencies, despite the shenanigans of the registration meetings and single-candidate seats, it looked like a real election. Candidates campaigned in the streets, held meetings in housing estates, put up posters and handed out leaflets. Those whose work gave them access to printing presses or photocopiers enjoyed a distinct advantage, although the state paid for a basic minimum of posters for every candidate. In Lvov the director of a bus depot shamelessly draped buses with his election banners. Even more disgracefully, a well-known television correspondent who was standing in a Moscow constituency against a physically handicapped candidate used an eve-of-poll report on the main nine o'clock news to highlight the needs of handicapped people and demand that measures be taken to help them. His opponent, Ilya Zaslavsky, won, and went on to become a most effective radical deputy.

The dirtiest campaign of all was in the city-wide Moscow constituency, the country's largest, where Boris Yeltsin chose to stand, having been nominated in a dozen districts all over the country. This was his chance to make a comeback. After more than a year's enforced absence from the media, he used the campaign to publicise his ever more radical programme on television, in the press and at public meetings. He said the new parliament must be turned from a 'collection of extras' into an organisation that expressed the will of the people, not of the *apparat*. He called for the repeal of the current election law in favour of a simple democratic procedure. As usual he called for the abolition of the privileges of the élite – but this time he was heard by millions of television viewers. He said it was time to start discussing the possibility that the Soviet Union needed a multi-party system. At his registration meeting in the splendid Hall of Columns near the Kremlin, with its brilliant white pillars, ruffled curtains and glittering chandeliers, his stature as a one-man opposition soared. His voice boomed and he towered above the other nine candidates. Only Yeltsin and one other man received enough votes to be registered for the election. Ironically, his opponent was Yevgeny Brakov, director of the huge Zil motor works, which manufactured, among other vehicles, limousines for the ruling class.

The *apparat* used every means at its disposal to discredit Yeltsin. The central committee set up a special commission to inquire into whether some of his statements were 'anti-Party' – a move which must have increased his popularity. At his registration meeting there were apparently planted questions designed to embarrass him: how come his daughter had managed to improve her living conditions twice in the past two years; why did his granddaughter go to a special English-language school; would he be a despot if elected, as he had been as Moscow Party chief? But Yeltsin absorbed the insults and campaigned like a man possessed, his charisma growing at every meeting. His jokes grew better with the retelling, his sense of timing and twinkling smile ever more effective, until he began to look like an American president at the hustings.

The result was a landslide 89 per cent in his favour – a crushing blow to the *apparat* and its favoured candidate. This was people power, for in effect, five million people – the largest vote in the country – had displayed their contempt for the leadership.

Almost all of the score or so of well-known radicals were also elected. So, of course, were hundreds of conservative and mediocre candidates. But about thirty-five regional Party bosses and several other officials of equal rank, many of whom had stood unopposed, were not. That was a massive display of defiance by millions of voters, who entered the voting booths clutching their single-candidate ballot papers to do what they had never dared to do for seventy years: scratch out the name of an *apparatchik* who had the nerve to stand unopposed. The rout was most complete in Leningrad, where voters humiliated the six most powerful politicians, including the regional Party boss and candidate member of the Politburo, Yuri Solovyov. His deputy was also rejected, together with the head of the regional council, the mayor and deputy mayor of the city, and the city-level Party leader, who scraped up a mere 15 per cent of the votes.

Gorbachev appeared to view the result with equanimity. The losers, he said, were 'those who were slow to restructure', and who were guilty of 'inattentiveness [to ordinary people], mismanagement, and attempts to keep their bureaucratic offices as impregnable as fortresses'. He expected them to 'draw the correct conclusions' from the people's verdict.[2] Not all were inclined to do so. Some were furious.

ON 2 April, a week after the election, Gorbachev, Yakovlev and Shevardnadze – the entire liberal wing of the leadership – left the country for a visit to Cuba and Britain. The right-wing backlash began at once. The Leningrad party organisation held a post-mortem on the election at which they blamed their defeat largely on Gorbachev's policies. Their leader, Solovyov, reported later that the meeting had 'drawn political and practical conclusions' from the election defeat and had 'mapped out a programme to emerge from the existing situation'. But none of the six defeated leaders showed any inclination to resign. It was, after all, not they who were to blame for their defeat, but *perestroika*, with its informal political clubs which had carried out 'psychological warfare against the Party', the new co-operative movement which had indulged in 'legalised speculation', and a 'historical striptease' carried out in the name of openness. The city Party first secretary, Anatoly Gerasimov – the one who had received 15 per cent – complained: 'People are dissatisfied with the results of four years of *perestroika*; they are unhappy about mounting shortages, inflation, crime, the mistakes made in the co-operative movement, and the inconsistent way economic reform is being implemented.'[3] The Leningraders called for a full-scale plenum of the central committee to study the crisis – and presumably hoped to conduct it in the same critical, if not 'counter-revolutionary' spirit.

In the days following the election, while Gorbachev was out of the country, the final touches were being put to new laws on political crimes. For many months lawyers, and even the minister of justice, had been promising that one of the old laws most used against dissidents – Article 190-1 of the Russian criminal code, on defamation of the Soviet system – would be abolished completely, while the other – Article 70 on anti-Soviet agitation and propaganda – would be radically rewritten, making only public calls for the *violent* overthrow of the state punishable.[4] In fact, the new laws, which were given to Gorbachev for signature immediately on his return from London, took the country even further away from the internationally accepted norms to which it claimed to aspire.

The rewritten Article 70, known as Article 7, replaced the concept of anti-Soviet agitation and propaganda with a new crime of 'calls for the overthrow or change of the Soviet state and social system'. Since Gorbachev himself was constantly calling for changes to the Soviet system, this theoretically made him guilty of a crime. The other article, 190-1, far from being repealed, was replaced by a more repressive law, Article 11-1, which prohibited 'insulting or discrediting state organs and public organisations' or even officials.[5] This appeared to give *carte blanche* for a fresh crackdown on dissidence.

It is not known who exactly was behind the new laws, but they bore the mark of Viktor Chebrikov, the former KGB chief who was now the Politburo member in charge of legal policy. Just two months earlier he had delivered a tirade against 'so-called informal associations' which were causing 'considerable harm' to society by 'pushing the masses towards anarchy and lawlessness, towards creating structures – legal and illegal – in opposition to the Party'.[6] The wording of the laws surprised even the lawyers who had been drafting them, and outraged most radicals. Although Gorbachev's signature was on them, he was clearly opposed to them; and just two months later he would support moves in the new Congress of People's Deputies to have Article 11-1 repealed and Article 7 reworded, in line with what had been promised before the April 'coup', to 'public calls for the *violent* overthrow of the system'.

On the day he signed the decree, however, Gorbachev probably gave little thought to the conservatives' legislative machinations. He had much graver things on his mind. For during his absence in London his colleagues had taken decisions which were to lead inexorably over the next twenty-four hours to a bloody massacre of peaceful demonstrators in the Georgian capital, Tbilisi, and one of the gravest crises of Gorbachev's rule.

During the week tens of thousands of nationalist demonstrators had gathered daily in the square in front of the Georgian government building, calling for independence. A group of hunger-strikers lay on the steps of the building, and a wave of strikes was spreading. The Georgian leader, Dzhumber Patiashvili, sent encoded telegrams to the Kremlin, and also spoke directly to Chebrikov (whose remit included nationalities matters), requesting help. On 7 April, before

Gorbachev's return, Ligachev called a meeting of selected Politburo members, including Chebrikov and the minister of defence, General Yazov, but not the prime minister, Ryzhkov. (Gorbachev had not asked Ligachev to deputise for him, as he used to do, but Ligachev claims his authority gave him the right to call this meeting.) The group considered Patiashvili's request and agreed to order interior ministry troops normally stationed in Georgia, who had been sent to Armenia, to return to Georgia to assist the regular army troops there. Yazov then telephoned Patiashvili to tell him he was putting General Igor Rodionov, the ultra-hardline commander of the Transcaucasian military district, in charge of the operation.

When Gorbachev, Shevardnadze and Yakovlev returned from London that evening, they were met at the airport by Politburo colleagues. Chebrikov informed them of the situation and told them that they had 'satisfied the requests from the Georgian comrades for help in maintaining order'. Evidently fearing a violent outcome, Gorbachev categorically stated that the situation in Tbilisi must be resolved by political means and through dialogue.[7] Events were already taking a different course, however.

The following morning, Ligachev left Moscow on holiday, and appears to have had no more to do with the affair.[8] Gorbachev, one assumes, believed his instructions about a 'political settlement' were being heeded. In Tbilisi, meanwhile, the Party leadership met and decided to clear the square. Patiashvili says he obtained assurances from Rodionov that there would be no violence and that the troops would be armed only with shields and truncheons. In fact they were armed with sharpened shovels and poison gas.

Tension among the demonstrators on the square reached snapping-point as rumours of impending military action reached them, but there was no violence: the protesters chanted freedom slogans, sang songs, said prayers, and heard the patriarch of the Georgian Church ask them to disperse because he feared the worst. They listened to him in awed silence, but refused to go away. At 3.30 a.m. on the 9th, Rodionov called Patiashvili at home and told him his troops were ready for action. Patiashvili says he suggested putting off the moment since the crowd was so large – still several thousands strong. But half an hour later armoured vehicles started moving up Rustaveli Avenue from Lenin Square. As they reached the crowd the troops went into action, wielding their spades and firing canisters of gas. In a frenzy of violence, soldiers pursued fleeing women into side streets and even into blocks of flats. At the end of the operation twenty were dead and hundreds injured. Some of the victims were Georgian policemen who tried to shield the demonstrators from the troops.

The arguments over who was ultimately responsible for the tragedy have never subsided, despite inquiries carried out by the USSR and

Georgian Supreme Soviets. Claims by some writers in the Soviet press that the whole chain of events was a conspiracy aimed against *perestroika* seem far-fetched. Ligachev and Chebrikov almost certainly did not foresee that the actions they initiated would lead to such a bloody conclusion. But there is little doubt that they intended to deal decisively and quickly with what they saw as nationalist extremists, and that they overstepped their authority in sending troops without consulting either Gorbachev or the prime minister. The action was fully in line both with the spirit of Chebrikov's public call for a decisive rebuff to 'extremist leaders' of informal organisations, and with the new anti-dissident decrees. When the truth about the affair began to be established, Chebrikov was dismissed from the Politburo (in September 1989), and Rodionov transferred to head a military academy. But in the meantime a *Pravda* editorial blamed the deaths on 'self-appointed leaders' and 'extremists' who had been trying to 'subvert the foundations of our society'. The new laws, said *Pravda* – making the link that convinced many people that there was indeed a conspiracy – should be 'uncompromisingly implemented' to punish such subversives.[9]

Bolstered after their election defeats by this reassertion of their power, the conservatives approached a central committee plenum on 25 April in combative mood. Unusually, *Pravda* printed long excerpts from the speeches, in which hardliners vented their grievances. Yuri Solovyov, the Politburo member who had been blackballed by Leningrad voters in the general election, lamented the 'ideological spinelessness which has infiltrated the ranks of Party organisations' and the tendency of young people to regard the Communist Party as 'a party of errors and crimes'. He then came up with an ingenious new idea to 'correct' the election result, which had filled only 18.6 of the seats in parliament with 'workers' (whereas the old-style Supreme Soviet had had a fixed quota of 35 per cent). Demanding an increased role for the working class (and implicitly criticising the leading role played in *perestroika* by the intelligentsia), Solovyov proposed convening an all-Union congress of workers' delegates – apparently as a counterweight to the new parliament.[10]

But while the conservatives let off steam, it was Gorbachev who won the day. Since the central committee was elected in February 1986 a paradoxical situation had arisen: about a quarter of its members had lost the posts which entitled them to membership, many of them in disgrace, yet they were still able to vote on crucial matters. On the eve of the plenum Gorbachev called in 98 of these 'dead souls' and coaxed them into signing a collective letter of resignation. As an incentive to go quietly they were allowed to keep their pensions and privileges, such as the use of official dachas and chauffeur-driven cars from the central committee pool. As one senior official pointed out, many of them were probably only too happy to resign: they saw it as a protest. Be that as it may, the manoeuvre reduced the size of the central committee to 251 full members, which Gorbachev would from now on regularly top up at crucial meetings with extras of his own choice. The membership was still hardly radical, but at least it would be less of a rival to the new parliament.

IT was at this time that a top crime investigator with a dubious reputation and an unpronounceable name emerged as the latest unlikely hero of *perestroika*. Like Yeltsin, Telman Gdlyan benefited from a clumsy campaign waged against him as part of the conservatives' rearguard action.

Gdlyan had been in charge of the investigation into corruption in Uzbekistan which began under Andropov in 1983 and led to the conviction of many senior officials, including Brezhnev's son-in-law, Yuri Churbanov (who was sentenced to twelve years' imprisonment at the end of 1988). Gdlyan first came to public notice, however, only in June 1988, just before the Nineteenth Party Conference, when he and his assistant Nikolai Ivanov published an article in *Ogonyok* alleging that the Uzbek delegation to the Conference included several people under investigation for bribery, and also that they had encountered political resistance to their work: it had taken more than a year, for instance, to obtain agreement for Churbanov to be brought to court.[11] The allegations were hotly denied at the Conference, but apparently substantiated later when three Uzbek delegates were arrested and removed from their positions.

Things came to a head in the spring of 1989 when, according to Gdlyan, the investigations were leading so high up into the Kremlin leadership that a campaign was begun to discredit and put a stop to them. In April Gdlyan spoke publicly for the first time about 'irregularities' in the Churbanov trial, and claimed to have evidence of connections between bribe-takers in Uzbekistan and officials of the Public Prosecutor's office, the court and the ministry of internal affairs. A week later, on 25 April, the USSR Supreme Court posthumously rehabilitated an Estonian inventor and entrepreneur, Johannes Hint, saying he was the victim of an earlier investigation by Gdlyan, who had 'violated socialist legality' by fabricating charges of embezzlement and holding Hint in jail for two years in the hope of forcing him to confess. The Court recommended that Gdlyan should no longer be used on important cases. Five days later *Pravda* published complaints about Gdlyan's conduct of the Uzbek investigation, saying he had arrested the families of bribe-takers and kept people in prison for years without trial. Gdlyan responded by claiming he was being victimised to stop his probe into the affairs of 'Moscow bribe-takers'.

On 12 May, Nikolai Ivanov, who was standing as a candidate in an election in Leningrad, revealed just how high their investigations had taken them: on a live television show he said that the names of Ligachev, former Politburo members Romanov and Solomentsev, and the former head of the Supreme Court Vladimir Terebilov, had all cropped up in the course of their work. He did not accuse any of them of any specific offence. Solomentsev and Terebilov were among those who had recently signed the collective letter of resignation from the central committee. The next day *Pravda* accused Gdlyan and Ivanov of making 'provocative statements about violations of legality allegedly committed by certain political leaders' and announced that a special commission had been set up to investigate *their* violations of legality.[12]

By now Gdlyan and Ivanov were popular heroes. Whatever dirty methods they may have used in the past to extort confessions (and a parliamentary commission later discovered considerable evidence of this), they were widely regarded as knights in shining armour, unjustly persecuted because they dared to penetrate the 'mafia' which was commonly believed to stretch right to the top of the Politburo.

Ivanov romped home in his election to the Congress of People's Deputies with 60 per cent of the vote against 27 other candidates. Gdlyan had already been elected in the first round in March. Now their names joined Yeltsin's on banners at protest demonstrations. Gdlyan-Ivanov Defence Committees were set up all over the country. As MPs, they now had an even higher forum in which to make their damaging allegations.

THE first session of the Congress of People's Deputies opened on 26 May 1989 in the spirit of insubordination and openness that was quickly to become its hallmark. No sooner had the chairman of the electoral commission declared the new parliament open than an unknown bearded figure, looking rather like Karl Marx, bounded up to the podium and interrupted the speaker with a call for a minute's silence in memory of those killed in Tbilisi. Deputies looked taken aback but reluctantly got to their feet. When they sat down again, the bearded man, who gave his name as Tolpezhnikov, from Riga, went on: 'On the instructions of my electorate, I demand a report, now and for all to hear, at the Congress of People's Deputies, about who gave the order for the slaughter of peaceful demonstrators in Tbilisi on 9 April 1989 and for the use against them of toxic substances.'[13]

This set the tone for perhaps the most momentous event in the Soviet Union since the 1917 Revolution. It was the moment the people, through their elected representatives, seized back power from those who had usurped it for seventy years. Gorbachev and his colleagues wanted the Congress to do little more than elect a president and 542-member Supreme Soviet from its own ranks, and then leave them to get on with the task of legislating. But a considerable number of deputies were determined to turn the Congress into more than a mere electoral college. They did so in a whirlwind of free debate that scattered every known communist taboo. Frankenstein-like, the institution that Gorbachev had created took on a life of its own, however hard he tried to dominate it.

Radical deputies had persuaded the leadership to permit full, live transmission of the event on television, and the population watched every minute, enthralled. During the two weeks of the first session of the Congress, industrial production fell by 20 per cent, while in most offices and academic institutions, no work was done at all. The country's old rulers, the Politburo, watched from a side balcony, looking oddly suspended from a wall of the cavernous Palace of Congresses, isolated from the main body of deputies and virtually excluded from the debate.

For a few minutes after Tolpezhnikov's disruption, the proceedings returned to the pre-arranged plan: a list of 18 presidium members was endorsed, and they took their places on the platform. Gorbachev, not yet elected to any post, then broke the constitutional requirement that the first session be chaired by the electoral commissioner, by instantly taking the chair himself. An agenda was then read out and approved, but before they could move to the first item on it several deputies jumped the gun and began making speeches. The first to address the Congress was Andrei Sakharov.

What he said – that he supported Gorbachev's candidacy for president[14] but believed there must be alternative candidates and that they should all put forward their programmes before the vote, rather than after, as envisaged by the agenda – was less important than the symbolism of the occasion. With his nervous, halting delivery and burred pronunciation, typical of the old Petersburg intelligentsia, he would not have looked out of place in the pre-revolutionary Duma. Other radicals followed him to the podium, and it was they who principally determined the course of debate during the next two weeks, even if, due to their small number, they could not influence the outcome of most votes. It turned out that the Congress included about 250 committed and active radicals, a similar number of active conservatives, and a huge grey middle group with no pronounced views, able and willing to be swayed by emotional speeches and – especially – by Gorbachev. This main group, reminiscent of the old-style Soviet parliament, was memorably described by the liberal historian, Yuri Afanasyev, as the 'aggressive obedient majority'.

The radicals challenged everything. Gorbachev, it is true, was elected president of the Supreme Soviet (head of state) as planned at the end of the long first day, but only after he had been required to answer questions from deputies on matters ranging from his knowledge of the events in Tbilisi to the construction of government dachas in the Crimea. He also unexpectedly faced a challenger: Alexander Obolensky, a 46-year-old engineer, nominated himself, admitting he had no chance of defeating Gorbachev but insisting that the precedent of multi-candidate elections for such posts be set. The majority, however, saw no need for such a precedent: two-thirds of the Congress voted against even putting Obolensky's name on the ballot paper, so Gorbachev stood alone – and won 95.6 per cent of the vote.

The rather gentle grilling that Gorbachev faced before his election matured into something similar to American congressional hearings for candidates to other top state and government posts. Gorbachev nominated his friend Anatoly Lukyanov for the post of deputy president, and Nikolai Ryzhkov to continue as prime minister. Both underwent an inquisition by deputies before being approved. Later, every member of Ryzhkov's government had to appear before hearings in parliamentary committees and in the Supreme Soviet, and several of his nominees were rejected – something unheard of under the old system.

Meanwhile the Congress continually found itself distracted from its agenda, as deputies took the floor with 'points of order', which were actually speeches, on every conceivable subject. At the start of the second day, for example, as the presidium tried to push on to the election of the Supreme Soviet, the radical sociologist Tatyana Zaslavskaya got up to say that some of her constituents had telephoned her at midnight to report an ugly incident. A group of citizens who had gathered – illegally – in Pushkin Square and set off towards the Kremlin to meet their deputies at the end of the first day's session had allegedly been 'dispersed', and some arrested, by the hated OMON riot police. Zaslavskaya called for the suspension of the two decrees promulgated the previous summer which gave the grey-bereted OMON the right to break up unsanctioned meetings.[15] Gorbachev instantly called the interior minister, Vadim Bakatin, to the podium to account for his men's behaviour. It was the first time such a thing had ever happened to a minister, and Bakatin recalls how nervous he was, although he was able to report there had been no arrests.

After a short discussion, Gorbachev put the question of suspending the decrees on demonstrations to the vote, and again the illiberal majority defeated the motion – whereupon Gorbachev took things into his own hands: he reminded deputies that the decrees did not actually prevent demonstrations from being held, and asked Moscow city council to see to it that meetings could be held unhindered throughout the Congress at one of the traditional meeting-places, Luzhniki, near the Lenin sports stadium. He promised that the decrees themselves would be debated later.

For the two-chamber Supreme Soviet, the new working parliament, the deputies had to elect 542 members from their own ranks, according to a complicated quota system designed to ensure fair representation for the various nationalities. Within these constraints, delegations from different regions were able to choose their own methods of nominating candidates. Most of them put forward precisely the number of candidates required for the seats to be filled, and there was no choice. But the more democratically-minded delegations, such as the Moscow one, insisted on having more candidates than places (in their case, 55 for 29 seats), and as a result several leading radicals failed to be elected. The Russian Federation was entitled to eleven seats in one of the chambers; and Boris Yeltsin, having himself insisted on there being at least twelve candidates for the sake of choice, predictably received the largest number of no-votes, and came twelfth. This caused an uproar. Yeltsin, after all, had the biggest popular mandate of any deputy, from virtually the entire adult population of the capital city, and would now be absent from the main legislature.

When the result was announced on the morning of the third day there was a furore. It was now that Yuri Afanasyev coined his celebrated phrase about the 'aggressive obedient majority' in Congress, which had thrown out all the decisions expected of them by the people, and elected a 'Stalinist-Brezhnevite Supreme Soviet'. And indeed, the Congress had thrown out some of the leading lights of perestroika: Tatyana Zaslavskaya, Gorbachev's erstwhile adviser, who received the biggest no-vote of all – 1558 – and only 591 votes for; the liberal agriculture expert, Vladimir Tikhonov (1519 against and 630 for); the economist Gavriil Popov (1142 against and 1007 for); and the popular young historian Sergei Stankevich, backed by the Moscow Popular Front (1343 against and 806 for). There were many others. A worker named Nikolai Travkin, who was regarded as the epitome of perestroika man (and praised by Gorbachev for his initiative), failed even to make it on to the ballot papers.

By contrast, dozens of nonentities from obscure regions, of whom the vast majority of deputies had never even heard and who may never have said anything of note in their lives, received as little as 20 or 30 votes against them, and sailed through.

Gorbachev must have been thoroughly depressed by this outcome, though the only way he could show it was by urging Afanasyev to continue with what he called his 'serious remarks' (about the aggressive obedient majority) when that majority tried to drown him out with jeers and slow handclapping. What Afanasyev said was undeniably true: the general level of qualifications and professionalism of the deputies elected to the Supreme Soviet was quite inadequate for the complex legislative tasks facing the new parliament.

Speaking calmly above the cat-calls, Afanasyev continued: 'We can carry on working like this. We can be obedient, and hand up little notes to the platform like good boys, instead of queuing up at the microphones. We can be meek, as Father Pitirim [a deputy from the Church hierarchy] exhorted us to be. But let us not forget for a minute about those who sent us to this Congress. They sent us here not to behave meekly but to change the state of affairs in this country in the most decisive manner.'

It was the boldest speech of the Congress, and perfectly summed up the depressing outcome of Gorbachev's compromise reform, which had allowed the *apparat* to fill most of the new parliament with its obedient servants. Yet, as Boris Yeltsin points out in his memoirs, the overall effect of the Congress was epoch-making nonetheless. The debates, he wrote, 'gave the people more of a political education than seventy years of stereotyped Marxist-Leninist lectures multiplied a millionfold and flung at the Soviet people in order to turn them into dummies. On the day the Congress opened, they were one sort of people; on the day that it closed they were different people . . . Almost the entire population was awakened from its state of lethargy.'[16]

The evening after the Supreme Soviet election results were announced, an angry rally took place at Luzhniki. Afanasyev's catchphrases were on dozens of banners. The speeches were primarily anti-Gorbachev. There were calls for a 'one-hour warning strike', and demands that Yeltsin somehow be included in the Supreme Soviet. It was one of the biggest demonstrations Moscow had seen, with people of all ages, including old women standing in the warm sunshine, knitting, and cheering at the most anti-Soviet comments booming over the public address system.

Who knows what might have happened had not an unknown deputy, Aleksei Kazannik, come to the rescue of democracy at the next sitting of the Congress by offering to give up his seat in the Supreme Soviet in favour of Yeltsin. Everyone realised there was something not quite constitutional about this, but it was agreed to, with Gorbachev's encouragement (all he had to do was reach into his pocket for his mandate-card to indicate which way he was going to vote, and the obedient majority followed suit).

The Congress achieved three tangible results. First, it shone the light of *glasnost* on untouched, and untouchable, subjects. The liberal academic Yuri Karyakin called for the rehabilitation of the exiled writer Alexander Solzhenitsyn and for Lenin to be taken from his Red Square tomb, where 'tanks roll past, shaking his body, and scientists and artists remodel his face', and given a decent burial. A former weightlifter, Yuri Vlasov, delivered a stunning denunciation of the KGB as an 'underground empire' which surrounded itself with privileges and virtually ran the country, accountable only to the *apparat*. He said that state violence, fear, intolerance and cruelty had become the norm in Soviet life, and called for the KGB to be cut down to size and removed from its Lubyanka headquarters in central Moscow to a more modest building somewhere in the suburbs. For decades, he said, the Lubyanka had been the source of orders for the 'elimination or persecution of millions. In the bowels of this building they tormented and tortured people – as a rule the best, the very pride and flower of our nation.' Another speaker, the agriculture specialist Yuri Chernichenko, broke the taboo on criticising Politburo members: he ridiculed Ligachev and wondered how it could come about that 'a man who knows nothing about [agriculture] and who failed in ideology was put in charge of a politically vital area which will determine the future of *perestroika* ?'

Since all this had been said in parliament, and broadcast on television, it became fair game henceforth for the press to start writing openly about Lenin, the KGB, members of the Politburo, and all the other previously unmentionable topics explored at the Congress.[17] Of course, there were equally hard-hitting speeches from 'the other side'. They also contributed to the 'political education' of which Yeltsin wrote.

A second important achievement was that the Congress and Supreme Soviet, for all their faults, did start introducing more liberal legislation. The repressive anti-dissident laws which had been proclaimed just after the election were repealed or amended. Later, the requirement for election candidates to go through the filter of registration meetings was abolished, and the Supreme Soviet even voted to do away with the reserved parliamentary seats for officially approved organisations. The republics were given the right to decide whether to copy the all-Union parliament, with its indirectly elected Supreme Soviet, or to have a directly elected single-chamber legislature. In general, the Supreme Soviet turned out to have more teeth than expected, and was particularly rigorous in its vetting of government ministers.

Thirdly, the Congress not only sidelined the Politburo, but brought a whole new generation of leaders to the public eye. Few had heard of Anatoly Sobchak, Sergei Stankevich or Gavriil Popov. Suddenly, it turned out that the country had a stock of capable parliamentarians, who could knock spots off the *apparatchiki* in any debate. They were free-thinkers, unencumbered by Marxist gobbledegook. Sobchak, a Leningrad lawyer, particularly impressed people with his clean looks and razor-sharp arguments. 'He could be a prime minister,' people murmured.

Such figures formed the core of the country's first formal parliamentary opposition. Shortly after the elections, in April, twenty-two radical deputies from Moscow began meeting regularly to prepare for the Congress. Soon they were joined by other deputies, elected by public organisations but resident in Moscow. On the eve of the Congress they scored two successes: the authorities agreed that the Congress would last longer than three days, as originally planned; and that it would be broadcast live on television.

Gavriil Popov, the editor of the journal *Questions of Economics*, had emerged as *de facto* leader of the Moscow Group, and it was he who on the third day of the Congress, after the election of the Supreme Soviet, first mooted the possibility of setting up a faction of 'democratically-minded' MPs (causing a storm of protest from the right-wingers). By the end of the first session of the Congress 256 deputies had joined the Inter-regional Group, as it became known. Among their successes they counted the setting up of a number of parliamentary commissions (on the Molotov-Ribbentrop pact, the Tbilisi massacre, the Gdlyan affair, and on Party privileges) and the decision to hold the next session of the Congress of People's Deputies in the autumn, rather than a whole year later. Throughout the summer the Inter-regional Group would work hard to draw up its political programme, based on two main premises – the multi-party system and radical economic reform. It was to play a crucial role in forming public opinion and in pressing parliament to adopt the deep reforms it believed the electorate wanted. Its joint chairmen were Yeltsin, Afanasyev, Popov, Sakharov and Viktor Palm, an Estonian professor of science.

The first session of the Congress ended as it had begun, with a speech by Andrei Sakharov. In the intervening period he had repeatedly gone to the podium, harrying Gorbachev with requests and reminders, as befitted the nation's conscience. The bulk of deputies soon stopped trying to hide their impatience with his punctiliousness and hesitant delivery. On 2 June a young Afghan veteran and Komsomol leader gave the crowd what it wanted: he attacked Sakharov for having claimed that Soviet helicopter gunships had fired on their own men in Afghanistan to prevent their being taken prisoner. This unleashed a stream of abuse against Sakharov from other deputies. Sakharov tried to defend himself, pointing out that he had never insulted Soviet soldiers, only those who 'committed the crime of sending Soviet troops to Afghanistan', and that he too had won an 'award' for his action – seven years' exile in Gorky. But he was scarcely heard above the jeers of the mob. It was the ugliest scene of the entire Congress.

Gorbachev's relationship to Sakharov seemed complicated. On the one hand, he gave Sakharov the chance to speak whenever he requested it, and on the final day of the Congress, when members of a commission to draft a new constitution were chosen, he agreed at once to include Sakharov, without putting it to the vote as he did with other proposals. But on the other hand, he too lost patience with him. As the Congress drew to a close Sakharov asked for fifteen minutes to read a major prepared speech, including the proclamation of a 'Decree on

Power' which he hoped the Congress would adopt. The 'Decree' was a fundamental statement on how the country should be governed: it proposed the abolition of Article Six of the Constitution on the Party's leading role; that the Congress, not the smaller Supreme Soviet, be the sole legislative body; and that the KGB limit itself to external security matters. There was more, but Sakharov was not given a chance to explain the rest. Once again, the slow-handclapping began, and Gorbachev rudely interrupted, telling Sakharov he had spoken too long already.

Sakharov insisted on continuing, and Gorbachev snapped at him: 'Comrade Sakharov, do you respect the Congress?'

'I respect the people,' replied Sakharov with dignity amid the uproar, 'and I respect humanity.' When he tried to go on, Gorbachev switched off the microphone.

And so, bar a little more shouting, ended the Soviet Union's first trial run at parliamentary democracy.

THE political revolution was accompanied by an economic one. It too, in the absence of real reform of the state sector, came mostly from 'below', in the private sector. By the end of 1988 there were about 77 500 co-operative businesses in operation, and by mid-1989, some 133 000, employing almost three million people, mainly in services and small manufacturing outfits.[18] Most had a modest turnover and employed only a few workers. They tended not even to try to compete with the state sector, preferring to look for holes in the market, where the state failed altogether. This allowed them to charge high prices and, in some cases, to neglect quality. As a result public resentment burgeoned, probably encouraged by ideological opponents. The authorities were flooded with complaints about high prices, shoddy workmanship and poor service – and, of course, about the fabulous sums which it was popularly believed all co-operative owners earned.

Some, it is true, did very well for themselves. Artyom Tarasov became one of the first millionaire businessmen. After starting up in mid-1988, he soon had 1000 employees on his payroll, involved in a complex business operation which helped hundreds of state enterprises to acquire Western computers, quite legally, but more cheaply than the state could provide them and with much less red tape. He achieved this by barter. His co-operative bought up unwanted materials from Soviet state enterprises. They collected the materials from all over the country (huge quantities of aluminium fuel drums discarded in remotest Siberia, for example) and shipped them abroad, organising their own transportation by sea, leasing berths at ports and paying good wages to teams of cargo loaders to get the job done efficiently. The goods – anything from scrap metal to tomato paste – were sold abroad and the money was used to buy computers. The co-operative itself installed business programmes in the computers, and sold them to Soviet enterprises, at half the official price. By January 1989, after only five months in business, they had made 70 million roubles' profit.

Tarasov says the entire operation was above board: none of the items they dealt in were subject to restrictions or bans. But then he heard that the ministry of finance was planning to introduce new legislation in February 1989 which would allow co-operatives to withdraw only 100 roubles a day from their bank accounts, except for salaries. At the time Tarasov had signed 142 contracts with enterprises which had paid in advance for their computers. His daily cash flow was well in excess of 100 roubles. So he decided to withdraw large sums of money allegedly as salaries, but in fact to pay for goods and shipping. He and his deputy received January 'salaries' of three million roubles, and other employees also received large sums. His deputy, being a Party member, had to pay three per cent of his salary as dues, and when the Party received 90 000 roubles from him, alarm bells started ringing: inspectors were sent to investigate, their bank account was seized, and all their contracts were frozen. At the end of a six-month trial it was established that they had done nothing illegal, but in the meantime their business was ruined. According to Tarasov, Gorbachev himself had referred to them on television as swindlers and demanded they be punished.

Tarasov believes the co-operative movement faced two threats. 'One was the Communist Party. They suddenly felt that with the emergence of co-operatives they were losing power. What kind of power could they exercise over a private company?' The other was from ordinary people. 'Here in the Soviet Union it has always been considered shameful to be rich. The rich were always considered to be thieves and swindlers.'

By offering wages on average three times as high as state enterprises, the co-operatives proved to be a magnet for skilled and enterprising workers. It was partly for this reason that the authorities soon started to shackle them. The economist Vladimir Tikhonov says that in mid-1989, when the co-operative movement was proliferating at an unexpectedly high rate, the state-monopoly economic system suddenly felt endangered by 'a real competitor, which was independent of state and Party power'. A clampdown began, especially in areas previously infamous for their corruption: 'In Krasnodar, Ivan Polozkov [the hardline regional Party leader] put out the cry "Follow the people's will, not the law" and started the mass annihilation of co-operatives. In Uzbekistan hundreds of co-ops were broken up, leaving tens of thousands out of work. And the then mayor of Moscow, Saikin, issued a decree aimed at banning co-operatives completely.'[19] Tikhonov lists several general measures aimed at curbing the co-operatives: prices for resources were set at higher levels for co-ops than for state enterprises; the tax system was changed three times, causing nervousness and instability; more and more restrictions were placed on the kind of activities in which co-ops could engage; and they were suddenly forced to pay extortionate duties on imported consumer goods. As a result, 465 000 people were put out of work, and the production of co-operatives, which had risen from 6.1 billion roubles in 1988 to 40.3 billion roubles in 1989, suddenly dropped by 20 per cent in the first quarter of 1990. The virtual elimination of trading co-operatives in Krasnodar region contributed, according to Tikhonov, to losses of 60 per cent of the fruit and vegetables grown in the area.[20]

For a time much official encouragement was given, verbally at least, to the idea of leaseholding in industry, whereby workers would pay rent for the use of machinery and premises while keeping the profits from their activities. The idea was pioneered by Mikhail Bocharov, the manager of a plant producing construction materials at Butovo, near Moscow. Bocharov himself was a model of the kind of business-man the Soviet Union needed to transform its economy – energetic, ambitious and free of dogma. He believed the only control the state should exercise over enterprises was by its taxation policy; he proposed eliminating the State Planning Committee altogether; he campaigned for the creation of a stock exchange; and he took his leasehold project a big step forward by establishing the country's first 'corporation', known as Butec, which amalgamated twenty-five enterprises, with no state ownership.[21] In 1989 he was elected to the Congress of People's Deputies and joined the Inter-regional Group. But his lease-holding initiative failed to catch on in more than a tiny proportion of Soviet enterprises, despite Gorbachev's support.

Leasing was also supposed to be the salvation of unprofitable collective farms, and Gorbachev put his weight behind the idea in numerous speeches. But his agriculture secretary, Ligachev, was less enthusiastic. He praised leasehold arrangements *within* existing collective farms, but opposed breaking them up (even if they were loss-making) into autonomous 'tenant farms'. He even declared – just two weeks before a central committee plenum which was formally to approve the idea – that 'it was not for this that we established Soviet power'.[22]

While Gorbachev clearly saw leasing as the principal way to improve the food situation, he repeatedly stressed that to *force* peasants to lease land would be as counterproductive and immoral as Stalin's enforced collectivisation of agriculture had been. He spoke of ensuring that all forms of ownership should have equal rights, apparently believing that competition would force unprofitable collective farms to close down and encourage peasants to lease land. But the two forms of ownership were in no sense equal. The management of collective farms had entrenched interests of their own, and no reason to give up their land to individual farmers. They also had the weight of a huge bureaucracy behind them, which guaranteed supplies of equipment, seed and fertilisers which the individual farmer had no means of acquiring. Peasants themselves feared that if policies were reversed, they could be branded *kulaks*, like their grandparents had been, and sent to Siberia. Who could blame them, when Ligachev was constantly asserting that 'the foundation of solving food questions is the development, by every means, of collective and state farms.'[23]

While the economic revolution from below – the growth of a private sector of co-ops and leaseholders – was half-stifled, Gorbachev's reform of the state sector was even less successful. The main plank of the reform was the Law on State Enterprises, launched back in June 1987. Two years later, it was showing catastrophic results. The law was intended to make 'self-financing' state enterprises work in a quasi-market situation by removing the central planners' total control over inputs, production quotas and trade, and making factories work instead to orders from customers. The main snag was that the state turned out to be customer number one. The *goszakaz* or 'state order' was soon damned as the old plan dressed up in new clothes. 'Self-financing' remained a myth: 15 per cent of enterprises were loss-making, kept afloat only by huge state subsidies, while another 50 per cent only just broke even.

The most disastrous effect of the Law on State Enterprises stemmed from the incompatibility of two of its parts. On the one hand, workers' wages were made dependent on output – a seemingly sensible incentive scheme. On the other, enterprises were given more control over their product-mix, and since output was measured in roubles, it became simpler not to increase output but to drop production of cheaper goods and concentrate on expensive items. The result was higher wages, and even fewer goods in the shops – the classic recipe for inflation. The government was forced to print money to pay the higher wages, and thereby incurred an ever-increasing budget deficit. Meanwhile, enterprises found that while the centre had stopped acting as a go-between, planning all their supplies and deliveries, there was no functioning wholesale market to take over the task; they had to resort to barter to obtain crucial raw materials and machinery.

In short, the economy lost the security of centralised planning without gaining the stimulus of market forces. An essential step towards a market economy ought to have been a top-to-bottom reform of prices, to bring them closer to world levels and to make them reflect the real cost of goods. This was strongly advocated in 1987 by Gorbachev's adviser, Abel Aganbegyan, but, he says, Gorbachev got cold feet – particularly over the most sensitive issue of raising food prices. Nothing was done about it. 'We have been reaping the fruit of this ever since,' says Aganbegyan.

Even ideas that looked good on paper ran into the ground. In an attempt to link the Soviet economy more closely to the outside world, and to provide better goods for the domestic market, it was decided to encourage Western firms to set up joint ventures with Soviet partners. But the fine print scared off many Westerners. First, the Western partner would not be allowed to own more than 49 per cent of the venture (and to begin with the legislation even insisted that all enterprises must have Soviet managing directors). Secondly, there were no provisions to allow the Western firm to repatriate its profits in hard currency. A firm would either have to sell its Soviet-made goods abroad for hard currency (bringing no benefit to the Soviet consumer) or indulge in complicated barter trade, selling on the Soviet market for roubles, then using those roubles to buy some Soviet commodity such as furs or timber to resell abroad. Convertibility of the rouble remained a distant prospect, so there was no point in just saving up roubles in the hope of eventually cashing them in for dollars. By the end of 1989, 1274 joint ventures had been set up, but only a tiny number involved major Western firms, and scarcely any produced consumer goods.[24]

There was no shortage of advice coming from professional economists. At the Congress of People's Deputies in June 1989, Nikolai Shmelyov advocated a return to normal sales of alcohol to reduce the budget deficit; a one-off $15 billion spending spree on imports of consumer goods to soak up the estimated 150 billion roubles of savings which he said were 'burning' in people's pockets, waiting to be spent; a freeze on imports of machinery for use in useless projects (billions of dollars worth of imported machinery was already lying idle, waiting to be installed in factories not yet built); a cut in subsidies to client states like Cuba; a major sell-off of state property – land, flats, lorries, tractors; and sales of shares in state enterprises and high-interest loans to soak up savings.

Gavriil Popov recommended that the government should study Keynesian economics. He said that half of the economy should be privatised, and that only one-fifth of the state sector should be controlled in Moscow, the rest being devolved to the republics and local councils.

But it was neither Popov, nor Shmelyov, nor even Abel Aganbegyan, Gorbachev's early adviser, who was listened to. Leonid Abalkin, the reformist director of Moscow's Institute of Economics, was now chief economic guru, and in June 1989 Nikolai Ryzhkov appointed him deputy prime minister in charge of economic reform. The appointment may have reflected the first disagreements between Ryzhkov and Gorbachev. Abalkin recalls that a year earlier, at the Nineteenth Party Conference, after he had incurred Gorbachev's wrath by making a speech critical of his handling of the economy,

Ryzhkov demonstratively came up to him and shook his hand. After that Ryzhkov started inviting Abalkin to give talks at the Council of Ministers, and they spoke regularly on the telephone. At the end of 1988 Abalkin's institute was given the task of drafting a 'concept' – an integrated, costed recovery programme – for the economy.

Under Abalkin's influence, the principle of the market finally began to be accepted. But there was no logic in the timetable for introducing it. Ryzhkov and Abalkin argued that the situation was too bad for the transfer to the market to begin immediately. The starting date was put off until 1993, by which time it was hoped that the economy would be 'improved' – by using precisely those central-planning methods which were plunging the country into a deepening crisis. In the summer Ryzhkov announced that the number of ministries dealing with various branches of the economy would be reduced from fifty-two to thirty-two. But it was still the ministries – demoralised, maligned, and under constant threat of cutbacks – that were expected to restore health to the system *before* the market would take over.

Paradoxically, the longer the government postponed radical reform, the harder it became to contemplate it, because the steadily worsening economic situation eroded public confidence and made people less willing to put up with any austerity programme. Gorbachev's leadership was judged mainly by the state of the shops, and on that count, by mid-1989, it was a failure.

Food supplies had grown perceptibly worse in the years of *perestroika*, and from about the middle of 1988, thanks to the adverse effects of the reforms, basic household and consumer goods began to disappear from the shops. Razor-blades, soap, washing powder, combs, cups and saucers, televisions, refrigerators – all became virtually unobtainable.

ON 10 July 1989 the people ran out of patience. Coalminers in a pit at Mezhdurechensk, in Western Siberia, found they could not wash after a shift because there was no soap. It was the last straw: they staged a sit-in. A massive strike movement, the first organised industrial unrest since the Revolution, soon spread to other mines in the Kuzbass coalfields of Western Siberia; and from there to Kazakhstan, to Vorkuta in the far north, and to the country's biggest coalmining region, the Donbass in the Ukraine. Over the next two weeks some 500 000 miners went on strike.

At first, the miners' demands were for better working and living conditions, improved supplies of food, a share in mine profits, greater local control over the pits, and curbs on the unpopular co-operative movement. This was bad enough for ideologues like Ligachev, who believed it was 'absurd' for workers in a workers' state to 'strike against themselves'.

But even more worryingly, as the strike spread, the miners added political demands. These varied from region to region, but included a call for independent trade unions along the lines of Poland's Solidarity, an end to official privileges, and a new Soviet constitution, with an end to the Party's leading role. In Kazakhstan, miners demanded the closure of the nuclear weapons test site at Semipalatinsk.

Whole towns were brought to a standstill as miners and their families held mass meetings in the main squares and outside Party and government offices. Like Solidarity in Poland, the first strike committees displayed great self-discipline and organising capabilities. They banned alcohol, helped the police maintain order, and ensured that essential services and food supplies operated normally. A Soviet newspaper reported at the end of the first week from Mezhdurechensk, where the first strike broke out, that the strike committee was 'in command of the town'.[25] They grouped together into regional committees, which negotiated with government teams led by the coal minister, Mikhail Shchadov, and Politburo member Nikolai Slyunkov.

Gorbachev and Ryzhkov addressed emergency debates in the Supreme Soviet. By 19 July the government, apparently panicking at the scale of the protests, caved in to thirty-five of the Kuzbass regional strike committee's forty-two demands. There was to be a sweeping reorganisation of the industry, and full economic and legal autonomy for all mines, including the right to sell above-plan output abroad for foreign currency.

By the end of July the miners had all gone back to work. But the strike committees, instead of disbanding, turned themselves into workers' committees as a kind of alternative to the official trade unions, which throughout the Soviet period had seen their role as helping the Party to implement its policies, rather than defending the workers' interests. (The chairman of the national trade union organisation had negotiated with the miners on the government side.) The new workers' committees were a dangerous challenge to the authority of both the Party and the Party-dominated local soviets. Yeltsin referred to them as 'embryos of real people's power'.

There may have been some, small, sense in which Gorbachev also welcomed the strike, and the committees which evolved out of it, as means of putting more pressure on conservative local officials and on the inert official trade unions. But the developments were fraught with the danger of anarchy, a conservative backlash, and, worse, of the initiative for change slipping irrevocably out of Gorbachev's hands.

There were now two serious challenges to the Soviet leader's authority and ability to control the pace of reform: the new parliament with its influential radical minority, and a new working-class movement which had flexed its muscles and found it had the strength to obtain concessions from the government almost without trying.

A third, growing, grass-roots revolution threatened not just the power of the Communist Party, or Gorbachev's personal grip on things, but the very survival of the Soviet empire.

# CHAPTER FIVE

# The Empire Cracks Up

ON 23 May 1989, a young man entered the colourful bazaar in the Uzbek town of Kuvasai, in the fertile Fergana valley. It was a typical central Asian scene: peasant women in brilliant reds and oranges, stubble-faced men wearing buttonless padded coats and embroidered *tyubeteika* skull-caps, a babble of voices – Uzbek, Russian, Kirghiz, Turkish – and mounds of fresh, local fruit and vegetables.

The young man approached a peasant woman and asked how much her home-grown strawberries cost. When she told him, he swore at her, and swung his fist at the plate on which she had neatly piled a kilogram of the reddest berries, scattering them on the ground. The young man was a Meskhetian Turk. The peasant woman was an Uzbek. A brawl broke out in the marketplace. The next day a bigger fight took place in the main square, which left one man dead. Large groups of young Meskhetians and Uzbeks, armed with iron bars, clubs, bicycle chains and hatchets, then attacked each other, and dozens of Meskhetian homes were burnt down. In early June the rioting spread to the city of Fergana, where Uzbek youths went on the rampage, setting fire to houses and cars, mutilating passers-by, and even taking the regional Party leaders hostage. In the city of Kokand the rioters armed themselves with automatic weapons and besieged the police station. At the end of a two-week orgy of violence, a hundred people had been killed, most of them Meskhetians, and a thousand injured. Over the next few weeks almost all the Meskhetians living in Uzbekistan – some 60 000 people – were evacuated to Russia.

That the Meskhetian Turks lived there at all was the result of yet another of Stalin's crimes. He had deported the entire Meskhetian population from their homeland in southern Georgia in November 1944. The same fate was suffered by the Soviet Germans, whose autonomous Volga Republic, set up by Lenin in 1924, Stalin abolished, and by the Tatars of the Crimea and several other ethnic groups who were banished from the Caucasus. The Crimean Tatars were the first, under *perestroika*, to demand to be allowed to return to their homeland: in 1987 they demonstrated in Red Square, and as a result a commission was set up to look into their demands. The two million Germans, now living mostly in Kazakhstan and central Asia, set up an 'informal' society – *Wiedergeburt*, or 'Rebirth' – in 1989 to press for the restoration of a national homeland.

The ethnic feuding in the Fergana Valley was the prelude to a long, hot summer in which the Soviet empire appeared to be pulling apart at every seam.

No sooner had interior ministry troops restored a semblance of order in Uzbekistan, than riots erupted in the town of Novy Uzen, in Kazakhstan. This time it was local Kazakhs who were demanding the expulsion of non-Kazakhs from the town and the closure of co-operatives – particularly those run by immigrants from the Caucasus (Georgians, Azeris and Armenians), who have a reputation throughout the Soviet Union for sharp practice. This time, four deaths were reported. Moscow took the opportunity to give the republic a Kazakh leader once again, to replace the Russian whose tactless appointment in 1986 had sparked the first violence of the Gorbachev era.

A week or so later, thousands of Tajik and Kirghiz villagers clashed over land and water rights.

In July 22 people were murdered in bloody clashes in the Black Sea town of Sukhumi, capital of Abkhazia, which is situated within the republic of Georgia. Abkhazians, who comprise only 15 per cent of the population of their autonomous republic, had been campaigning for some months for it to be detached from Georgia and given full republic status. The much larger Georgian population's fears of discrimination were one of the reasons for the ill-fated demonstrations in Tbilisi in April, and now they led to virtual civil war in Abkhazia itself, with well-armed gangs staging shoot-outs in the centre of Sukhumi, a popular holiday resort.

Several republics took steps to give their national languages official status. When Tajikstan declared Tajik to be the state language of the republic, 10 000 people of other nationalities left the capital, Dushanbe, to settle elsewhere, rather than face the prospect of having to learn Tajik. When Moldavians demonstrated for their language (which is identical to Romanian) to be given official status and for it to be written in the Latin script again (instead of the Cyrillic imposed by Stalin), this provoked strikes in the Russian-populated parts of the republic.

The restoration of local language rights was one of the chief demands of the popular fronts which were set up in most republics during 1989, following the example of the three Baltic republics in 1988. In every case they encountered opposition from the Party. The

Belorussian Popular Front had to hold its founding congress in Vilnius in Lithuania because the authorities would not permit it to take place in the Belorussian capital, Minsk. The Ukrainian grass-roots movement, *Rukh* ('Movement'), and the Uzbek popular front, *Birlik* ('Unity'), faced ferocious propaganda campaigns in the official media. Some of the biggest demonstrations mustered by any popular front were in Baku, the capital of Azerbaijan, where crowds half-a-million strong demanded greater local autonomy, the legalisation of the popular front, and continued Azeri control of Nagorny Karabakh.

The conflict over Nagorny Karabakh simmered on throughout the year, despite the imposition of 'special administration' – effectively, direct rule from Moscow – in January 1989. After a campaign of strikes and demonstrations by Armenians, most of the members of the Karabakh Committee, who had incurred Gorbachev's wrath during his visit to the earthquake zone in December, were released from prison. But much of Armenian life, including reconstruction after the earthquake, came to a standstill as a result of an almost total rail blockade by Azerbaijan, through which Armenia received 87 per cent of its supplies. Throughout the summer the death toll continued to rise in sporadic outbreaks of violence. At the end of November the direct rule experiment was judged to have failed, and Nagorny Karabakh was returned to Azerbaijani rule – and stalemate. By now most Armenians living in Azerbaijan had fled the republic, and there were few Azeris left in Armenia.

The most persistent erosion of Soviet power went on in the Baltic republics. Since the creation of the popular fronts the previous autumn, the local communist parties, and therefore the republican parliaments, had fallen heavily under their spell. Lithuania and Latvia passed declarations of sovereignty similar to Estonia's (which had been declared illegal by Moscow), giving them the right of veto over Soviet laws. At an emotional ceremony on a misty February morning, Estonia's president, Arnold Rüütel, raised the national blue, black and white tricolour for the first time from Tallinn's highest tower, to mark the anniversary of the creation of the bourgeois Estonian republic. The Balts refused to hold registration meetings to filter out candidates in the elections in March – and the Popular Front swept the board. The Estonians then passed an election law which required non-Estonians to have spent a minimum of two years in the republic before gaining the right to vote. All three republics reasserted their identities by moving into the Finnish time-zone, declaring Christmas a public holiday, permitting religious education and broadcasting, preparing citizenship laws, and a host of other measures.

On 23 August – the fiftieth anniversary of the Molotov–Ribbentrop Pact – some two million Balts joined hands to form a human chain linking Tallinn, Riga and Vilnius. Their action evoked a chorus of angry comment in Moscow, even though the Supreme Soviet commission on the Pact had just unofficially admitted the existence of its secret protocols and recommended that they be declared null and void. (These draft conclusions were not signed by the commission's chairman, Alexander Yakovlev, under pressure from the Party.)

The nationalist and intellectual bias of the popular fronts in the Baltic republics and elsewhere prompted an anti-intellectual (working class) and Russian counter-reaction. The Estonian Popular Front, for example, was opposed by an 'internationalist' organisation known as Inter-movement; in Latvia its equivalent was the Interfront. These groups represented the immigrant populations, primarily Russian and proletarian, who appealed for 'international friendship', by which they meant the restoration of the Brezhnevite–Stalinist colonial *status quo*. As a Lithuanian newspaper editor caustically remarked to me, 'I am bilingual, and they call me a nationalist, while they, who have spent perhaps twenty years here and never learnt a word of Lithuanian, are "internationalists".'

The rise of militant Russian working-class groups in the republics coincided with the rise of nationalistically inclined organisations in Russia itself. In July a United Workers Front was set up in Leningrad, with the participation of the conservative local Party leadership. This was clearly intended as a counterweight to the Leningrad Popular Front whose campaign had helped to humiliate the Leningrad leaders in the elections. The United Workers Front's first proposal was to change the local election laws to ensure that two-thirds of deputies were elected by workers at factories rather than by the electorate at large. This was strikingly similar to the call by the Leningrad leader, Yuri Solovyov, for a workers' congress to balance the too intellectual Congress of People's Deputies. It also corresponded to Ligachev's criticism of suggestions 'that the class composition of the soviets of people's deputies is of no importance'.[1]

In early September the various Russian workers' groups got together to found a United Front of Workers of Russia, its principal aims being to fight against market-oriented reforms and against the national movements in the non-Russian republics.

So 'nationalism' had many facets. In the Baltics, it was essentially progressive and democratic; in central Asia and Transcaucasia it brought racial passions to the surface; and in Russia itself it made common cause with all the conservative, anti-reform forces called into life by *perestroika*.

THE summer's events were not just the result of ethnic hatred. They had economic, and ultimately colonial roots. Yuri Afanasyev says the Soviet Union is 'constructed like a single factory or conveyor belt, where whole regions are like separate shops or units of the production-line. For example, Kazakhstan was turned into an accessory supplying raw materials for all the other republics. Central Asia was given over to the cultivation of cotton. The result was an ugly deformation of the natural state of each region – mutilated land and suffering people.'[2]

Unemployment is a big problem in central Asia (unlike almost everywhere else in the Soviet Union), and the riots in Uzbekistan and Kazakhstan are believed to have been caused mainly by poor living conditions, with the local inhabitants merely venting their frustrations on ethnic minorities in their regions. In much of central Asia, Moscow dictated that other crops be neglected for the sake of cotton-growing. The Fergana Valley, for instance, produces one-quarter of the country's cotton, but at a huge cost to the local environment and population. The people there consume less fruit and vegetables than in other parts of the country, and suffer higher rates of disease and infant mortality because of the dangerous chemicals used on the cotton.

Speaking at the Congress of People's Deputies, the Turkmenian Party leader, Saparmurad Niyazov, gave a textbook description of colonial exploitation. 'The economic structure of the republic is considerably distorted. The *per capita* production of consumer goods is three times lower than the USSR average. Though Turkmenia has the largest *per capita* production of cotton, it is hard to find cotton fabrics in our shops. No more than five per cent of the cotton grown in the republic is processed there.'[3]

How did Gorbachev react to this fever of unrest? As far as treating the disease was concerned, he did nothing, pending a central committee plenum on the nationalities question which was first scheduled for July 1989, and finally took place in September. All he could do in the meantime was treat the symptoms – by sending in interior ministry troops to quell violence and confiscate arms, and by evacuating persecuted minorities.

The nationalities plenum seemed doomed from the start. For one thing, its planning was largely in the hands of the former KGB chief, Viktor Chebrikov, whose insensitive statements about 'nationalist extremists' all summer made him the least suitable person to treat such an epidemic. It was he who drafted an aggressively worded central committee statement on 26 August which described nationalist movements in the Baltic republics as 'reminiscent of political formations of the Nazi period', with no support among the 'common people'. The slogans held aloft by the human chain of 23 August were alleged to have been 'foisted upon' the two million participants. The statement said that 'things have gone too far' and warned of 'impending disaster'.[4]

Inexplicably, instead of addressing the plenum when it opened on

19 September, Chebrikov was sacked at it – but not, one must assume, because of deep disagreements with Gorbachev over nationalities policy. Gorbachev's own speech showed how hard he found it to overcome his Russocentric view of the empire.

Apart from the age-old panacea – 'Lenin's national policy' – Gorbachev offered only some degree of economic autonomy for the republics, while making it clear that his concept of this was significantly more limited than that of the Balts. Similarly, he supported republican state languages, but effectively gave Russian precedence over them by proposing that it be the state language of the Soviet Union as a whole. He insisted that the Baltic nations had entered the Soviet Union of their own free will – a statement which was untrue and deeply offensive to them. He produced figures to prove how integrated the economies of the republics were, without realising that such proof of the 'colonial production line' would cut no ice in the Baltics. Secession, he said, was something contemplated only by 'adventurists' and 'demagogues', while boundary changes, such as those demanded by the Armenians of Nagorny Karabakh, 'would only make a difficult situation worse.'[5]

There was little in this for anyone except the Russians. The long-awaited nationalities plenum, eighteen months in preparation, did nothing to ease the fundamental problems. Gorbachev's determination to hold the federation together at all costs, in its existing shape, overrode any sympathy he may have had for the national aspirations of the country's 100-odd peoples. Such thinking was strikingly at odds with his policies abroad.

STALIN'S empire stretched as far as the Elbe, the Danube, and Checkpoint Charlie. Khrushchev defended that empire in 1956 when he invaded Hungary to stop the anti-communist revolution. Brezhnev did the same in 1968 in Czechoslovakia. His assertion of the Kremlin's 'right' to intervene to prop up communist regimes in any of the allied countries was dubbed in the West the 'Brezhnev doctrine'.

Gorbachev's empire stopped at Brest-Litovsk, the frontier town between the USSR and Poland. Within the borders of the Soviet Union he gave short shrift to national moves towards secession. But beyond, nations were free to follow their own paths of development, even to leave the socialist camp. Foreign ministry spokesman Gennady Gerasimov, the Kremlin's chief wit and propagandist, dubbed this the 'Sinatra doctrine': allowing each country to 'do it their way'. Gorbachev had outlined the theory in numerous speeches, most notably at the United Nations, but it was only in the autumn of 1989 that he got the chance to prove he meant it.

All East European regimes were unpopular for two reasons: they were unelected communist dictatorships; and they were regarded as vassals of a foreign power. The Hungarian communists were the first to seize the opportunity afforded by *perestroika* to try to give themselves legitimacy by, first, displaying their independence of Moscow, and, secondly, turning themselves into a humane socialist party, willing to submit itself to public scrutiny in free elections. The Brezhnev-era leader, Janos Kadar, was sacked. The Party declared its aim to be the establishment of a multi-party system and a Western-style market economy. The leading reformist Imre Pozsgay admitted for the first time that the events of 1956 were a 'popular uprising'. The executed leader of the uprising, Imre Nagy, was given a ceremonial reburial. The Communist Party renounced its constitutionally guaranteed 'leading role' in society. In March the prime minister, Miklos Nemeth, went to Moscow to check that they were not overstepping the limits. Gorbachev sang the Sinatra tune: 'Every ruling communist party solves tasks in accordance with its historical conditions and national values, and works out its policies in a sovereign fashion.'[6]

The Hungarian communists were the only ones to understand that legitimacy comes only through the ballot box. The Poles, by contrast, tried to subvert democracy by holding half-free elections in June which guaranteed the Communist Party a majority (much as Gorbachev had done in the Soviet Union). But the communists suffered such a massive moral humiliation, losing every freely contested seat to candidates supported by the newly legalised Solidarity trade union, that in August they were forced to succumb to the people's judgment and allow a leading Solidarity journalist, Tadeusz Mazowiecki, to become the eastern bloc's first non-communist – indeed anti-communist – prime minister.

Meanwhile the Hungarian government – the only regime which was liberal enough not to require a prison wall along its borders to prevent a mass exodus of its citizens – literally pulled the plug on its neighbours. On 2 May soldiers snipped away the barbed wire 'iron curtain' between Hungary and Austria. During the summer, increasing numbers of East Germans, ostensibly holidaying in Hungary, found they could slip across the border at night and make their way to West Germany, where Bonn automatically guaranteed them citizenship. In September Hungary cocked a snook at the dinosaur regime in East Berlin by allowing East Germans to travel unhindered to the West. Tens of thousands left.

In East Germany pressure mounted for radical reforms that might help to stem the haemorrhage. Groups such as New Forum called for 'humane socialism', but were declared illegal. Thousands of people began to demonstrate every Monday evening in Leipzig. In this, its hour of humiliation, the regime tried to celebrate the German Democratic Republic's fortieth anniversary on 7 October, with singing, dancing, speeches and torchlight parades for the assembled guests, including Mikhail Gorbachev. That afternoon Gorbachev held talks with the entire East German Politburo, and warned them of the consequences facing hardline regimes which ignored the mood of the people: 'He who is late will be punished by life itself,' he said. Gorbachev was speaking from bitter experience: the consequences of his own tardiness were only too plain at home.

'He did not utter a harsh word,' says his aide, Georgy Shakhnazarov, who sat at Gorbachev's side during the meeting, 'nor accuse them of being too conservative. He said: "Look at the situation in the world – everything changes, and we cannot act as before. For many years we used to say the West was stagnating and would collapse. But they've overtaken us in terms of technology, and socially they have done much more than we have. You live close to them and must feel this."'

But his host, Erich Honecker, ignored this homily, and repeated his view that the GDR had no need to change its successful course, brushing aside Gorbachev's remarks with such discourtesy that two other Politburo members – Berlin Party chief Günter Schabowski and the state security chief, Egon Krenz – apologised afterwards to members of the Soviet delegation.[7]

Schabowski and Krenz had been plotting Honecker's removal ever since the crisis began. They did not discuss their plans with Gorbachev; they did not have to – his views were evident. At a reception that evening the Soviet leader was shown on television demonstratively kissing the prime minister, Willi Stoph, but not Honecker. Outside, Gorbachev's prophecy was already coming true. A large group gathered in the dusk near the Palace of the Republic. Inside, behind the copper-coloured reflecting windows, the celebrations of 40 years of communist rule were in full swing. On the square, a collective feeling of disgust welled up in the people's throats, and a huge crowd set off through the streets of East Berlin, chanting 'Freedom', 'Gorby' and 'We are the people'. The crowd swelled to many thousands – the biggest demonstration in the capital since the workers' uprising of 1953. Riot police closed off the streets, cornered the demonstrators, beat some of them up, but could not stop them. They marched on late into the night. Honecker's celebration party was ruined.

He almost took his revenge on the Leipzig demonstrators two days later, but Krenz moved swiftly to prevent a bloodbath. In the next ten days he and Schabowski persuaded their colleagues to act, and on 18 October Honecker was removed from power and replaced by Krenz. But this did not stop the demonstrations, and thousands of people continued to leave the country every day. The government resigned on 7 November, and a new one was formed under Hans Modrow, the reformist Party leader from Dresden, who was apparently Moscow's choice, and had had clandestine meetings at the Soviet embassy. Two days later the Berlin Wall was opened up to allow unrestricted travel to the West. On that joyous night, millions of Germans celebrated freedom and the end of the post-war division of Europe.

Thereafter, the cancer cells quickly spread around Eastern Europe. On 10 November, Todor Zhivkov, who had ruled Bulgaria since 1954, was ousted. The new leadership soon promised free elections and the abolition of the Party's leading role. A week later, the brutal dispersal of a student demonstration in Prague led to daily mass demonstrations on Wenceslas Square, and they in turn brought about the resignation of the entire Czechoslovak Party leadership on 24 November. Here too the Party's 'leading role' was deleted from the Constitution. In December a coalition government with non-communists in the majority was formed, and just before the year's end Vaclav Havel, the country's leading dissident, was elected president.

A week earlier the revolution had even penetrated the Stalinist stronghold of Romania. After demonstrations in the western city of Timisoara were bloodily suppressed, the people rose up against the tyranny of Nicolae Ceausescu, and with the help of the army, overthrew him. He and his wife Elena were executed, and a National Salvation Front took power, promising free elections and a return to democracy.

At no stage did Gorbachev offer even a hint of support to his beleaguered colleagues. On the contrary his only advice was that unless they started their own *perestroikas* they would suffer. Only with Ceausescu did he raise his voice, according to Shakhnazarov. The Romanian leader wanted the Warsaw Pact to overthrow the Mazowiecki government in Poland, and even threatened to act without the Soviet Union. Gorbachev gave him a 'serious warning', says Shakhnazarov.

Within the Soviet Union, many senior politicians and military men saw the 'loss' of Eastern Europe as a disastrous defeat. Marshal Akhromeyev, the chief of the general staff, felt deep regret at the fate suffered by his personal friends who had run Eastern Europe for so many years. 'Do you think it was pleasant', he asked, 'for me to watch the destruction of, say, the Czechoslovak regime, and of this judgment being passed on the communists? I am a communist and don't intend to leave the Party. It was a bitter thing to see those regimes fall. I fought for them, I knew the leaders personally – both the military and the political. They are my friends. In East Germany, for example, they were all my good friends, starting from Honecker down. I don't believe the things they say about Honecker now (about his corruption and abuse of power). He is a man of crystal-pure honesty.'

At the same time, Akhromeyev pointed out that this did not mean that 'I or some other general was about to march off with our guns . . . You can't prop up a party if it loses the faith of the people.'

But by no means all his military colleagues agreed with that. Some even said so publicly. General Albert Makashov, commander of the Volga-Urals military district, lamented that, 'because of the victories, the so-called victories, of Soviet diplomacy, the Soviet Army is being driven without a fight from countries which our fathers liberated from fascism.'[8] There were critics of the policy in the political leadership, too. Ligachev complained that West Germany was simply 'devouring' the GDR, and that there could be no better proof of the continuing 'class nature' of international relations. 'What we are seeing is a major retreat from socialism,' he told a central committee plenum, 'but I am an optimist and think that in historic terms this is a temporary defeat. They say that as a result of the changes that have taken place in Eastern Europe opportunities are opening up for the creation of a united civilisation. Maybe! But something quite different is happening. I, of course, am in favour of developing peaceful co-operation among different states, but not by rolling back socialism and strengthening the international positions of capitalism. Yet that is the direction everything is going in. The NATO bloc is strengthening, while the socialist community is falling apart.'[9] Remarkably, however – as Ligachev also pointed out – the question was never discussed properly in the Politburo. Gorbachev simply allowed events to take their course.

In a ringing defence of this policy, the foreign minister, Eduard Shevardnadze, later gave the following answer to an unnamed Communist Party critic of the 'serious defeat for Soviet diplomacy': 'Soviet diplomacy did not and could not aim to prevent the elimination in other countries of administrative-command systems and *totalitarian regimes which were forced upon them and alien to them* [my italics]. That would have contradicted the logic of our own actions and the principles of new thinking. Furthermore, even if what was happening in Eastern Europe had conflicted with our interests, we would still have ruled out any interference in the affairs of these states.' Asked whether he and the top Soviet leadership knew in advance how things were going to develop in Eastern Europe, he hinted that Gorbachev had ignored pleas for help from the old leaders and connived at their overthrow: 'Yes, we basically forecast the changes and felt their inevitability. When the time comes it will be possible to show transcripts of conversations which Mikhail Sergeyevich had, and the telegrams which came from the capitals of those countries. We sensed that if there were not serious changes and reforms, events could end tragically.' As for the unification of Germany, Shevardnadze admitted that Moscow used to see the division of the country as a guarantee of security, 'but can a guarantee be reliable if it is based on the artificial and unnatural division of a great nation?'[10]

THESE events had a tumultuous effect back in the Soviet Union, where people saw the entire revolution played out on television. As each 'fraternal' communist leader was ousted, the Soviet press began to refer to him as a dictator and to praise the establishment of 'democracy'. Portentous questions begged to be answered. If the pluralist, multi-party systems now being set up in Eastern Europe constituted 'democracy', then why should the Soviet Union not also have such a democracy? If the old communist regimes were now branded as unpopular dictatorships, what about the present Soviet regime? If East Europeans could throw out the communists, why could not the Soviet people? If the 'leading role' of the Party was being abolished in country after country, why not in the Soviet Union?

In late November, Gorbachev wrote an article in *Pravda*, in which he sought to demonstrate the difference between his leadership and the regimes being overthrown in Eastern Europe.[11] The aim of *perestroika*, he said, was to build socialism 'with a human face' – precisely the phrase associated with the 1968 Prague Spring, which Brezhnev's tanks had crushed. Because of opposition within the leadership, he still could not openly advocate a multi-party system for the Soviet Union. But he indicated clearly for the first time that it would come eventually. The one-party system, he wrote, was 'expedient' as a means of 'consolidating society and focusing all its healthy forces on the difficult tasks of *perestroika*' – but only 'at the current complex stage'.

This did not go far enough for the radicals. They regarded the 'leading role of the Party', as enshrined in Article Six of the Constitution, as being incompatible with the creation of a civil society, because it made every public and state institution subordinate to the Party rather than to society. It meant that the Party not only had power, but had wealth and assets rivalling – or even greater than – those of the state. The finest buildings in the land belonged to the Party, as did most of the newspapers and publishing houses. The KGB and the army were answerable not to the government or parliament but to the Party, on whose Politburo their bosses sat.

The Inter-regional Group of deputies made the abolition of Article Six its prime goal, but failed in its efforts to have the issue included in the agenda for the second session of the Congress of People's Deputies, which was due to start on 12 December 1989. At a central committee plenum on the eve of the session, Vadim Bakatin, the progressive interior minister, also tried to persuade the leadership that it was time to recognise that a multi-party system was in any case already taking shape. He argued that the Party's insistence on keeping Article Six in the Constitution 'handed points' to the opposition.

That Gorbachev failed to come to his side was not surprising, given the hostility of the other speeches at the plenum, which showed how the *apparat* was still smarting from its election defeats, the chaos in the republics and the coalfields, and the 'loss' of Eastern Europe. Far from being able to push ahead with his masterplan for the introduction of a multi-party system, Gorbachev had to fight for his survival in the face of a ferocious attack on his record by hardliners. The transcript of this turbulent meeting of the Party's 400 top functionaries shows that the assault was led by Alexander Melnikov, the Party first secretary in Kemerovo region, where the summer's coal strikes had started.[12] Melnikov was a long-standing close associate of Ligachev's, and had been defeated in the March elections.

Melnikov observed that the Party's attempts to solve all the problems besetting the country reminded him of 'reading fire regulations when the whole house is already in flames'. He went on, in a passage that particularly infuriated Gorbachev: 'You will note that the whole bourgeois world, all our former and present enemies, praise us for the critical situation that exists in the country, and the Pope blesses us.' Melnikov claimed that 'separate groups in the Politburo' (apparently he meant the Gorbachev-Shevardnadze-Yakovlev group) had a monopoly on decision-making. He was applauded when he criticised the press for directing 'our ideological weaponry' at ordinary Party workers. Workers and secretaries of Party organisations – the *apparat* – were fed up with being blamed for the mistakes and shortcomings of the leadership, he said: 'We haven't taken any decisions, nobody asked us – the "charge" was ordered from above. Those who took the decisions and made the mistakes must take the blame personally for what has taken place over the past four years.'

Gorbachev was shaken by the vehemence and directness of this attack. 'We will have to think about comrade Melnikov's thesis that "the bourgoisie and even the Pope praise what we are doing in the country." What he means is that we are not going in the right direction, that we've taken the wrong road.'

Gorbachev stunned the hall into silence with a dramatic offer of resignation: 'This is very serious, comrades. It turns out, we're going in the wrong direction. So we're mistaken. If that's the way you feel, comrades, you'll have to elect a new Politburo and a new general secretary . . . I for one cannot associate myself with such an assessment of our policies. What I have been doing is what is necessary for our country – I am certain of this! You have to decide. Let everyone make his views plain. If that's the way the question has been put, it has to be resolved, comrades. Resolved! What are we going to do?'

Two speakers later, the Minsk Party secretary, Anatoly Malofeyev, let slip the phrase, 'We must bring *perestroika* on to the right path', and Gorbachev hit the roof. 'Here's another one saying we're not going in the right direction!' he exclaimed, and amid what the transcript describes as 'commotion in the hall', he shouted: 'Come on, then, let's deal with this! Let's deal with this! Let's deal with this!'

In the end, no one dared to call for a vote of confidence in Gorbachev, but it was clear that he could not ask this audience to agree to abolish Article Six of the Constitution.

As he wound up the proceedings, Melnikov took the floor again to ingratiate himself with Gorbachev, but the general secretary once more flew off the handle, recalling those words about the bourgeoisie and the Pope. The transcript ends like this:

> GORBACHEV: I reject this. I do not accept it! It is casting aspersions on everything we are doing.
> VOICES: (*commotion in the hall*)
> GORBACHEV: Does anybody else want to speak?
> VOICES: No.
> GORBACHEV: I declare the plenum closed.

On 12 December the second session of the Congress of People's Deputies opened. When Andrei Sakharov tried to hand Gorbachev a petition demanding the abolition of Article Six, Gorbachev rudely brushed him aside, and bullied the deputies into voting not to include the matter in the agenda. Two days later, after making an emotional speech in which he criticised the slow pace of reform, Sakharov suddenly died. He was praised by Moscow radio as 'our conscience', and Gorbachev joined mourners in condemning Sakharov's seven-year exile in Gorky as a 'gross injustice' and calling his death 'a major loss for Soviet society'. He may well have reflected that he himself had met many of the demands for which Sakharov was banished in 1980, and would gladly have accelerated the pace of reform, were he not surrounded by Ligachevs and Melnikovs.

THE lessons of Eastern Europe were most keenly understood in the Baltic republics. The three nations regarded themselves as equal to the Poles or Czechs: they had been incorporated into the empire at about the same time, the only catch being that they had ended up inside the borders of the Soviet Union and were thus denied even the limited sovereignty accorded to the rest of Eastern Europe.

Free elections to the republican parliaments were looming. In Lithuania they were due as early as 24 February 1990, and the majority of Lithuanian communists, led by Algirdas Brazauskas, saw their only hope of survival in following the Hungarian model – that is , in asserting their national identity and adopting liberal-socialist (or social democratic) policies. (They could not know at that stage that even the thoroughly reformed and renamed Hungarian communist party would be trounced by voters in the first free election.) Having moved closer and closer to the Sajudis movement, which itself was by now campaigning for outright independence, the Lithuanian Communist Party held a special four-day plenum just before Christmas

1989. Headed by Brazauskas, 82 per cent of the delegates voted to leave the Soviet Communist Party and set up as an independent party with their own Programme and Rules. The Party split, with the remaining 18 per cent and their supporters declaring that they were still loyal to Moscow.

This was no internal Lithuanian matter: it struck at the very heart of Gorbachev's policy. Gorbachev had ruled out the federalisation of the Communist Party. Only the Party, in his view, could overcome the strengthening centrifugal forces in the country and keep the federation from falling apart.

Immediately after the Lithuanian party's decision, he called an emergency plenum of the CPSU central committee in Moscow, on 25-26 December. The acrimonious debate demonstrated that the disintegration of the empire was perhaps the rawest nerve so far exposed by *perestroika*. A few exerpts give the flavour of the discussion: of the accusations hurled at the Lithuanian breakaway leader, Brazauskas; of the desperate fears of the Moscow leadership; and of Brazauskas's attempts to wriggle out of an impossible situation.

> GORBACHEV: Do you think you will take part in further work on Party policy?
> BRAZAUSKAS: It's hard to say. Our Congress only ended two days ago.
> GORBACHEV: So you will not take part in our central committee plenum any more?
> BRAZAUSKAS: I will if you invite me. We as the independent Party of Lithuania will take an active part in the political life of the Soviet Union . . . because we are an integral part of the USSR.
> VOICES [*protests in hall*]
> GORBACHEV: Comrades, don't get upset. We must understand each other and decide what to do. . . . Do you think other republican communist parties should do the same as you have done?
> BRAZAUSKAS: Yes.
> GORBACHEV: So how does that fit with your statement that you are trying to avoid splitting the CPSU?
> BRAZAUSKAS: We must avoid it.
> GORBACHEV: You have left the CPSU. Others will do the same. Let's think logically – what is left?
> BRAZAUSKAS: The whole of the Soviet Union is left.
> VOICES: [*Noise, laughter in hall*]
> GORBACHEV: The fact that the Soviet Union is left is clear. But what about the Party?
> BRAZAUSKAS: We are small. Just one per cent.
> GORBACHEV: No, wait. What if the communists of Russia, of the Ukraine, and all the others start leaving?

BRAZAUSKAS: Where are they leaving? They are not leaving.

GORBACHEV: What if they leave the CPSU . . .?

BRAZAUSKAS: But everyone is staying in the Soviet Union.

GORBACHEV: I'm not talking about that. If everyone leaves the CPSU, that will be the end of the Communist Party.

VADIM MEDVEDEV [Politburo member]: I want to ask a simple question. Are you still a member of the Soviet Communist Party, or have you left it?

BRAZAUSKAS: It's a difficult question, of course. We represent the reconstructed Party of Lithuania. We are all communists. Those members of the CPSU who want to be members of the Lithuanian Communist Party will join it, and those who can't agree will be in a separate organisation . . . [noises in hall] I personally will be with the majority . . . [noises] in the Communist Party of Lithuania.

ALEXANDRA BIRYUKOVA [deputy prime minister]: I have in front of me an address adopted by the Lithuanian Party. It says '[Our] aim is the same as the aim of the rest of Lithuania – to create the independent state of Lithuania.' How can we interpret that? You yourself have been talking about *remaining* within the Soviet Union.

BRAZAUSKAS: Yes, but what is the word 'independent'? It is the same as 'sovereignty'. [noises] Let us look it up in the dictionary. You will see that it is the same; at any rate, it is in Lithuanian. The sovereignty of individual republics is enshrined even in the out-dated Soviet Constitution which is still in force, and we are now turning that into reality.

BUROKEVICIUS [leader of pro-Moscow faction of Lithuanian Party]: The Communist Party of Lithuania is in the grip of national egotism, its leaders are in the grip of megalomania. The defeatist tendency has given in to anti-socialist, separatist and nationalist forces. A historic tragedy has hit the Communist Party of Lithuania.

NAZARBAYEV [first secretary of Kazakh Communist Party]: The communists who sing along with those who blacken the Party and set the public against it are fifth-columnists. There will be nothing left of the Party's authority if we tolerate this destructive activity, if we calmly watch the betrayal of our comrades. We cannot allow people who don't share our aims and ideals, and who sell the Party's and the nation's interests for the sake of their political ambitions, to remain in our Party.

YELCHENKO [secretary of the Ukrainian Communist Party]: The Lithuanian precedent is dangerous not only for the Party but for the whole of our federation.

VADIM MEDVEDEV: The Lithuanian Communist Party has given in to mass pressure and social psychosis. The nationalist forces felt the weakness of the leadership, and in order to achieve its aims of secession from the Soviet Union they worked through the Communist Party. And I must say they have succeeded.

GORBACHEV: It's a Trojan horse.

LIGACHEV: The last obstacle in the way of the separatists has been removed. What kind of *perestroika* is it, comrade Brazauskas, if you announce that the main aim of your party is to set up an independent state? You have found yourself at the head of the separatist forces, whose aim is the destruction of the Soviet federation. That is the political logic. [*applause*] The anti-socialist, nationalist and separatist forces are turning their words into subversive actions aimed at undermining the basis of socialism.

IVASHKO [first secretary of Ukrainian Communist Party]: It's not just a question of the Lithuanian Party. Those who prompted Brazauskas to organise the split understand perfectly well that they can't succeed without starting a chain reaction in other republics.

MASLYUKOV [Head of State Planning Committee]: Comrades, we must remember the defence of the interests of the Soviet Union. What shall we do with the defence installations in Lithuania? Should we just disarm? And another thing – there are 200 000 non-Lithuanian families living in the republic. They will want to leave. There will be a problem of refugees – even bigger than the one we have with Armenians, Azeris, Meskhetian Turks . . .

GORBACHEV: Comrades, we must not allow that. We must get rid of those adventurers, those who ignore reality, who want to trample over the lives of millions of people. [*applause*]

GEDRAITIS [former secretary of Lithuanian Communist Party]: I would like to say that comrade Yakovlev [the liberal Politburo member] carries some of the responsibility. He visited Lithuania and did not evaluate the situation soberly.

SOKOLOV [Belorussian Party leader]: This has been a long time in the making. The central committee must have known about it. Yet look at how Sajudis was praised in the papers! It was on television – how enthusiastic the reports were! They were showing us a new experiment and saying: 'comrades, follow their example, act!'[13] Who is responsible for our press and television? Comrade [Vadim] Medvedev [ideology secretary], you must share the blame for everything together with the Lithuanian comrades. [*enthusiastic applause*] I suggest we should first of all order the dissolution of Sajudis. And I support the proposal to expel comrade Brazauskas from the Party. I cannot be in the same party as him!

At this point Gorbachev intervened to try to cool passions, but he himself talked in riddles and muddles, apparently thrown off his stride by what he called the 'bloodthirsty atmosphere' at the plenum. He accused the previous speakers of acting as if they were at a timber yard, 'chopping wood' irresponsibly, instead of talking things through calmly and seriously. 'Today in this Kremlin hall,' he reminded them, 'the fate of the world is being decided. Where do we go after this plenum? A great deal depends on that – the fate of the country, the fate of socialism, the fate of the world. . . . I think the Communist Party's main aim is to avoid a shoot-out . . .[14]

The plenum ended inconclusively, deciding only to send a delegation, headed by Gorbachev, to Lithuania to study the situation, and then to reconvene and study the matter further.

In January Gorbachev spent three days in Lithuania and came face to face, for the first time, with the true feelings of a captive nation with only one concern in the world: freedom and independence. Secession was the issue, not just the disloyalty of the republic's Communist Party. Gorbachev had done his homework, and tried to prove to the Lithuanians, in set speeches and pavement chats, how bad things had been during the years of independence and how much they had gained from Soviet power. Major reforms in the pipeline, he said, would give them all the sovereignty they needed within the Soviet Union. He confused many by both rejecting the idea of leaving the Union and promising a new law which would regulate the mechanics of secession.

In one televised incident, Gorbachev lost his temper with an elderly worker during a visit to a factory. The worker was carrying a banner reading 'Total independence for Lithuania'.

'Who told you to write that banner?' Gorbachev asked.

'Nobody. I wrote it myself,' the worker replied.

'Who are you? Where do you work? And what do you mean by total independence?' said Gorbachev.

'I mean what we had in the 1920s, when Lenin recognised Lithuania's sovereignty, because no nation is entitled to dictate to another nation.'

'Within our large family, Lithuania has become a developed country,' said Gorbachev. 'What kind of exploiters are we if Russia sells you cotton, oil and raw materials – and not for hard currency, either?'

The worker interrupted: 'Lithuania had a hard currency before the War. You took it all away in 1940. And do you know how many Lithuanians were sent to Siberia in the 1940s, and how many died?'

Gorbachev lost his temper. 'I don't want to talk with this man any more. If people in Lithuania have attitudes and slogans like this, they can expect hard times. I don't want to talk to you any more.'

Raisa tried to calm him. He told her to 'be quiet'.[15]

Despite such behaviour, the Lithuanians in the streets did not seem angry with him. Rather, they just dismissed all his talk as if it were somehow irrelevant. They already had their minds set on the republican elections in February, confident of the result they would bring.

EVEN as Gorbachev tried to cajole and banter on the streets of Vilnius, Soviet power was virtually collapsing in Azerbaijan.

Over the New Year, thousands of Azeri rioters had pulled down the border fences between the Azerbaijani province of Nakhichevan[16] and Iran. A week later, tens of thousands of Popular Front supporters began to demonstrate in the capital, Baku, against renewed Armenian claims to Nagorny Karabakh and a decision by the Armenian parliament to extend election laws to cover the region, which was still legally part of Azerbaijan. On 13 January (Gorbachev's last day in Lithuania), 70 000 Azeris, assembled in the centre of Baku, were told that an Armenian living in the city had axed to death an Azeri who had come to evict him. A mob set off through the streets, hunting down Armenians and smashing up houses. In a horrific pogrom that lasted two days, they massacred some sixty Armenians. The two republics came to the brink of war. In some districts full-scale guerrilla warfare, with stolen army ammunition, armoured cars and even helicopters, did break out. A state of emergency was declared. Army and interior ministry troops were sent to the area at once, but found it impossible to enforce the law because of massive civil disobedience. Troops were unable to enter Baku because of road blocks erected on the outskirts of the city. For three days demonstrators held Baku under siege, demanding the resignation of the leadership. The Azeri government of the region of Nakhichevan, meanwhile, declared its secession from the Soviet Union and intention to set up an independent Islamic republic.

On 19 January, Gorbachev, now back in Moscow and firmly in control, ordered a military assault, by land and sea, to retake Baku from what he was told were Popular Front insurgents who were about to seize full power in Azerbaijan. Officially, eighty-three people were killed in street battles as tanks smashed through barricades. Nationalists claim the death toll ran into several hundreds. The action was taken against the wishes of the republican government: the president of the parliament condemned the assault and declared that her people would never forgive those responsible. As in Georgia, the people, the nationalist movement and the republic's government were drawn closer together as a result of bloody action ordered by Moscow. But this time, Gorbachev could not blame it on others. He took the decision, based on reports received from candidate Politburo member Yevgeny Primakov, who had arrived in Baku on 14 January, the day after the anti-Armenian pogrom. Primakov admits that the pogrom ended long before the Soviet army assault, thus confirming that the action had nothing to do with saving lives, as was claimed at first.

Primakov makes it clear that the aim was to crush the Popular Front: 'Many people here and in the West have the impression that the Popular Front is a democratic organisation. Maybe it is in other places, but not in Azerbaijan. One of their leaders, Panakhov, made a speech on the 13th – we have it on video tape – where he said that not a single Armenian should be left on the territory of Azerbaijan. Just 150 metres away a man was burned to death, and he did nothing – he continued his speech. They were beasts. What were their plans? In effect they already had power in their hands. They had three gallows erected in the central committee building. Outside there was a raving crowd of 25 000. I spoke to them. It was terrible . . .'

The contours of the Gorbachev doctrine were now clear. The nations of Eastern Europe were free to do things 'their way', but the nations of the Soviet Union, while they were free to raise the issue of secession, had to go about it '*his* way' – cautiously, peacefully, constitutionally, and not before every other option, including the gradual devolution of certain powers to the republics, had been given a chance to succeed. In the event of a direct threat to Soviet power, he was willing to send in tanks and spill blood.

He was truly to be pitied. Many countries have one or two problems with national or religious minorities. The Soviet Union has more than a hundred nations, living in territories defined, in the main, by Stalin. And even more than the troubles in the economy or the political and legal systems, this part of Stalin's legacy could not be conjured away at the stroke of a legislator's pen. Every move to satisfy one nation was guaranteed to offend several others.

And yet the aspirations of the republics were both natural and necessary. For without a fundamental reshaping of the relations between the centre and the republics, without the abandonment of the colonial structure, the crisis could only get worse.

# CHAPTER SIX

# The Climax of Perestroika

NIKOLAI Travkin was a working man and devout communist – the kind of person Yegor Ligachev considered the salt of the earth and the soul of the Communist Party. As the leader of a construction brigade he had made a huge success of the 1983 Andropov experiment in self-financing and self-management. He was held up as an example by Gorbachev, was awarded the title Hero of Socialist Labour, was elected a delegate to the Nineteenth Party Conference in 1988, and a year later entered parliament.

Then, in the autumn of 1989, he made his first trip abroad, to Sweden and the United States. His life was changed – not by the shops, which he soon got used to, but by the sight of the people, who seemed 'uninhibited, with good complexions, easily moving from one language to another, and confident of themselves – in contrast to our eternal Russian supplicants'. There were well-tended flower-beds in front of the houses, not the wilderness of weeds that surrounds most Soviet blocks of flats. Travkin was seized with 'powerless fury – the usual fury of a normal Russian abroad at the thought of his own ways'. Back home, he could no longer bear to hear the kind of clichés spouted by Party leaders about 'our people, who cannot imagine themselves outside the framework of the socialist choice'.[1]

At the end of May 1990 Travkin left the Communist Party and founded the Democratic Party of Russia, dedicated to burying the communist system and restoring private enterprise, democracy, and truth.

Travkin's transformation was typical of a new mood, hardened and cynical, that settled on the country from around the beginning of 1990. All the strands of disillusion were summed up for me by a taxi driver in Moscow in February. He said: 'For decades these communists have been telling us we were the most advanced country in the world. Now we see we're just about last. They've made fools of us. You can't even buy socks in the shops now. If they can get rid of them in Eastern Europe, so should we.'

Russians had always grumbled about shortages. What was new was the focusing of their anger on 'these communists', and the realisation that there was no immutable law which condemned them to live under communism for ever.

Several factors contributed to this change, apart from the almost ecstatic television and press coverage of the anti-communist revolutions throughout the Warsaw Pact countries. First, 4.3 million people travelled abroad on holiday or business in 1989, not just to the 'socialist countries' but to Western Europe and America.[2] Like Travkin, they lost their innocence and came back as 'adults', laden with as many consumer goods as they could carry and shaken by their first experience of freedom and plenty. They told their friends about it. Others experienced it vicariously on television, which by now made no attempt to pretend that Soviet-style socialism was a 'more developed stage of human development'. Western radio, no longer jammed, boomed in loud and clear with the same message.

Second, *glasnost* on Soviet history had moved into a new phase. Almost all the forbidden works of the Brezhnev period were being published, and those authors who had been banished to the West were welcomed back and interviewed on television. Even the most famous work of all, Alexander Solzhenitsyn's three-volume labour camp epic, *The Gulag Archipelago*, came out in full.

There was nothing much new in all this for the intelligentsia, but for millions of less aware citizens the truth about the West and about the Soviet Union's past came as a rude shock. What they had been told was imperialist propaganda turned out to be true. Stalin *had* murdered millions, Western schoolchildren really did learn to use computers, Soviet rates of infant mortality and life expectancy really were on Third World levels. In a word, the 'most advanced nation in the history of mankind' really was 'Upper Volta with rockets', as the Western press had dubbed it.

Worse than the truth itself was the humiliation of being duped. One of the features of totalitarian regimes is that by controlling all information they make sure that most of their citizens are not *aware* that they live in a totalitarian regime. It was only as they emerged from the dark that many Soviet citizens began to realise there was such a thing as light. They felt intensely bitter and ashamed to discover that they had believed half of the lies they had been fed since birth.

And now, to cap it all, the economy was simply grinding to a halt. Never mind complicated things like toothpaste and televisions, the great planned economy could not even provide its citizens with socks.

Above all, the same Party that had perpetrated these crimes and got the country into such a mess was still at the helm, begging for a last chance to get things right, and protesting piously that it had changed – even as it refused to remove Article Six from the Constitution.

IT WAS this mood that set the agenda for 1990, not any dim plans for controlled democratisation that Gorbachev might have devised two or three years earlier. By February, just two months after he had refused to allow Congress to discuss Article Six, the pressure on him to change his mind became overwhelming. Local and republican elections were just around the corner, and grass-roots revolts against conservative leaders in some regions at the start of the year gave a taste of the thrashing that the Party could expect.

The Party itself was in grave danger of splitting: on 20–21 January some 450 representatives of reformist communist groups from 78 cities met in Moscow to set up the Democratic Platform of the CPSU. Its aim was to turn the Party into a Western-style parliamentary party with social democratic policies, which would compete for power on an equal footing with other parties. Its leaders included many of the radical figures who had made names for themselves in the Congress of People's Deputies – Gavriil Popov, Yuri Afanasyev, Sergei Stankevich, Boris Yeltsin. Though scarcely represented in the top echelons of the Party (except, covertly, by Alexander Yakovlev), the Democratic Platform's voice was a powerful addition to the campaign against Article Six.

Gorbachev, however, felt that simply to declare the country a multi-party democracy would do nothing in itself to ease the crisis. Early in 1990 he began devising a whole package of new reforms to deal, in effect, with the adverse consequences of his previous ones – particularly the disintegration of the federation and the virtual collapse of the economy.

The trouble, he believed, was that while the country now had, in the Congress and Supreme Soviet, a reasonably effective central legislature, it was not backed up with an effective administrative or executive arm of government. This role had in the past been played principally by the Communist Party, with its strong vertical structure, but the Party had now been told to stop interfering in matters of government. Following Gorbachev's reforms of December 1988, the 42-member presidium of the Supreme Soviet was now the unwieldy collective head of state, while Gorbachev, as Chairman of the Supreme Soviet, had ended up as a glorified Speaker of parliament, with little real executive power.

The key element of the new package was therefore the creation of a presidential system of government to fill what Gorbachev's deputy, Anatoly Lukyanov, called the 'vacuum of executive power' and ensure that legislation, once passed, was effectively enforced. Six months earlier, Gorbachev had ruled out the idea of an executive presidency on the grounds that it would concentrate too much power in one person's hands and undermine his efforts to transfer power from the Party to the soviets and the government. Moreover, he told friends, he did not want it to look as if he had planned the entire reform just to make himself president. Partly at the urging of Alexander Yakovlev, he now changed his mind.

At the same time, Gorbachev wanted the party to accept a whole new programme befitting its role as a *part* of the political system, rather than its 'nucleus', as Article Six put it. In the Politburo in the first months of 1990, he hammered out a 'Platform' based on the principles of 'humane, democratic socialism', which he wanted to have adopted at the coming Twenty-eighth Party Congress. He had already advanced the date for the Congress (not to be confused with the Congress of People's Deputies, or parliament) from early 1991 to October; and now, with the pressure for change mounting daily, he proposed bringing it further forward to July 1990. The Platform included a commitment to the 'planned market economy' and a reformed federation which would ensure 'optimum relations' between the republics and the centre.

Gorbachev put his new proposals to the central committee at stormy plenums in February and March against a background of massive pro-democracy demonstrations, including the biggest unofficial rally seen in Moscow since the Revolution, attended by 200 000 people. Many carried placards with the number six crossed out, and speaker after speaker denounced the Party's continuing monopoly on power. Gorbachev broached the subject of the Party's leading role gingerly, arguing that the process of democratisation taking place in the country 'may at some stage lead to the creation of [other] parties', and that the Communist Party would have to fight for its 'vanguard role' in a democratic system, rather than having it guaranteed by the Constitution. He tried to mollify hardliners by insisting that 'at the present turning-point, the CPSU is capable of playing a consolidating, integrating role, and of ensuring the progress of *perestroika* for the good of the entire people'.

Once again, Gorbachev was accused of leading the country on to 'the wrong path'. The Soviet ambassador to Poland, Vladimir Brovikov, made perhaps the most vituperative and personalised attack that Gorbachev had ever heard: 'Reactionaries of every hue are slandering communists and singing a requiem for the CPSU, for Leninism and socialism. The worst thing of all is that nobody – neither the general secretary nor his closest colleagues – has taken measures to defend the honour and dignity of the Party. Either this is because it suits them, or because they themselves are afraid of the critics . . . They are trying to shove the Party on to the sidelines of political life, to turn it from a ruling party into a discussion club, or at best into a pawn in a parliamentary game. To let this happen would be a catastrophe for the country . . . One gets the impression that our leaders are rushing to cross out the Party as the leading force in society and to transfer the functions of the Politburo to the President.'

Brovikov called on his colleagues not to rush headlong into adopting Gorbachev's new reform package, recalling that they had allowed themselves to be rushed into accepting his last 'ill-considered' reforms at the Nineteenth Party Conference (when Gorbachev had sprung a speedy timetable on them in the closing minutes). A previous speaker had called on Ligachev to resign, but Brovikov retorted that 'not just Ligachev, but also comrades Gorbachev, Medvedev, Slyunkov, Yakovlev and Lukyanov should be held personally responsible for the crisis in the country'.[3]

The conservative diehards fought tooth and nail to keep a reference to the Communist Party, even if not its 'leading role', in the Constitution. In a working group on the new wording of Article Six, during the March plenum, Gorbachev defended the position of the hardliners. He proposed that instead of abolishing the article, it should be changed to read, 'The Communist Party of the Soviet Union and other socio-political organisations and mass movements . . . take part in the elaboration of the policies of the Soviet state, etc.' Thus, the 'leading role' of the Communist Party was eliminated – but, as the Kazakh Party leader, Nursultan Nazarbayev, pointed out, why mention the communists at all, if there was to be a multi-party system? 'People will ask: why is the Communist Party mentioned in the Constitution?' he said, and suggested the article should simply refer to 'parties, socio-political and mass organisations'.

Gorbachev replied that the Politburo had discussed this and decided 'after a long debate' (implying disagreement) that the Communist Party had to be mentioned. 'Does this contradict reality?' he asked. 'No, it doesn't. At the moment the CPSU is the only registered party. There aren't any others . . . so when we say "The CPSU and other socio-political organisations and mass movements . . ." it does not contradict reality.'

'But what about when other parties appear in a year's time?' objected Nazarbayev.

'Look at the text, please,' said Gorbachev. ' "The CPSU and other socio-political . . ." The formula embraces that eventuality.'

Another member of the group also objected to this: 'What if people say: "Let's write in the name of our party too"?'

Gorbachev persisted: 'The text we are adopting just now suits all cases that might arise. If new parties appear and, as it were, legally enter the political process, then they will come under the heading "other socio-political organisations".'

Whether Gorbachev himself really believed in such a patently absurd proposition will probably never be known. He may simply have felt obliged to plug the agreed Politburo line. Yegor Ligachev, for example, was uncompromising: 'If we give up our positions on this question,' he said, 'I fear that we shall give up a great deal. We have already given up much. That is my view. And we must not go further along that path.' He also insisted that they must not be swayed by the huge anti-Party demonstrations in Moscow: 'We must bear in mind that ten deputies [he meant the most outspoken radicals] is not the entire parliament. A mob is not the entire people. And a rally in Moscow is not the whole of Moscow – far less the entire country.'

He was supported by his Politburo colleague, Vitaly Vorotnikov, who said it was a 'matter of principle' that the words about the Communist Party be left in, though he admitted that parliament (which was to pass the amendment the next day) might turn down the idea.[4]

The minister of justice, Veniamin Yakovlev, in contrast, argued that 'it is not very modern or civilised to have the constitution of any state marking out one political organisation and giving it priority in political life, so we should not do it in our constitution'. But his advice was ignored. The revised Article Six proposed by the central committee and pushed through parliament on 13 March referred to the Communist Party 'and other parties'.

While the conservatives in the Party opposed the assault on Article Six, the radicals in parliament were equally critical of Gorbachev's presidential plans. The manner in which he drew up this major constitutional reform without consulting the Supreme Soviet's legislative committee, and then bulldozed it through parliament, only confirmed their suspicions of dictatorial tendencies. Many deputies accepted the argument that a strong hand was needed to hold the country together and maintain law and order. But Gorbachev was nonetheless forced to water down his presidential powers to obtain a majority. At the insistence of Baltic leaders, for example, it was made more difficult for the president to declare a state of emergency in individual republics. His power to veto legislation was curtailed, and he was deprived of the right he sought to appoint the chairman of the Supreme Court. These changes were thrashed out in hasty whispered conversations between Gorbachev and various advisers and emissaries who approached him on the platform, in full view of deputies and journalists.[5]

The amendments were passed by the Congress of People's Deputies on 13 March. There then followed a day of angry debate on whether Gorbachev should be allowed to stand unopposed for the presidency, and on whether to accept his proposal that the *first* president be elected by the 2250 members of Congress rather than directly by the people – as required by the amendment they had just passed. In the end, the Congress was swayed by deputies who argued that the urgency of the crisis in the country demanded the immediate election of Gorbachev to the presidency, and that a direct presidential election could 'lead to civil war'. Even some radicals such as Anatoly Sobchak understood that a direct election could have fateful consequences if Gorbachev, who was becoming more and more unpopular in the country at large, failed to win. As it was, Gorbachev barely scraped home in the election by Congress, though he was unopposed. He won the support of 59 per cent of the deputies – only 206 votes more than he needed.

On 15 March, in a hastily improvised oath-taking ceremony, Gorbachev was sworn in for a five-year term as the Soviet Union's first president.

Half an hour later, relaxing over tea in a private room with his wife Raisa and his aides, Shakhnazarov, Chernyayev and Frolov, he reflected on the irony of his situation. When he had come to power five years earlier he had gained truly dictatorial powers as leader of the Communist Party. He had since undermined those powers and placed himself under parliamentary control. 'Yet even now,' he said, 'some stupid people believe that I need the presidency so that I can order people around. If that was what I wanted I would just have remained general secretary [of the Party] and could have ordered people around for another ten or fifteen years!'

GORBACHEV had two new advisory bodies to help him as president – a Federation Council consisting of the parliamentary leaders of all fifteen republics, and a Presidential Council comprising the most senior government ministers and others of his own choice. He scarcely needed to consult the Communist Party leadership any more, and he planned to formalise the Politburo's diminished role at the Twenty-eighth Party Congress in the summer.

The Presidential Council was Gorbachev's 'cabinet'. Its most senior member was Alexander Yakovlev, whose influence on Gorbachev and on the country's future was decisive. Much of the credit for the radical change in attitudes towards religion, freedom of expression, and the rehabilitation of the victims of previous Soviet regimes, must go to him. As the most consistent advocate of the separation of Party and state bodies, Yakovlev set an example by at once telling his colleagues he would not stand for re-election to the central committee.

The other full-time members of the Presidential Council were Yevgeny Primakov, a former foreign-affairs journalist and, briefly, Yakovlev's successor as head of the Institute of World Economy and International Relations, and Grigory Revenko, until now Party chief in Kiev, whose new job was to help Gorbachev sort out his nationalities policy. Six government ministers were *ex officio* members: the prime minister, the ministers of foreign affairs, defence and the interior, and the heads of the KGB and the state planning committee.

The part-time members of the Council were of a representational nature: two writers (one Kirghiz, the other Russian), a farm chairman, professors of physics and economics, and a blue-collar worker.

In theory, Gorbachev now had great power and much more freedom to operate without the restraints of the Politburo. But the presidency was flawed from the start, partly because it lacked the legitimacy which direct elections would have given it. In his inaugural speech he promised to 'radicalise' economic reform and introduce the market speedily, and to start work on drawing up a new union treaty to define relations with the various republics within a looser federation. But instead of using his new powers as promised to act decisively to sort out the chaos, he became enmeshed in a new tug-of-war between the centre and the republics. The battle was the direct consequence of a round of republican and regional elections held in the spring of 1990, which returned national and local parliaments with real popular mandates to challenge Moscow and its new federal president.

ELECTIONS to republican parliaments and regional and local councils were held in most areas of the Soviet Union in February and March. In contrast to the elections to the federal parliament (the Congress of People's Deputies) a year earlier, which had been manipulated by the Party apparatus, these were generally free and fair, and brought radical – or even downright anti-Soviet – governments to power in several places.

The people of Lithuania, Latvia and Estonia took the opportunity to accomplish the Soviet Union's first – or Eastern Europe's last – gentle revolution. Elections in the three Baltic republics were effectively a referendum on whether or not to leave the Soviet Union, for in each case the Popular Front (or Sajudis in Lithuania) endorsed a list of pro-independence candidates, including members of the Communist Party. These candidates scored impressive victories in each republic – even in Latvia, with its relatively small indigenous population.

On 10 March the new Lithuanian parliament met for the first time and elected as its first president the leader of Sajudis, Vytautas Landsbergis – a music professor and a mild, intellectual anti-communist in the mode of Czechoslovakia's Vaclav Havel or Poland's Tadeusz Mazowiecki. The next day – by chance, the fifth anniversary of Gorbachev's accession to power – Lithuania became the first Soviet republic formally to declare itself independent of the Soviet Union. As the result of the parliamentary vote was announced – 124 for, none against and only six abstentions – deputies joined hands and chanted 'Lietuva' (Lithuania), while massive crowds in the streets broke into wild cheering and singing.

Carefully preserving the historical truth that Lithuania was occupied by the Soviet Union and never voluntarily joined it, the parliament voted not to *secede* but to restore its inter-war status and to invalidate the Soviet Constitution on its territory. The declaration read: 'Expressing the will of the people, the Supreme Council of the Lithuanian Republic hereby resolves and solemnly declares that the exercise of the sovereign rights of the Lithuanian state, violated by an alien force in 1940, shall now be restored and Lithuania shall henceforward once more become an independent state.'[6]

It was all very dignified and ceremonious. But even though it was necessarily more a declaration of intent than of reality, since thousands of ties between Lithuania and the Soviet Union had still to be severed, that was not how it was seen in Moscow. Gorbachev's first act as president, within hours of being sworn in on 15 March, was to send Landsbergis a Resolution of the Congress of People's Deputies declaring the Lithuanian move null and void, together with a curt order: 'Inform us within three days of the measures that will be taken to implement this Resolution.'

The Lithuanian leadership, however, was in no mood to heed ultimatums by a Soviet president. They already considered him to be the head of a foreign power with no jurisdiction over them. There followed a long dialogue of the deaf, to the accompaniment of the menacing rumble of tanks and the strident tones of propaganda and economic warfare.

Gorbachev refused to negotiate with the Lithuanians, saying Moscow negotiated only with foreign countries, though he held out the prospect of a 'mutually respectful dialogue' about ways by which Lithuania might eventually secede. Lithuania was not interested: it was a foreign country, it was independent, and did not need to secede.

A war of nerves began. On 24 March Soviet tanks rolled down Gediminas (formerly Lenin) Avenue, in Vilnius, in a show of strength. The pro-Moscow rump of the Lithuanian Communist Party called in Soviet paratroopers to seize control of Party buildings and printing plants. As the Lithuanian government told its citizens they were under no obligation to serve in any foreign army, Soviet troops began rounding up deserters. Five weeks after the independence declaration, Gorbachev cut off supplies of oil and gas, and imposed a crippling economic blockade on the republic, saying that this would 'let them see' what it was like to survive without the Soviet Union (although the Lithuanians had never suggested that they did not wish to continue trading with the Soviet Union). The Lithuanians took the blockade as a compliment, since it implied that they were a foreign country. The prime minister, Kazimiera Prunskiene, toured Western capitals in search of aid and recognition, but got only sympathy.

Gorbachev desperately tried to avert a repetition of the Lithuanian situation in Estonia and Latvia by offering them talks to establish looser links with Moscow. But he undercut this conciliatory move by pushing a Law on Secession through parliament, which made it exceedingly difficult for any republic to leave the Soviet Union. Secession became possible only if two-thirds of a republic's eligible voters said yes in a referendum – and then only after a transitional period of up to five years, during which other republics or ethnic minorities could raise objections. A second – binding – referendum, capable of overturning the decision of the first one, would have to be held during the last year of the transitional period if just one-tenth of the electorate requested it.[7]

As a result, both Estonia and Latvia also moved towards independence, though slightly less abruptly than Lithuania had done. Estonia's parliament voted not to recognise the sovereignty of the Soviet Union, and announced 'the beginning of the restoration' of its pre-war status. In early May, Latvia took a middle road, declaring independence, but keeping Soviet civil and criminal law in force for an unspecified transition period. The more Moscow pressed, the more united the three Baltic republics became. All rejected the need for a referendum, claiming the electorate had given their parliaments a mandate to restore independence. Spurred by Latvia's more radical move, Estonia caught up a few days later by also reinstating the key provisions of its old 'bourgeois' constitution, dropping the words 'Soviet' and 'Socialist' from its title, and abandoning all communist state symbols and the Soviet anthem.

After three months of stalemate, Gorbachev abandoned his blockade of Lithuania in the hope of drawing the republic and its neighbours into talks on a new Union Treaty. The Balts had been advocating such a treaty, under which the republics would delegate certain powers to the centre, rather than the other way about, for almost two years. But even as recently as September 1989, the central committee had refused to consider the idea. Half a year later, some kind of federal, or even confederal, framework for the country was being seen as the last hope of holding the hundred disparate nations of the Soviet Union together. In June 1990 a working group, under the auspices of the President's Federation Council, began drafting a union treaty.

GORBACHEV'S new-found willingness to countenance something akin to the 'loose confederation' which he used regularly to damn was inevitable, given the results of the republican and local elections. For it was not just the Baltic nations who chose radical governments.

Even the heavily Russified Ukraine was beginning to march under its once-banned national colours – blue and yellow, symbolising the sky and the wheatfields that once made it one of the breadbaskets of Europe. Candidates of the 'Democratic Bloc', backed by the nationalist Rukh movement, human rights groups and other radicals, won 149 of the 450 seats in the republican parliament in Kiev. They were outnumbered by official Communist Party deputies, but even the communists began to espouse the nationalist cause. The majority of radical deputies were elected in the western provinces, which, like the Baltic states, had come under Soviet control only after the war. In these areas, where politics were inextricably mixed up with religion, years of nationalist campaigning had already yielded fruit: Stalin had banned the Ukrainian Catholic (sometimes known as the Uniate) Church in 1946 and handed over its property to the Russian Orthodox Church; on 1 December 1989, as Gorbachev held talks with the Pope in Rome, the Council for Religious Affairs in Moscow announced that the ban on the Ukrainian Catholic Church was lifted.

This victory merely encouraged the western Ukrainians to fight for more. The local and regional councils elected in March were overwhelmingly nationalist, dominated by deputies who had run on overtly anti-Soviet, separatist tickets. In Lvov region, Vyacheslav Chornovil won a landslide victory and became head of the regional council – the first former political prisoner to attain such high office in the Soviet Union. Under Brezhnev, Andropov and Chernenko, he had spent fifteen years in Siberian labour camps and exile, working as a stoker in a factory boiler-room, for publishing underground articles about political repressions in the Ukraine. Now he calmly set about restoring capitalism in his region of 2.5 million people, passing resolutions on the privatisation of land, services, shops and housing at a time when the Soviet government in Moscow was still strongly opposed to such ideas. The Communist Party in Lvov was so poorly represented in the council that it scarcely deserved to be called an opposition party. Under Chornovil, the Lvov council, which included several other former inmates of the Gulag, removed Lenin's statue, flew the sky-and-cornfield flag from the town hall, and forbade the Party to interfere in the economy or make staff appointments in non-communist bodies. When the Party refused to give up either of the two newspapers which it owned jointly with the previous council, the new council set up its own, *For a Free Ukraine*, and allowed the market to put the communist papers out of business. In many enterprises, as Chornovil gleefully recounts, stroking his Lech Walesa moustache, 'the workers chucked the Party committees out and told them to find a room somewhere else for their work . . . For example, at the farm machinery factory in Lvov, they piled up all the commies' papers and volumes of Lenin on to a lorry, carted them out of the factory gates and dumped them!'

In elections in the Russian Federation, the biggest of the Soviet Union's fifteen republics, radical communist and non-communist candidates campaigned together in a coalition group known as Democratic Russia. They won big majorities in the Moscow and Leningrad city councils, effectively wrenching power in Russia's two greatest cities out of traditional Communist Party control. Two of the radical heroes of the federal parliament, Gavriil Popov and Anatoly Sobchak, became mayors of Moscow and Leningrad respectively. Both councils embarked on a careful programme of 'decommunisation' – to the extent that this could be achieved within the confines of the cities. They planned privatisation of services, restaurants and other state businesses, a sell-off of state apartments, and even the removal of Party control over local security forces. But trying to democratise and liberalise small units of a centrally controlled state was a thankless task, and by the end of 1990 they had little to show for their eight months in office.

They remained popular thanks mainly to the small things they achieved. Mayor Popov sanctioned the first-ever unofficial May Day demonstration in Red Square in 1990; after the official parade, when demonstrators armed with anti-communist slogans marched past Lenin's tomb, booing the leadership and chanting 'Down with Gorbachev', the Soviet president was forced to leave the reviewing stand, humiliated. Pre-revolutionary street names were restored. In Leningrad people started calling their city – even occasionally on television – St Petersburg, or simply 'Peter', as it is still fondly known. In one celebrated incident, the authorities tried to prevent Leningrad television from showing a planned interview with the prosecutor, Nikolai Ivanov, who wanted to show documentary evidence of his claims about corruption leading up to the Politburo; a large group of radical municipal councillors besieged the studios and virtually held the television chief hostage while the broadcast went out – for four hours!

In both cities the demoralised Communist Party had no positive power left – only negative power, to block council decisions through its continuing control of the administrative apparatus and of enterprises. In desperation, the *apparat* indulged in a frenzy of asset-stripping immediately after it lost control of the councils in Leningrad and Moscow, by handing over dozens of council buildings and computers to the Communist Party, free of charge, before they could pass into the hands of the new democratically elected authorities.

The biggest challenge to communist rule, and to the personal power of President Gorbachev, came in the Russian Federation itself – the vast backbone of the Soviet empire, with more than half of the country's population and three-quarters of its territory. Here, Boris Yeltsin made the ultimate comeback, not just as a rebel backbencher, as he was in the federal parliament, but as president of Russia, and arguably the second most powerful man in the Soviet Union. What is more, he achieved this in spite of Gorbachev's blatant interference in the election to try to foil his arch-rival's plans. It was not just a victory for Yeltsin, but an ignominious defeat for Gorbachev, who from now on could rule only with the blessing of the man whose political career he had tried to bury.

It was never a foregone conclusion that Yeltsin would come out on top, despite massive support from the electorate in his own constituency. The Democratic Russia bloc, which backed Yeltsin, did well in the elections to the Russian parliament, but not well enough to dominate it. When parliament opened on 16 May, Gorbachev urged Alexander Vlasov, the outgoing Russian prime minister and a candidate member of the Politburo, to stand against Yeltsin for the presidency (technically, the chairmanship of the Russian Federation's Supreme Soviet). In his first speech, Yeltsin proved once again his ability to see the way things had to develop long before Gorbachev did. While Gorbachev was still speaking of 'economic autonomy' for the Union's constituent republics, Yeltsin proposed full-blown political sovereignty for all republics, including Russia. All existing Soviet laws, statutes and decrees, he said, should become valid on the territory of the Russian Federation only if they did not contradict the republic's own laws. He was not suggesting that Russia should leave the Soviet Union, but that it should decide for itself which powers to delegate to the central authorities – the kind of thing for which Gorbachev had censured Baltic leaders.

Gorbachev intervened in the contest for the leadership of Russia with an abrasive attack on Yeltsin, whom he accused of 'trying to separate Russia from socialism'. He even held an informal meeting with 250 deputies (though constitutionally he himself had nothing to do with the Russian parliament) at which he told them: 'At this turning-point I would never take the risk' of voting for Yeltsin. He accused him of wanting to 'destroy the Union – its defence, its finances – destroy everything.' Evidently Gorbachev already saw that if Yeltsin both became president of Russia and implemented his radical version of sovereignty for the republics, he would become more powerful than Gorbachev himself, for the president of the Soviet Union would be little more than a figurehead.

Gorbachev's favoured candidate, Vlasov, withdrew from the race when it became obvious that he would come third to Yeltsin and the other contender, Ivan Polozkov, the Ligachevite Party chief from Krasnodar. Polozkov won applause from conservative deputies for his attacks on co-operatives and support for collective farms, law and order and the armed forces. In the first round of voting, Yeltsin fell just short of an overall majority.

In the second round, Polozkov withdrew and Vlasov entered the race again, but Yeltsin campaigned cleverly with a pledge to form a coalition government if elected. This was enough to win over the waverers, and Yeltsin won a small but comfortable majority, with 535 votes to Vlasov's 467.

In his new position, Yeltsin matured into a formidable politician. His popularity with the public soared, as even sceptical intellectuals had to admit they admired his skills in chairing the parliamentary sessions. There proved to be much more to Boris Nikolayevich than the blustering, blundering showman people had seen before. He had a concrete political programme, was a strong debater, and had two great virtues which many Russians appreciated because Gorbachev seemed to lack them – an ability to listen patiently and learn, and a willingness to appoint young, radical thinkers as his advisers and as key government ministers. Among the earliest moves for which he obtained the Russian parliament's assent were the removal of any reference to the Communist Party in the republic's Constitution, and a law which forbade anyone to head both a Party committee and a local council.

His election was a watershed in two ways. First, it gave him great power to challenge, block and radicalise Gorbachev's policies. Secondly, it helped to establish the supremacy of an elected parliament over the Communist Party in a way that the federal Congress of People's Deputies, with its 'obedient aggressive majority', failed to do.

Until 1990, Russia – unlike the other fourteen republics – had no Communist Party organisation of its own. But in response to the emerging trends of federalisation, Russian communists set about creating their own structures, within the CPSU. The initiative came mainly from the conservative wing of the Party, particularly the disgruntled and reactionary Leningrad organisation. Gorbachev at first opposed their moves, and came round to the idea only after the Leningrad communists had gone ahead with an 'initiative conference' of their own in April. In the spring of 1990 the movement gathered strength and Gorbachev threw his weight behind it, apparently aware that if it escaped from his control it could veer into the hands of extreme nationalists and conservatives. Such fears were borne out in June, when 2768 delegates from all over Russia held a founding conference in the Kremlin, dominated by right-wing speeches from embattled communist leaders and military men. In line with the conservatives' liking for positive discrimination towards the working class, 200 'workers' who had failed to be elected as delegates were allowed to attend anyway, to boost the proletarian image of the Party. Gorbachev faced repeated attacks from delegates who seemed overwhelmingly in the Ligachev mould. They gave rapturous applause to General Albert Makashov when he denounced Gorbachev's military cutbacks and complained: 'Patriotism takes centuries to foster, but it is destroyed in two years by the yellow press.'[8] Alexander Melnikov, Ligachev's protégé, won an ovation for saying, 'It is incomprehensible to me that President Gorbachev, in his recent speech, did not once use the words "Party" or "communists".'[9] The conference elected Ivan Polozkov, the conservative whom

Yeltsin had defeated for the presidency of Russia, as the Russian Communist Party's leader. (Gorbachev's position as leader of the *Soviet* Communist Party was not affected by this.)

The battle lines for power in the Russian Federation were now drawn. On one side stood a hardline Communist Party led by Polozkov, still in control of the administrative apparatus but bereft of popular legitimacy. This was the power of the past. On the other side was the power of the future – a democratically elected parliament, headed by Yeltsin and passing radical legislation.

The dramatic shift of power from one to the other was graphically illustrated on Soviet television, which soon began to cover Yeltsin's every public appearance and utterance. As for Ivan Polozkov, he made speeches, too; but nobody seemed to notice, or read them. It was enough to look at the manic, wild-eyed expression on his face, in a picture which some newspapers were particularly fond of printing, to understand what he was about.

IT WAS the power of the past, though, that continued to plague efforts to improve the economy. At the end of 1989 the prime minister, Nikolai Ryzhkov, won parliament's approval for a cautious 'economic recovery programme' which foresaw several more years of central planning – allegedly to stabilise the economy – before finally beginning moves towards marketisation in 1992-3. There would be no revision of retail prices (even by central decree, far less by exposing them to the market) until 1991 – and then only after 'nationwide debate'. Radicals said the programme was a non-starter.

In January, in a sign that he was seeking more radical solutions than his prime minister, Gorbachev took on a committed free-marketeer, Nikolai Petrakov, as his personal aide – the first full-time economics adviser he had ever appointed. Then in March, when he became president, he named an equally passionate advocate of the market economy, Professor Stanislav Shatalin, as a member of his presidential council. Significantly, Shatalin's appointment followed just days after he had declared at a central committee plenum – to conservative cat-calls – that he was a 'social democrat' and that he fully intended to 'push the Party leadership and the Party as a whole to accept the ideas that are close to me'.[10]

Shatalin had come to Gorbachev's notice in February when he argued publicly with Abalkin during a central committee debate which revealed the extent to which the Party preferred to cling to ideological totems than to seek real solutions to the economic crisis. The original draft of the Party's new policy platform had proposed recognising, for the first time, the right to private property, including private ownership of means of production – i.e. anything from a tractor to a factory.[11] But Abalkin, for all his commitment to the market, argued together with the conservatives that the platform must use the term 'individual labour-gained property' rather than 'private property', and that 'we must emphasise quite emphatically that the exploitation of man by man is impermissible'. Abalkin, then, wanted a market without what in the West are its normal concomitants – private property and the right to employ workers. Professor Shatalin, the social democrat, argued that there was nothing so terrible about private property, and that all the talk about 'exploitation of man by man' was nonsense. He brought Gorbachev round to the view that if either of them bought more shares in a joint-stock company, they could hardly be said to be exploiting workers.

Yet Gorbachev ended up siding with the conservatives as they deployed their panoply of dogma. Alexandra Biryukova, a candidate Politburo member, declared: 'I suggest that as well as saying that exploitation of man by man is impermissible, we should emphasise that "individual, collective and co-operative ownership must not employ hired labour". The whole trouble with the co-operatives today is because ten co-operative owners exploit the labour of 200–300 people. That's the start of the rot. Ordinary people don't understand the word "exploitation", but everyone understands "hired labour".'

Gorbachev retorted that there was no point in defining every principle in a Party policy document. Ligachev tried to be helpful: 'Mikhail Sergeyevich, maybe we should use Marx's words: "excluding the private-property form of appropriating hired labour and the labour of others"?' At which Gorbachev exploded, and finally gave in to shouts from the hall to use Abalkin's formula, which had the merit of simplicity even if it was ideologically blinkered.[12]

The sterility of the debate well indicated why Gorbachev felt obliged to look outside the Party – to radical academics such as Petrakov and Shatalin – for ideas. Yet for some reason he himself held back from the reform debate, other than to call for 'radical measures'. It was left to Ryzhkov and Abalkin to come up with something better than they had proposed in December.

In March, with official statistics showing a drastic deterioration in the economy and a record level of days lost in strikes, Abalkin and a team of sixty specialists set themselves up at the government dacha at Sosny, west of Moscow, to work out a new scheme. They toyed with the idea of 'shock therapy' – a sudden leap into the full market economy, like that undertaken by the Solidarity-led government in Poland – but shied away from it on the grounds that the Soviet leadership did not enjoy the confidence and popularity which allowed the Polish government to impose a harsh cure. Opinion polls showed that most Soviet citizens neither trusted nor understood the market economy, and associated it with high prices and unemployment rather than full shops. (Writers such as Vasily Selyunin wrote that the answer was not to water down the policies but to elect a new Soviet 'government of national trust'. His advice was not heeded.)[13]

In mid-April the Ryzhkov-Abalkin team took its first draft to the Presidential Council, which rejected it as incompetent.[14] A month later they produced a new version, which envisaged a three-stage transition to a 'regulated market economy' (the latest terminology). Like the ill-fated December plan, the switch would take five years overall, but it brought forward the timetable for price reform: bread prices would be tripled almost immediately, from 1 July, and there would be drastic increases for other foodstuffs and transport from the new year. The idea was greeted with derision on almost every side. Marketeers said that it preserved central planning – even the price rises were to be dictated not by the market but by central decree, while nothing would be done to change the *system* until 1993. The official trade unions complained that it put the burden on to ordinary workers. Many agreed that the plan administered a 'shock' without any 'therapy'. In a panic, Abalkin compounded the impression of incompetence by announcing that the price rises would take place only after a referendum – as if there was the slightest hope that people would vote for a 'reform' which appeared to involve nothing but swingeing price rises.

The Presidential Council unenthusiastically allowed Ryzhkov to present the plan to parliament on 24 May. Immediately a wave of panic buying swept across the country, forcing the Moscow city authorities to ban food sales to out-of-towners.

Ryzhkov's position as prime minister was looking decidedly shaky as the plan was rejected by parliament. To undermine his confidence further, Stanislav Shatalin let it be known that Gorbachev did not wholly endorse the Ryzhkov plan, and that more radical proposals were already being drafted by his own team. Shatalin promised that a programme for the introduction of private enterprise and direct foreign investment would be ready by September.[15]

THE economic crisis was one reason Soviet communists felt deeply demoralised as they approached the landmark Twenty-eighth Congress of their Party in July 1990. But it was not the only one. Power was slipping from their hands, the Party was split into at least three factions, members were leaving in droves (especially after the depressingly conservative mood that prevailed at the founding conference of the Russian Communist Party and the election of Ivan Polozkov as its leader), and the whole system of values that they believed in was coming under intensive fire.

A devastating film was released shortly before the Congress. Its title, ironically, echoed the words that Gorbachev says went through his mind as he was poised to take over the leadership in 1985: *Tak zhit'*

*nel'zya* ('We cannot go on living like this'). The film, made by
Stanislav Govorukhin, both reflected the new mood, and intensified it
by exposing huge audiences to a powerful denunciation of communism. It showed contrasting images of Soviet and Western shops, and
dwelt upon the problems of alcoholism and the steeply rising crime
rate in the Soviet Union. But it soon emerged that the real subject was
not murder and robbery, but a much greater crime – the evil perpetrated over seventy years by the Communist Party. The film even suggested that a Nuremberg-style trial was needed to establish the guilt,
not just of individuals, but of the whole system. Over images of dese-
crated churches and magnificent marble Party buildings, the commentary condemned the Godlessness and immorality of a regime
which had reduced a great nation to poverty and lawlessness, while
enriching its élite. How could a regime be any good, the commentary
asked, if it started out by murdering the innocent daughters of the last
Tsar? People emerged from the cinemas sad, humiliated and angry.

More puzzling was the Party's own lemming-like rush to destroy its
image. A document published for the first time in the central committee's own journal in April revealed the founder of the Party and Soviet
state, Vladimir Lenin, to have been a bloodthirsty bigot with little
concern for ordinary people. It was a letter written by Lenin himself in
1922, urging the confiscation of Church valuables – on the pretext of
using the proceeds to help famine victims, but in fact as an excuse to
crush the clergy 'with such cruelty that they will not forget it for decades'. Lenin went on: 'Famine is the only time when we can beat the
enemy over the head. Now, when people are being eaten in famine-
stricken areas, we can carry out expropriation of Church valuables
with the most furious and ruthless energy.'[16] So much for the man to
whose humanist values Gorbachev was constantly urging a return.

GORBACHEV planned the Twenty-eighth Congress as the culmination of the Second Russian Revolution – the final showdown. Most
elements of the new order were already in place, or at least legislated
for: a working parliament, the presidency, a multi-party system, and a
decision in principle to switch from central planning to a market economy (even if the details still needed working out). One goal remained:
to persuade the Communist Party to give up its still burning pretensions to a monopoly on power.

To this end, Gorbachev wanted to bring about another stage in the
separation of Party and state by removing all government ministers
and members of his Presidential Council from the Party's central
committee. He also planned to turn the Politburo into a broad-based,
representative body (including the first secretaries of the fifteen
republican Party organisations) which would meet only once a month
to formulate Party – not government – policy. A new central commit-

tee, preferably full of reform-minded people, would be elected. Gorbachev himself would remain leader of the Party to ensure it remained under control, but there would be a new official post of deputy leader to take charge of the day-to-day running of its affairs. Finally, conservatives such as Ligachev would bow gracefully out of politics.

It is unlikely that many of the 5000 delegates saw things that way. Radicals – supporters of the Democratic Platform, who wanted to go even further than Gorbachev – were in a tiny minority. There was a large pugnacious element which was determined to prevent the Party being pushed aside. They aimed to get rid of reformers like Yakovlev and Shevardnadze and return it to the safe hands of conservatives such as Ligachev and Polozkov. In the centre was a mass of delegates of a generally conservative disposition, but with no pronounced views, who could be swung in either direction. This group loudly applauded anyone who criticised the leadership and the failures of *perestroika*. On several occasions during the 12-day Congress, their herd instincts led them to the brink of disaster. Gorbachev, exasperated and angry, had to call on his prodigious powers of persuasion to make them grasp what he was trying to do and force them to retract decisions which threatened to bring down the entire fragile edifice which he had constructed. It was high noon in the Kremlin – Ligachev's last stand.

In his opening address on 2 July Gorbachev delivered his strongest ever condemnation of the system inherited from the past, and the clearest ever statement of his intentions. It is worth quoting at some length as a reminder of how much had changed in just five years – and also to understand why it earned the frostiest reception of any speech he had ever made.

'A civil society of free people is replacing the Stalinist model of socialism,' he said. 'The political system is being radically transformed, genuine democracy is being established, with free elections, a multi-party system and human rights, real people's power is being reborn. The system of production relations, which alienated workers from property and from the fruits of their labour, is being dismantled; and conditions created for the free competition of socialist producers. There has begun the transformation of a supercentralised state into a real alliance based on self-determination and the voluntary unity of nations. Instead of ideological dictatorship there are freedom of thought and *glasnost* – a society of open information.

'The USSR has become a country open to peace and co-operation, evoking not fear but respect and solidarity. Since April 1985 we have told people the truth, we have swept away false conceit and admitted that we were incapable of providing them with a decent life. We have resolutely condemned the crimes of the authoritarian, bureaucratic system. We have restored the good names of many thousands of victims of the illegal repressions.

'One hears voices – indeed there is a widespread view – that *perestroika* is to blame for all our present woes. Forgive my bluntness, but that is plain rubbish . . . We inherited an extremely difficult legacy. The ruination of our countryside, our agriculture and processing industry – did that just happen yesterday, after 1985? The lamentable condition of our forests and rivers, the millions of acres of fertile land flooded because of our former energy policies – was that caused in the last few years? The grave ecological situation – more than 100 towns in disaster areas, over a thousand enterprises shut down because of this; the drama of Baikal, Aral, Ladoga, the Azov Sea [all seriously polluted]; Chernobyl, other accidents and catastrophes on our railways and gas pipelines – is not all this the consequence of policies carried out in previous decades?

'Is it not the case that the structure of our economy, in which only one-seventh of our industry produces consumer goods, was formed in the thirties, and has been kept like that ever since? And everything that has flared up in inter-ethnic relations – is that not rooted in the past? Not to mention the militarisation of the economy, which has devoured colossal resources – the best material and intellectual resources available . . . So when people say "Lay off criticising the past" and blame all the troubles on *perestroika*, I can't agree.'[17]

In his defence of *perestroika*, Gorbachev claimed they had broken the 'ideological vice' which had gripped people's minds. The Party had stopped meddling in culture, the intelligentsia's role had increased, the press had revolutionised society, and the Politburo commission on Stalin's legacy had rehabilitated thousands of victims of the Terror.

He could scarcely have written a speech better calculated to enrage this particular audience. When, at the end of his tirade against Stalinism, he made his customary remark about being 'against the wholesale denigration of everything done in our country in the past seventy years', the hall responded with lukewarm ironic applause. By the time he started saying that artists should not be subject to censorship but merely feel 'moral responsibility to the people', he had lost most of his audience.

Whenever he fed them a line which could have pleased them ('No one has the right to forbid Party members to organise cells in enterprises'), he horrified them in the next breath: 'We don't claim an exceptional position here: this is the natural right of *all* parties which will be legally registered in our country.' This even applied in the army, he said – and a perceptible shudder went through the uniformed section of the audience.

The question of 'depoliticising' the armed forces – i.e. removing them from Communist Party control – was one of the demands of the reformist Democratic Platform, and here Gorbachev came close to their stance. He also appeared to embrace their position on turning the Party into a parliamentary one. 'Its vanguard role,' he explained, 'cannot be foisted on society . . . The CPSU will carry out its policies and fight to retain its mandate as the ruling party through the democratic process of elections to legislative organs in the centre and in the regions. In this sense it acts as a parliamentary party.'

Such candour terrified the conservatives and even many of the uncommitted. At the end of the third day's proceedings, Gorbachev held a meeting with a large group of city and district-level secretaries – many of them epitomising the unreformed *apparat*. It was a sobering experience. One said: 'Judging from your opening speech, I understand that we are closer to capitalism than socialism.' Another said: 'If I made a speech as weak as that [at my district meetings] I would be drummed out of the place. Stop blaming your predecessors. Start strengthening discipline. Let's have less talk. You weren't much help to us in the elections.' According to an eye-witness, Gorbachev 'had probably never been spoken to like that in the whole of his political career'.[18]

Gorbachev almost lost control of himself. According to the eye-witness, he snarled back: 'If my speech was so weak, worse than district-level, send me yours – I'll have it photocopied and handed out at the Congress for comparison.' The heckling continued, and Gorbachev angrily shouted: 'Okay, let's elect you as general secretary. I'll sit down, and you can talk!' And he really did sit down for a few minutes, unable to control the crowd. At one point he foolishly ventured: 'What are you saying, then? Is our entire course wrong?' To his astonishment the crowd of first secretaries yelled back: 'Yes! Yes! Yes!'

During the next days the Congress required each member of the Politburo to give a speech accounting for his work over the past five years, and then answer questions from the floor. But even this was not enough to satisfy the more extreme conservatives who were determined to punish those who had 'led the Party astray'. They proposed that each member of the leadership should be 'personally assessed' on a scale of one to five. Gorbachev advised against it, but democratically put the idea to a vote. The result was the first crisis of the Congress.

At the end of the morning session on 7 July a majority of delegates, swayed by the bloodlust of the conservatives, voted in favour of giving individual assessments of each Politburo member. It is no exaggeration to say that, had this gone ahead, it might have meant the end of *perestroika*, for the best 'marks' would have gone to conservatives such as Ligachev, while Yakovlev would certainly have come last, and Gorbachev himself might not have received a 'pass mark'. In effect, it would have been a vote of no confidence, and it is doubtful whether

Gorbachev could have continued as leader of the Party in such a situation.

During a long lunch break Gorbachev held crisis talks with his closest colleagues. He returned for the afternoon session clearly furious. In a voice laden with sarcasm, he began: 'Well, I suppose it's time to call in the jury, is it? You haven't forgotten about your decision this morning? No? You did it consciously, eh? Consciously?' He drew a breath and continued: 'If you want to split and bury the Party, then let's carry on this way. . . You'd better think again. Think, and think hard.'

After leaving them to think for an hour or so, and reading out some notes from delegates to support his thesis that the assessments would amount to mob law, Gorbachev put a new proposal to the vote – that there should be only a 'collective assessment' of the entire central committee. The motion was passed, and the first crisis was over.

Even though deprived of the weapon of assessment, delegates continued to make their feelings known about their leaders and the course of *perestroika*. Ligachev faced hostile questioning from radicals, but it was the conservatives who made the running, with particularly fierce criticism of Shevardnadze and Yakovlev.

On the ninth day of the Congress Gorbachev took the floor for an unscheduled impromptu speech – one of his most powerful performances – to ram home the message that the conservatives had failed to grasp: that hankering after the past would only ensure the demise of communist rule in the Soviet Union. 'I am deeply worried by the lack of understanding here. We shall never move forward, shall never strengthen the Party's position and offer society an effective policy, to lend dynamism to *perestroika*, unless we realise that *everything in the past* is largely outmoded and unacceptable. I have noticed in the atmosphere of the Congress, in many speeches and in the manner in which some delegates conduct the discussion, that by no means everyone has understood. The Party is living and working in a different society, and we need a different, renewed Party, with a different style of work. We are not changing our line, our choice, our allegiance to socialist values. But believe you me, the Party's success depends on its grasping that society has changed. Otherwise it will be pushed aside by other forces, and we will lose ground.'[19]

The speech was well received, and seemed to win round many of the wavering delegates. But the very next day his authority was challenged again – this time by none other than Yegor Ligachev.

It was the day they elected the deputy general secretary of the Party. This was a new and crucial post, for with Gorbachev concentrating on the Presidency and restricting his Party duties to the chairmanship of monthly Politburo meetings, the deputy leader would effectively run the Party. (The old unofficial position of second secretary had disappeared in the reorganisation of September 1988.) Nominations were made during the lunch break. Gorbachev then read out the list of names, and pointedly indicated that his preference was for Vladimir Ivashko, until recently the Ukrainian Party leader.[20] All the other candidates had withdrawn from the race, Gorbachev said, with one exception – Ligachev.[21]

Ligachev had never dared to defy Gorbachev so openly before. But he now had nothing to lose. Earlier in the day he had clashed openly with Ryzhkov over agricultural policy – the first time two Politburo members had ever disagreed in public. In his various speeches to the Congress he had made no secret of his unhappiness about foreign and economic policy, and the fact that the Politburo was no longer consulted before major decisions were taken. Moreover, he knew that Gorbachev had no intention of allowing him to be elected to the central committee, far less the new Politburo. His only chance of remaining in politics was to persuade the Congress to elect him deputy leader.

Some delegates tried hard to stop Ligachev by proposing an age limit of 60 or 65 for the post (Ligachev was 69) but this was turned down. Gorbachev himself dug out a hitherto unused 'instruction' which enabled delegates to vote for the removal of any candidate from the ballot paper. First they voted in favour of removing Ligachev; then, amid protests, they voted again and Ligachev went forward. Yet in the end, Gorbachev need not have feared. Ivashko won the vote by an overwhelming majority of 3109 to Ligachev's 776. Evidently Gorbachev's own clearly stated position – and Ligachev's unconvincing performance in answering questions – had persuaded the floating voters to give Gorbachev what he wanted.

Gorbachev's ability to make delegates change their minds and vote against their instincts was uncanny. One speaker likened him to a television hypnotist, Kashpirovsky, who was then enjoying great popularity in the country. Gorbachev would need his magic touch one more time before the Congress was over.

On the final day, a new central committee was elected. To avoid mishaps, Gorbachev proposed a list of exactly 398 candidates for the 398 places on the committee. He did not foresee that delegates would then start putting forward other names, as a result of which the ballot papers included fourteen extra candidates. When the votes were counted, it turned out that all fourteen newcomers had sailed through, while fourteen from Gorbachev's original list, including several of his key supporters, came last.

Gorbachev proposed that, since all the candidates had received more than 50 per cent, they should all go through, and the central committee would be a little larger than planned. A vote was taken, and Gorbachev's suggestion was turned down. Once again, there was an uproar. And again Gorbachev had to resort to blatant manipulation. 'If you do this,' he warned the delegates, 'everything we have achieved at this Congress will go down the drain.' Another vote was taken: this time they decided to include all the candidates.

The next day the new central committee held its first plenum, at which it chose a new senior Party leadership – Politburo and secretaries. The average citizen would scarcely have recognised any of the names. That, indeed, was the measure of Gorbachev's success at the Congress. The well-known people who were really running the country – Yakovlev, Shevardnadze, Ryzhkov and the senior ministers – were now members only of the Presidential Council, not of the Politburo. Gorbachev, in other words, had succeeded in separating the Party from the government, leaving the top bodies of the Party a mere talking shop, able to propose policies, but with no means of implementing them other than by persuading the Presidential Council or parliament.

This was not enough to satisfy radicals, however, who still regarded the Party as dominated by the *apparat* and resistant to reform. Boris Yeltsin spectacularly announced he was leaving the Party. Popov and Sobchak, the mayors of Moscow and Leningrad, followed suit, while the leaders of the Democratic Platform called on members throughout the country to sign up with their faction, so that they could later leave *en masse*, taking with them their share of the Party's property and assets to help the foundation of a major opposition party. They criticised Gorbachev for choosing to stay in the Party, placing unity above his principles. But it is hard to see what else Gorbachev could have done. Had he left, or sided with the radicals, the conservative *apparat* would have been strengthened, not weakened. For without him, the Party would have fallen into the hands of people like Polozkov and Ligachev, and thus posed a much greater threat to *perestroika*.

THE emasculation of the Party now continued apace. More drastic cuts in the size of the *apparat* were immediately ordered. In 1989 the central committee bureaucracy had already lost 536 of its original 2029 officials; now it was to lose another 603 – a total reduction of 56 per cent.[22] The work of the Party leadership became introspective, concerned with sorting out the structural changes and staff cuts, and drafting a new programme. One of the new Politburo members, Gennady Yanayev, who was put in charge of foreign policy, admitted in August 1990 that his department's main task was to work out 'alternative policies' – as if the central committee was now in opposition to the government. He confirmed that the Party now played no role in selecting diplomats to work abroad – something which had previously been a central committee prerogative.[23]

In several republics – not just the Baltics, but also Armenia, Moldavia and Georgia – power had effectively passed to nationalist or popular front organisations, and the Communist Party considered itself to be in opposition. The Tomsk regional Party committee – Ligachev's old power base – simply disbanded itself, and in several other places Party buildings were handed over to the soviets, as town or district committees moved into shared premises.

The Democratic Platform's hopes of splitting the Party and keeping its share of the assets failed to materialise, but all over the country Party members were handing in their membership cards, spurred by the example of Yeltsin, Popov and Sobchak. In 1990 at least 2.3 million members left, compared to 137 000 the previous year and only 18 000 in 1988.[24]

The Soviet Union was now undeniably an embryonic multi-party state, with new parties sprouting up almost every day – Constitutional Democrats, Social Democrats, Liberal Democrats, Socialists, Anarcho-Syndicalists, the People's Party and so on. Few, it is true, seemed destined to survive the rigours of pluralism, apart from those backed by recognisable names, such as Nikolai Travkin's Democratic Party of Russia. But the radicals' umbrella organisation, Democratic Russia, had the makings of a real opposition party.

Gorbachev took advantage of the Communist Party's disarray to assert himself as president. In the weeks following the Party Congress he took a number of decisive steps – usually in the form of presidential decrees – which had been impossible while he was still beholden to the Politburo. He ended the Party's monopoly over radio and television broadcasting. He ordered the 'political organs' of the armed forces, through which the Communist Party controlled the military, to transform themselves into politically neutral arms of the state. He received Chancellor Kohl of West Germany and dropped all objections to the incorporation of a reunited Germany into NATO. He issued a blanket rehabilitation of *all* of Stalin's victims, and restored Soviet citizenship to a group of dissidents who had been expelled in the Brezhnev era or even in the early part of his own period in office, including Alexander Solzhenitsyn. His ally Yakovlev, referred to the latter decrees as 'acts of repentance'.

This was the high point of *perestroika*. Gorbachev clearly felt he had the conservatives on the run and was keen to win back the support of the radicals. At Gorbachev's request, his aide, Shakhnazarov, met a group of prominent liberals with a view to establishing a 'left-centre coalition'.

The culmination of this process was the president's sudden decision to side wholeheartedly with the free-marketeers – and at the same time to bury the hatchet with Boris Yeltsin.

Gorbachev had grown increasingly impatient with the blundering attempts of the Ryzhkov–Abalkin team to put together a plan for the switch to the market economy. Yeltsin's Russian Federation government meanwhile, had drawn up a detailed programme for a transition in just 500 days. Its chief author, Russian deputy prime minister Grigory Yavlinsky, soon realised that it would be impossible to implement the programme in Russia alone, if the rest of the country was still lumbered with central planning. He discussed the problem with Gorbachev's economics adviser, Nikolai Petrakov, and shortly before Gorbachev left for his August holiday, Petrakov showed him a memo in which Yavlinsky briefly explained his ideas.

Gorbachev was very excited by the memo, read it out loud to the others in the room, and demanded an immediate meeting with its author. Within hours, Gorbachev had become a total convert – persuaded above all, perhaps, by the argument that genuine economic links would hold the republics together better than any political structures imposed by the centre. The plan also seemed to be proof that Yeltsin was not, after all, intent on breaking up the Soviet Union. Within twenty-four hours a momentous deal was struck. Gorbachev telephoned his old rival Yeltsin, who was on holiday at Jurmala, on the Latvian coast, and they decided to set up a thirteen-man team of radical economists (whose average age was only 32) under the chairmanship of Stanislav Shatalin, to draft a '500 Days' marketisation programme for the entire Soviet Union.

Throughout August, the Shatalin team worked day and night at a dacha outside Moscow. Gorbachev rang several times a day from the Crimea to check progress. Everyone who talked to him testifies to his tremendous excitement and commitment to a crash programme which would (it seemed then) launch the Soviet Union within months on the road to a market economy and an end to communist central planning. On 21 August he broke off his holiday early, held a seven-hour meeting with the team, and then spent three days combing through every detail of the 600-page programme with his adviser, Petrakov.

The following week Gorbachev had five hours of talks with Yeltsin himself – their first substantive meeting for almost three years. Afterwards, Gorbachev admitted to Petrakov: 'You know, it was easier for me to talk to Yeltsin than to many of our officials.' Gorbachev promised his full support to the programme. The presidential spokesman said: 'We are now on the threshold of a major decision, a real change in the economic structure and relations of the union itself.'

For just a few days, a mood of optimism flickered in the country.

# CHAPTER SEVEN

# The Old Order Fights Back

THE word backlash has been used often in this book to describe the waves of conservative reaction after each of Gorbachev's liberalising reforms. But what happened between the autumn of 1990 and August 1991 was no mere backlash. It was the revenge of a mighty coalition of forces, representing all those sections of the Soviet establishment whose vital interests were under assault. Alexander Yakovlev had predicted it in December 1988 when he said that if *perestroika* failed, then 'within two to three years' a 'triumphant, aggressive and avenging conservatism' would come to the fore.

This chapter records the death throes of communism in the Soviet Union during the months leading to the hardliners' final desperate attempt, in August 1991, to turn the clock back by overthrowing Gorbachev.

By mid-1990, the 'revolution' was far from complete, but it already amounted to a deadly assault on the vested interests of the most powerful groups in Soviet society – the Communist ruling class, the Party and state bureaucracy, the barons of centralised industry and farming, the KGB, the military, and the military-industrial complex. All stood to lose their jobs, their power, and their influence. Many would surely find no place at all for themselves in the kind of free, non-communist, market-oriented society which loomed ahead. The fate of their erstwhile colleagues in Eastern Europe, already on the social scrapheap, terrified them.

● The Party élite was furious at its impotence: the Politburo no longer governed, and local communist bosses were forced to face elections – at a time when the mass media seemed to be deriding everything they stood for. Communists now formed the parliamentary opposition in six of the fifteen republics and in several regions and cities. Statues of Lenin were being taken down all over the country.

- The *apparat* not only faced big redundancies, but had been forbidden to 'meddle' in the running of the country.
- The decision to move to a market system threatened the livelihoods of those who ran the centralised economy – the managers of state industries and collective farms.
- The KGB had lost its ability to control society, thanks to the liberalisation of the press and the opening up of the country's borders. A priest consecrated a monument to the victims of the communist terror right in front of the Lubyanka.
- The military had lost its East European buffer zone. Soviet security strategy was in tatters, the Warsaw Pact dead. Officers and men were returning home to an acute housing shortage, forced, as one disgruntled colonel put it, to live in 'tents in the snow'. The break-up of the union was a further blow to the military's interests: an independent Lithuania, for example, would literally sever the strategic outpost of Kaliningrad, an enclave of the Russian Federation, from the rest of the Soviet Union. Half of the rebellious republics were talking of setting up their own armies, and critical numbers of young men were refusing the draft.
- Most crucial of all, perhaps, was the opposition of the 'military-industrial complex', which was threatened by three of the central elements of *perestroika*: the market, federalisation and foreign policy. The great swathe of industry that serviced the armed forces was highly centralised and lavished with resources. So none of Gorbachev's policies were in its interests – neither the ending of the arms race, nor the move to the market system (and the conversion of many enterprises from military output to consumer goods production), nor the devolution of power to the republics. The all-union ministries which ran the military-industrial complex had enterprises in every republic, including those trying to secede from the USSR. They refused even to disclose details of these enterprises' activities to the freely elected republican governments, far less give up their ownership of them.

In 1990, these interest groups found their voice in parliament, in a new faction known as *Soyuz* ('Union'). Soyuz found support among deputies from the armed forces, from the Russian-speaking minorities in other republics, from the *apparat* and managerial circles, and among all those who opposed the disintegration of the Soviet Union and the loss of central control. By the end of the year they had some 600 supporters in the Congress of People's Deputies.

The growth of the hardliners' discontent has been chronicled in earlier chapters. To begin with, it expressed itself in isolated outbursts – the attacks on Gorbachev for 'taking the wrong path', on Yakovlev for allowing the press to become anti-Soviet, and on Shevardnadze for 'losing' Eastern Europe. In the summer of 1990 the different strands of opposition came together, galvanised by the sidelining of the Party after the Twenty-eighth Congress and by Gorbachev's espousal of the market.

It was a propitious moment to mount a concerted attack on *perestroika*. The country was in such disarray that large sections of the public were demanding a strong hand to take control again. The country was becoming ungovernable, for while the structures of the old political order had been scrapped, no new ones had replaced them. Instead, there was chaos, most often described in the Soviet press as 'paralysis of power'.

Gorbachev discovered that his presidential power was only one force, no stronger than the sum of all the others. Through the summer and autumn of 1990 most republics, and even districts, declared 'sovereignty' of one sort or another. Many republics wanted to have their own armies, currencies, budgets and laws. Presidential decrees were generally ignored or resisted (including one which decreed that his decrees should be obeyed), and the Presidential Council, lacking an 'apparatus' of its own, could not enforce them. The centre and the republics waged a 'war of laws', each side insisting its legislation took precedence over the other's. Meanwhile, enterprises had no idea who was supposed to be running them – the local authorities, the republic, or Moscow.

The traditional links in the economy were disrupted, and replaced, if at all, by primitive barter arrangements. Republics and regions started withholding supplies to other areas except in exchange for deliveries. Individual farms refused to deliver to the state, preferring to send a consignment of wheat, say, to a factory which could supply it with a load of cement or consumer goods in return. The 1990 grain harvest was the best since the record year of 1978, but a tenth of it was lost in transportation and storage – as much as the country had to import from abroad for hard currency. Food became a political weapon with the Party hardliners, who still held sway in much of the countryside, withholding supplies from cities such as Moscow and Leningrad to undermine confidence in their radical leaders. Racketeers hoarded supplies to push up prices. The black market thrived as never before.

The most basic goods and foodstuffs became scarce. Even bread was hard to find in Moscow for a few days in the summer. Riots broke out in several towns when cigarettes disappeared. Prices – and wages – soared. But there was nothing to buy. Money lost its value, except for the growing mass of poor people.

As Gorbachev's popularity reached rock bottom, the conservatives began a war of attrition – first against his policies, then against the liberals in his entourage whom they held responsible for the chaos.

★ ★ ★

THE first casualty was the '500 Days' plan for the transition to the market economy. Even as the 'presidential group', under Shatalin, worked on the programme throughout August, with Gorbachev constantly encouraging them by telephone, his prime minister, Nikolai Ryzhkov, tried to ensure it would not succeed. Ryzhkov was widely regarded as the chief representative of the military-industrial complex. His own team, led by deputy prime minister, Leonid Abalkin, also worked through August to produce an alternative programme which envisaged a much slower move to the market and the retention of far greater powers for the centre vis-à-vis the republics. The finance minister, Valentin Pavlov, in effect sabotaged the work of the presidential team by refusing to supply essential data about government spending.

At the end of August Gorbachev presented the Shatalin programme to a joint two-day session of the Presidential Council and the Federation Council. Ryzhkov spoke four times, declaring he would refuse to implement it. Abalkin, a few days later, said that if the 500 Days plan was adopted, 'we will publish the government programme and move into battle'.

Gorbachev called in his first adviser, Abel Aganbegyan, to try to amalgamate the two plans. He soon produced a 'presidential programme' which was, he said, '99 per cent Shatalin', with just a few figures taken from the Ryzhkov plan. Ryzhkov kept up an almost daily torrent of criticism of Shatalin's 'shock therapy', which he said would cause mass unemployment, lead to the closure of thousands of factories and collective farms, and bring about the collapse of the union. Gorbachev began to bend under the pressure. He himself was afraid of allowing the country to disintegrate, and was only half-committed to Shatalin's privatisation plans (he was resolutely opposed, for example, to private land ownership).

Other representatives of the military-industrial complex lobbied Gorbachev directly. His economics adviser, Nikolai Petrakov, attended a meeting between Gorbachev and twelve managers of major state enterprises, eleven of whom represented military factories. Throughout the meeting, Petrakov recalls, Gorbachev argued in favour of the Shatalin plan, but the industrialists, led by the ultra-conservative Alexander Tizyakov, president of a recently created 'Association of State Enteprises', told him bluntly that any transfer to the market was unacceptable.

In mid-September, Gorbachev caved in to the pressure. He asked the Supreme Soviet to grant him special powers to impose a reform programme by presidential decree, but at the same time set up yet another commission to find a compromise between the Shatalin and Ryzhkov plans. Yeltsin protested that this was like 'trying to mate a hedgehog with a snake', and indeed, when the commission produced its version, in mid-October, it turned out to be an unworkable crossbreed. Parliament, weary of months of indecision, endorsed it. But in reality, the conservatives had killed off any hopes of a swift introduction of the market economy.

PARLIAMENT then went into recess. When it reconvened, in mid-November, Soyuz delegates immediately demanded that Gorbachev make a 'state of the nation' speech detailing how he intended to put a stop to the chaos and paralysis of power. On the evening of 15 November, he conferred with his radical personal aides, Georgy Shakhnazarov and Nikolai Petrakov. In a last attempt to save the situation, they pleaded with him to announce that he was giving up the position of Communist Party leader, and that he would hold a direct presidential election the following year.

Gorbachev listened – and ignored them. The next day he delivered a long and lacklustre speech which satisfied no one, neither radicals nor conservatives.

That night Gorbachev once again underwent a sudden and mysterious transformation, and made a fateful turn to the right. He abandoned all his radical colleagues and, according to Stanislav Shatalin, consulted instead his old comrades from the Party leadership. The next morning he made a 20-minute statement to parliament in which he announced unprecedented constitutional reforms which stunned even his closest colleagues.

Prime Minister Nikolai Ryzhkov was at his desk that morning when Gorbachev telephoned him from his car as he drove to the Kremlin, to tell him that he intended to make 'some changes that the country needs'.

'What changes? When are you going to announce this?' asked Ryzhkov.

'Right now, at 10 o'clock,' replied Gorbachev. He informed Ryzhkov that his Council of Ministers was to be replaced by a smaller 'Cabinet of Ministers', directly subordinate to the president rather than to parliament. Ryzhkov was furious. A few weeks later he suffered a heart attack and was replaced.

The Presidential Council was also abolished. Alexander Yakovlev, Gorbachev's confidant for the past seven years, did not even know he was intending to make a speech. Suddenly, he learnt that Gorbachev had announced he was getting rid of the only body on which Yakovlev sat. The Presidential Council itself had never discussed the idea.

Gorbachev's other innovations in this November shake-up were: greatly increased personal powers for the president; a revamped Federation Council to give the republics a greater say in central decision-making; a new 'Security Council' with seats for the KGB, army and police; and the creation of the post of vice-president, in charge of a new 'state inspectorate'.

The changes were intended to increase the president's authority and help restore law and order. But Gorbachev's actions no longer seemed to be governed by careful planning. He was improvising – thrashing around for ways to salvage something constructive from the ruins of communism. Worse, as far as the supporters of radical reform were concerned, he was becoming more and more authoritarian as the situation deteriorated. While still repeating his dedication to reform, he sought refuge in the traditional pillars of the communist state – the KGB, the *apparat*, and the threat of force – rather than in speedy moves towards a new order.

Events now seemed to be rolling uncontrollably towards a crackdown. At the end of November he appointed Leonid Kravchenko – the man who claims to have taught him his television techniques – as head of the state television and radio service, with a brief to cut off the oxygen of publicity from the radicals.

On 1 December Gorbachev issued a presidential decree authorising the use of troops to enforce the call-up of army recruits in the recalcitrant republics.

The next day he sacked his liberal interior minister, Vadim Bakatin – and admitted to him privately that he had no alternative because the conservatives were demanding it. Seven Soyuz deputies, led by two colonels, Alksnis and Petrushenko, had stormed into Gorbachev's office a month earlier to demand that he sack Bakatin, mainly because of his leniency towards the secessionist republics. In the following weeks Gorbachev told Bakatin that he was being bombarded with complaints about him from the right. Finally, he succumbed. He appointed in his place Boris Pugo, a right-wing *apparatchik*, and provided him with a deputy who was the very epitome of military muscle – General Boris Gromov, the last commander of Soviet troops in Afghanistan. One of Pugo's first acts was to sign a secret joint order with the defence minister, Yazov, setting up military patrols on the streets of Soviet cities.

Vladimir Kryuchkov, the KGB chief, meanwhile revived the rhetoric of the Cold War in a series of speeches in which he laid the blame for most of the country's problems at the door of Western secret services, which he accused of economic sabotage and stirring up ethnic unrest.

At the Congress of People's Deputies, which held its fourth session in the last days of 1990, it was no longer the Inter-regional Group that called the shots, but Soyuz, with its shrill demands for decisive measures to restore order and maintain the unity of the Soviet state. Gorbachev himself declared he would not shrink from using his widened presidential powers to crush nationalist movements and install a state of emergency or martial law in rebellious republics.

All the signs of an inexorable drift to the right were dramatically confirmed by no less a figure than Eduard Shevardnadze, the foreign minister and, together with Yakovlev, the only member of Gorbachev's leadership constantly urging him towards more liberal reform. In an emotional speech to the Congress on 20 December, he announced his resignation 'in protest at the advance of dictatorship'. Shevardnadze's decision was taken suddenly, overnight, and he did not forewarn Gorbachev. But it came as no surprise to those who knew him. His aides say that for at least a year he had been deeply unhappy with the criticism of his diplomatic efforts by individuals in the army and military-industrial complex. He was embarrassed by attempts to undermine international agreements which he negotiated. (He learnt from the *French* foreign minister that the Soviet army had removed thousands of tanks east of the Urals to circumvent the historic 1990 treaty on Conventional Forces in Europe.) Until mid-1990, his aides say, Shevardnadze was consistently supported by Gorbachev in his disputes with the military, but since then that support had vanished.

Whether Shevardnadze was warning of a personal dictatorship by Gorbachev or of a 'creeping coup d'état' by military and right-wing forces, using Gorbachev as a figurehead, was not clear – and mattered little. His message was that the reforming spirit of the Second Russian Revolution had been betrayed – by its initiator and leader. It was the gloomiest day since Gorbachev came to power.

Gorbachev had now lost four liberal allies – Shevardnadze, Yakovlev, Bakatin and Shatalin. At the end of the year Petrakov also resigned. The president's new team of grey men included Gennady Yanayev, appointed vice-president, and Valentin Pavlov, the prime minister. Yanayev, a Party functionary and opponent of the market economy, appalled many television viewers by answering a parliamentary question about his state of health as if it referred to his sexual abilities: 'I'm a normal bloke,' he replied. 'My wife has no complaints.' Pavlov was the man who, as finance minister, had tried to sabotage the presidential group's work in the summer.

The first weeks of January 1991 brought events which many people interpreted as the beginning of the end of *perestroika*. Glasnost – Gorbachev's only indisputable domestic achievement – suffered a grave blow when the radicals' flagship television show, *Vzglyad*, was taken off the air, after trying to put out a programme explaining Shevardnadze's resignation. The main television news programme returned to a pre-*glasnost* diet of official communiqués. The commitment to peace seemed to vanish, as Gorbachev won parliament's approval for a defence budget for 1991 amounting to more than one-third of all central government spending (96.5 billion roubles, as opposed to 71 billion in 1990).

Finally, all respect for democracy crumbled, as Gorbachev accused the freely elected government of Lithuania – in language he had not used for five years – of aiming to bring back the 'bourgeois' system, and demanded that they restore the Soviet constitution in the republic. Mysterious 'national salvation committees', sponsored by the pro-Moscow communists, appeared in Lithuania and Latvia, calling on Gorbachev to impose presidential rule. Soviet tanks then rumbled into Vilnius and began occupying key government buildings. On 13 January 14 people were killed as paratroopers seized the Vilnius television station. A week later, four died in Riga, as 'Black Beret' riot police stormed the Latvian interior ministry. In each case it looked like a dress rehearsal for the overthrow of the elected republican governments – or even for a nationwide clampdown. Perhaps only the huge international outcry prevented that from happening.

Gorbachev gave the appearance of having lost control. There is no evidence to suggest that he personally ordered the use of force in the Baltics (indeed, Bakatin, who spoke to him the morning after the Vilnius killings, says Gorbachev was unaware of exactly what had happened there). Yet in a disastrous parliamentary performance he blamed the republican governments for what had happened, and failed to condemn either the shadowy 'salvation fronts' or the army for taking its orders from them. It was beginning to look as if the hardliners now in charge of the army, interior ministry and KGB – Yazov, Pugo and Kryuchkov – could get away with anything.

In another blustering, red-faced appearance in parliament, Gorbachev condemned the media for lacking 'objectivity' in their coverage of the events, and even suggested suspending the press law which had allowed hundreds of independent newspapers to flourish since August.

The Communist Party's central committee held a plenum at the end of January at which, for the first time in at least two years, there was scarcely a word of criticism directed at Gorbachev. At last, it seemed, he was doing what the hardliners wanted him to do.

Both Shakhnazarov and Yakovlev optimistically described Gorbachev's swing towards the conservatives not as the end of *perestroika*, but as a major tactical manoeuvre. Shevardnadze seemed to be indicating the same in his resignation speech when he said that Gorbachev and he were 'of a like mind' – implying that Gorbachev's basic inclinations were and remained reformist, but that he was being pushed by the right.

Gorbachev himself no longer seemed to know where he was going. Asked by journalists whether he was moving to the right, he admitted, only half-jokingly, 'Actually, I'm going round in circles.'

★ ★ ★

IN the spring Gorbachev recovered from his dizzy spell. The continuing 'war of laws' between the centre and the republics (Russia and six other republics were refusing, for example, to transfer any tax revenue to the central budget) made it essential to bring talks on a new union treaty to a speedy conclusion. On 17 March the views of ordinary people were sought in a referendum on 'the preservation of the union'. But the wording of the question put to voters throughout the country was pure compromise, and therefore guaranteed to produce a confusing result.

Voters were asked: 'Do you consider necessary the preservation of the Union of Soviet Socialist Republics as a renewed federation of equal sovereign republics, in which the rights and freedoms of an individual of any nationality will be fully guaranteed?'

In effect, this was several questions rolled into one. It was impossible to vote for the union without also saying yes to a union of *socialist* republics; if one voted 'no' to the preservation of the union, did that mean one was also against guarantees of human rights? Even from the point of view of logic, it was hard to see how a 'renewed' federation (i.e. one that did not yet exist) could be 'preserved'. To add to the confusion, several republics either amended the wording slightly, or added other questions of their own, about the desirability of more autonomy or sovereignty. In several places, a majority appeared to be in favour both of a 'renewed federation' *and* of republican independence! The referendum was not held at all in republics which had already decided to leave the union.

The overall result – a 76 per cent yes vote – was hailed by the conservatives as a victory, although what exactly the vote was in favour of was hard to guess. In practice it meant nothing, and did not bind Gorbachev, or the republics, to any commitment.

Apparently emboldened by having thrown this scrap of meat to the conservative lions, Gorbachev began to proceed with a number of more radical moves.

From 23 April he held a series of meetings at his Novo-Ogaryovo country house near Moscow with the leaders of just nine of the fifteen republics. Together they hammered out the principles of an entirely new state structure for the Soviet Union. The 'Nine plus One' agreement foresaw the creation of a 'union of sovereign states', omitting any reference to socialism, and effectively recognised the right of the other six republics (Lithuania, Latvia, Estonia, Moldavia, Georgia and Armenia) to secede. Most importantly, it envisaged that as soon as the treaty was signed, a new constitution would be drawn up, and fresh parliamentary and presidential elections held. (The Supreme Soviet, led by its chairman, Anatoly Lukyanov, objected both to the terms of the agreement, which they said ignored the results of the referendum, and to the plan for a new parliament to be elected.)

The agreement meant that Gorbachev and Yeltsin, who only two months earlier, in the wake of the Baltic crackdown, had publicly called for Gorbachev's resignation, had once again buried the hatchet. Yeltsin's authority continued to rise. In early April he had won emergency powers from the Russian parliament, just days after tens of thousands had marched in his support through Moscow, defying both a ban on such demonstrations and a massive display of military force. He now used his influence to bring a two-month coalminers' strike to an end, by transferring the pits from central control to the jurisdiction of the Russian Federation. On 12 June he won a direct election to the newly created presidency of Russia. A few weeks later he enraged conservatives by decreeing an end to all Communist Party activities at workplaces throughout the Russian Federation.

On the economic front, Gorbachev gave his blessing to the so-called 'Grand Bargain', a blueprint for massive Western aid in return for deep Soviet reforms, drawn up by the radical economist Grigory Yavlinsky (co-author of the earlier 500 Days Plan) together with economists at Harvard University.

Gorbachev further tested the hardliners' patience by welcoming the creation of a new Movement for Democratic Reform in July. The Movement, which was expected to transform itself into a major political party – the first viable opposition to the Communist Party – counted among its leaders several of Gorbachev's former liberal comrades: Shevardnadze, Yakovlev, Shatalin, Petrakov and Volsky, as well as the radical mayors of Leningrad and Moscow, Anatoly Sobchak and Gavriil Popov.

As for the Communist Party itself, Gorbachev forced it, at a plenum of the central committee on 25-26 July, to accept a new Programme which entirely abandoned Marxism-Leninism. He even suggested it ought to rename itself a 'socialist' or 'social-democratic' party.

All these developments brought Gorbachev into almost open confrontation with the hardliners. Throughout the spring and summer of 1991 they repeatedly tried to embarrass or undermine him. According to Alexander Yakovlev, 'Step after step was taken to create an atmosphere in which the introduction of a state of emergency would seem necessary.'

In April, Gorbachev faced such a barrage of criticism at a central committee plenum that he strode to the podium and offered his resignation as Party leader. 'Seventy per cent of the speakers are criticising me, not from a personal point of view, but on behalf of the people. I propose to resign,' he said. He had done this before, though in less stark terms, and it had the same effect again, of shocking the central committee into refusing to accept his resignation.

In June, the conservatives attempted a 'constitutional' coup d'état. The prime minister, Valentin Pavlov, asked the Supreme Soviet to grant him emergency powers, rivalling the president's. Gorbachev angrily opposed the suggestion, but the idea was supported at a closed session by three of the men who would shortly plot to overthrow him – defence minister Yazov, KGB chief Kryuchkov and interior minister Pugo.

The timing of some of the hardliners' moves suggested a coordinated campaign. As the president flew to Oslo to receive the Nobel Peace Prize, the Soviet prosecutor issued a report exonerating the troops who had massacred civilians in Vilnius in January. As leaders of the G7 group of leading Western countries were weighing up whether to invite Gorbachev to their economic summit in London in July, with a view to offering Western economic aid, the military staged a show of force in Vilnius. Pavlov meanwhile pulled the rug from under Yavlinsky's 'Grand Bargain', saying he did not believe Gorbachev had any new plan to present to the G7 leaders: 'It's high time we stopped producing programmes. As far as I know, Gorbachev is not working on any new programme, certainly not for his trip to London.' And as President Bush arrived in Moscow at the end of July, eight Lithuanian customs officials were gunned down.

The conservatives' public arguments were becoming increasingly desperate, with Pavlov claiming a plot by Western banks to flood the USSR with roubles, and Kryuchkov alleging that offers of Western economic aid were all part of a decades-old CIA plot to undermine the Soviet Union, while Western intelligence services were working out plans 'for the pacification and even occupation of the Soviet Union under the pretext of establishing international control over its nuclear potential'.

Privately, their arguments were focused on Gorbachev himself. Four men regularly met to discuss their grievances: Kryuchkov, defence minister Yazov, Oleg Baklanov (deputy head of the defence council) and Valery Boldin (the president's chief of staff). According to Yazov, they came to the conclusion that 'Gorbachev had exhausted himself as an active statesman', that he was allowing the USSR to fall to pieces, and selling the country out to the USA, and that he acted too often without consulting them. They were outraged that they were not even informed of the contents of Gorbachev's report to the G7 leaders in London. 'Until then,' said Yazov, 'we at least used to discuss all these things in the Politburo, or in the Presidential Council or Security Council.'[1]

The 'ideological preparations' for a final move against Gorbachev were completed with the publication in the right-wing *Sovetskaya*

*Rossiya* of a 'patriotic' appeal entitled 'Word to the People', signed by 12 leading conservatives. Appearing on 23 July, just three days after Boris Yeltsin's decree banning Party cells at workplaces, it described Gorbachev's rule as 'six tragic years', during which the Party, which was 'being destroyed by its own leaders', had ceded power to 'frivolous and clumsy parliamentarians who have set us against each other and brought into force thousands of stillborn laws, of which the only ones that function are those which enslave people and divide the tormented body of the country into pieces.'

THE situation was now so tense, and the leadership so polarised, that Gorbachev ought to have known better than to leave Moscow for his usual August vacation. The precedents, after all, were ominous: Ligachev's repeated attempts to change the course of *perestroika* during Gorbachev's absences, not to mention the overthrow of Khrushchev in 1964, while he was on holiday in the south.

On 16 August Alexander Yakovlev resigned from the Party, echoing Eduard Shevardnadze's earlier warning of an imminent right-wing takeover. It was the most astute and timely observation of his career. But Gorbachev ignored it. He remained with his family in his new holiday dacha at Cape Sarych near Foros in the Crimea, with his closest advisers at a nearby health resort – all too far from Moscow to be aware that the most senior men in his entourage were plotting to stop his reforms.

Gorbachev was putting the final touches to a speech he would make on the 20th, the day the new Union Treaty was due to be signed. He was helped by his aides, Georgy Shakhnazarov and Anatoly Chernyayev, who were staying at the Yuzhny sanatorium, seven miles away. The presidential aeroplane had already arrived at a military airfield in the Crimea to take Gorbachev back to Moscow for the signing ceremony. It was precisely this event – the imminence of a treaty that would spell the end of the old centralised Soviet Union – that determined when Gorbachev's enemies would act.

On Saturday evening, 17 August, as KGB staff began to drift home from the Lubyanka, Kryuchkov rang three of his most trusted allies and invited them to a top-secret meeting at a military base in the southern outskirts of Moscow, at the end of Lenin Avenue. The three were Yazov, Baklanov, and Oleg Shenin, a hawkish secretary of the Communist Party's central committee. They decided to send a delegation to the Crimea the next day to put an ultimatum to Gorbachev. Yazov would provide a military plane. The delegation, it was decided, would consist of five men: Shenin (to represent the Party), Baklanov (for the defence industries), Boldin (Gorbachev's chief of staff and trusted long-time associate), General Valentin Varennikov (Yazov's deputy in the defence ministry), and General

Yuri Plekhanov (who as head of the KGB department responsible for the security of Soviet leaders knew his way around Gorbachev's dacha complex).

At 4.50 p.m. on Sunday 18 August, Gorbachev was surprised to be told that a group of people had arrived and were demanding a meeting with him. He was not expecting visitors. His surprise turned to suspicion and fear when he tried to make a telephone call, and discovered that all his lines, including the safe Kremlin line, were cut.

Before agreeing to see the visitors, Gorbachev summoned his family – Raisa, their daughter and son-in-law – and warned them that something was afoot, that he feared an attempt to blackmail or arrest him, and that he was determined not to yield to any pressure. But before he could invite the visitors in, they barged straight into his office. According to Raisa, 'They broke in, without even telling us beforehand. They were escorted by Plekhanov, and all the guards saluted him. It was like a bolt from the blue. I was sitting in an armchair, and they cruised by as if they didn't see me.'[2]

Gorbachev immediately demanded to know who had sent them. 'The committee,' came the answer.

'What committee?'

'The committee set up for the state of emergency in the country.'

According to the constitution, only the president and the Supreme Soviet had the right to declare a state of emergency – and neither had been consulted. The delegation demanded that Gorbachev either issue the necessary decree to legitimise the 'committee's' state of emergency, or hand over power to vice-president Gennady Yanayev. Gorbachev categorically refused.

He later told Chernyayev that General Varennikov had been the 'pushiest', and that Shenin had kept quiet during the meeting. When Boldin (whom Raisa described as almost one of the family) ventured, 'Don't you realise we [the country] are in a terrible plight?' Gorbachev rudely cut him short: 'You prick, shut up! Don't come to me with lectures on the situation in the country.'

Gorbachev warned the group that what they were attempting was a coup d'état, that their 'committee' was unconstitutional, and that their adventurism would lead to bloodshed and civil war.

While this was going on, Vyacheslav Generalov, the deputy head of government security, appeared at Chernyayev's office, in a separate building next to Gorbachev's dacha. Generalov told him he had been ordered to keep everyone there. He said there was a triple semi-circle of guards around the dacha complex, from one seacoast to the other, that the roads were all blocked, and that three warships were cruising along the shoreline.

Chernyayev asked Generalov what would happen on Tuesday, the day the Union Treaty was to be signed. He was told: 'There will be no signing. The aircraft that came to pick up Gorbachev has already been sent back. Garages with his limos have been sealed and are under guard – not by my people, but special units, with machine-guns.'

The delegation left after an hour, taking with them Vladimir Medvedev, the president's personal aide-de-camp, who for years had never been more than a few yards away from Gorbachev – his thinning hair and alert expression were seen in the background of almost every picture of the Soviet leader.

The siege had begun. For 72 hours, Gorbachev and his family and advisers, together with 32 bodyguards, would be kept under house arrest. They had no external communications and knew what was happening in the country only from television – which immediately came under total control of the Emergency Committee – and from foreign radio stations, once Gorbachev's guards managed to rig up an old receiver with proper aerials.

THE delegation returned to Moscow (apart from Varennikov, who travelled to Kiev to put pressure on the Ukrainian leader, Leonid Kravchuk). The other four – Boldin, Baklanov, Shenin and Plekhanov – went straight to a meeting in the Kremlin with the other conspirators.

The meeting, at the long, green-baize table in prime minister Pavlov's office, from which Lenin had once ruled the country, began at around 9 o'clock. It was attended by Vladimir Kryuchkov, KGB chief; Gennady Yanayev, vice president, who was to take over Gorbachev's functions, and who signed the official documents on the state of emergency; Boris Pugo, interior minister; Valentin Pavlov, prime minister; Dmitry Yazov, defence minister; Anatoly Lukyanov, chairman of the Supreme Soviet (he arrived later, having been flown in specially from his holiday dacha at Valdai, at Pavlov's request); and Alexander Bessmertnykh, foreign minister, who also arrived late, at about 11 o'clock. (He says he was invited along as an afterthought, because the hardliners wanted a liberal in their team to lend it more credibility.)

As the conspirators conferred, they consumed coffee and whisky. Yanayev was drunk throughout the meeting – 'quite merry, in fact', according to Yazov. Pavlov, who had already been drinking with his son at his dacha before being summoned by Kryuchkov, became so inebriated that – according to his own testimony – he ended up flat on his back and had to be carried out to his limousine. (He appears to have remained drunk over the next days, when he was declared too 'ill' to perform his duties as prime minister.)

The core group of conspirators resorted to blatant lies to intimidate their weaker-willed colleagues into supporting the coup. Boldin and Baklanov, for example, opened the meeting by reporting that they had allegedly found Gorbachev at his dacha in a terrible state of health, with 'no proper grasp on reality', having suffered either a heart attack or a stroke.

Kryuchkov and the security chief, Plekhanov, then alleged that an 'emergency' had arisen: they had information that a military coup would be attempted within hours and that gangs of thugs were already gathering round key buildings, armed with an assortment of weapons including mortars. They showed four lists of people whom the alleged plotters intended to liquidate immediately, and claimed that they had only hours to act in order to pre-empt them.

Most of those present went along with Kryuchkov. Six of them – Yanayev, Pavlov, Pugo, Baklanov, Yazov and Kryuchkov himself – actually joined the Emergency Committee. Lukyanov did not, but he agreed to write a statement, harshly critical of the Union Treaty, which was circulated and broadcast the following morning, alternately with the Emergency Committee's own announcements. It was later alleged that he was not merely deeply involved but was in fact the 'chief ideologist' of the coup.

Foreign minister Bessmertnykh declined to join the Committee, saying that if he did, 'it will be the end for all our foreign dealings'. But he did not actively oppose them: his ministry sent out instructions to embassies abroad to inform foreign governments of the change of power, as though it were perfectly constitutional.

The following morning two extras were invited on to the Committee – Alexander Tizyakov, the head of the Association of State Enterprises who had lobbied hard against market reforms, and Vasily Starodubtsev, chief representative of the country's collective farm chairmen. Both had signed the 'Word to the People' in *Sovetskaya Rossiya* the previous month.

The heads of TASS and Soviet television were called in and ordered to put out the necessary announcements. The plotters did not sleep that night. Overthrowing the president of a country the size of the Soviet Union was no easy matter. Instructions had to be issued to local authorities, local Communist Party organisations, army units, the KGB. Radical newspapers had to be banned, radio stations prevented from operating. During the night, lists were drawn up of people to be arrested, headed by the Russian leader, Boris Yeltsin. Blank forms were printed for mass arrests and deportations. A factory in Pskov was even ordered to produce 250,000 pairs of handcuffs.

As early shift workers got out of bed on the morning of 19 August, they heard the Committee's clumsily worded statements, read out over and over again on radio and television: 'In view of Mikhail Sergeyevich Gorbachev's inability, for health reasons, to perform the duties of president of the USSR, and the transfer of the president's powers, in keeping with paragraph 7, article 127 of the USSR Constitution, to Vice President Gennady Ivanovich Yanayev, . . . we resolve to declare a state of emergency in parts of the Soviet Union from 4 a.m. Moscow time on 19 August 1991.'

Despite the attempt to legitimise the coup by reference to the Soviet Constitution, the Committee's 'Address to the Soviet People' made it plain that the declaration of the state of emergency was anything but constitutional, and that the aim, far from being to 'continue with Gorbachev's policies' (as Yanayev was to claim at a press conference later in the day) was to put an abrupt end to them.

The Emergency Committee declared that the policies of *perestroika* had come to a dead end. It spoke of a 'mortal danger' hanging over the country, which had 'become ungovernable'. It criticised almost every result of Gorbachev's reforms – the 'chaotic and uncontrolled slide towards the market economy', the 'war of laws' between the centre and the republics, the 'inevitable' prospect of famine, the 'unbridled personal dictatorships' of some elected leaders (apparently a reference chiefly to the Russian Federation president, Boris Yeltsin), the growth of crime and the 'propaganda of sex and violence', and, above all, the impending break-up of the USSR itself.

At nine o'clock, in heavy rain, tanks and troops began to pour into Moscow and took up position outside key buildings. It seemed to most Russians, and to people around the world, that *perestroika* had been snuffed out. Gorbachev's rule was over. The old order had reestablished itself.

# CHAPTER EIGHT

# *The August Revolution*

EVEN on the first evening of his house arrest, Gorbachev had to confront the most uncomfortable fact about the coup: he himself had hand-picked the men who staged it. He had prevailed upon the Supreme Soviet to endorse Yanayev as vice-president, after deputies had initially rejected him. His aide, Anatoly Chernyayev, reminded him as they walked in the darkness around the dacha: 'They are all your men. You cultivated them, promoted and trusted them.'

During the two days of isolation that followed – 19 and 20 August – there was little Gorbachev could do to save himself. During the first night his son-in-law, Anatoly, made a videorecording of his statement, condemning the coup. They unreeled the tape and cut it into four sections, to be smuggled out – but the opportunity to do so never arose. Gorbachev sent a series of demands – that his communications be restored and the presidential plane returned – via the aptly-named General Generalov, whom Kryuchkov had put in charge of the Foros compound. But to no avail.

Gorbachev received massage treatment for back-ache which, contrary to the putschists' claims, was the only ailment he had. He took his granddaughter, Anastasiya, down to the beach, until warned against it by his bodyguards. The family did not dare to discuss things indoors because every room was bugged. Their movements were observed by KGB-men from watchtowers all around the compound. Raisa fell ill.

But by the end of the first day they must have felt slightly encouraged. Soviet television broadcast a press conference given by the coup leaders, at which 'acting president' Yanayev's hands were visibly trembling. Moreover, the questions, especially those asked by foreign correspondents, clearly indicated that the putschists and their claims – about Gorbachev's state of health, for example – were not being taken seriously.

211

Although they had had months to think about it, the plotters proved inordinately inept in carrying out the coup. They argued among themselves, took decisions in a state of drunkenness, and made a series of blunders. In Yazov's words, 'We didn't think anything through, either long-term or short-term.' One of the first mistakes was to delay the introduction of troops into Moscow until after the announcement of the state of emergency. This allowed protest demonstrations to begin. Most crucially, Boris Yeltsin was not only not arrested, but calmly allowed to drive in from his dacha at Arkhangelskoye, outside Moscow, to the Russian parliament building on the embankment of the Moskva river – the so-called 'White House'.·

From here, he was able to lead the fight against the coup. In a brilliant piece of political theatre, he climbed on top of a tank that had taken up position outside the White House to address the crowd that had gathered there, many waving the white-blue-and-red tricolour of pre-revolutionary Russia. He denounced what he called 'a cynical attempt at a right-wing coup' and called for civil disobedience and a general strike. 'Soldiers, officers and generals,' he declared, 'the clouds of terror and dictatorship are gathering over the whole country. They must not be allowed to bring eternal night.'

The White House became the headquarters of the resistance. Radicals such as Shevardnadze and Yakovlev joined Yeltsin there. When the KGB closed down the independent radio station *Ekho Moskvy* and the Russian government's Radio Russia, an amateur station was set up inside the White House, broadcasting news of the resistance and Yeltsin's appeals under the call-sign Radio 3-Anna. Banned radical newspapers got together to produce a 'joint newspaper' (*obshchaya gazeta*) on desk-top computers and photocopiers. Protesters began erecting barricades to protect the huge white skyscraper, using building materials, girders, pipes, paving stones, planks, slabs of concrete, and trolleybuses with their tyres punctured. As the crowd around the White House swelled, tank crews from three divisions, sent to enforce the state of emergency, disobeyed orders and went over to Yeltsin's side. Ten 'friendly' tanks kept guard around the Russian parliament.

The coup leaders had underestimated Yeltsin's popularity and courage, as well as the new mood of the Soviet people, highly politicised by six years of *perestroika*. Up to 200,000 Muscovites demonstrated in the Manege Square, next to the Kremlin, and a crowd of 5000 staged a vigil in front of the White House in heavy rain throughout the night. In Leningrad, where the mayor, Anatoly Sobchak, persuaded the local commandant not to introduce troops, even bigger crowds held protest rallies.

By Tuesday evening there were already signs of dissent among the coup leaders. Pavlov was 'sick'. There were rumours that Yazov and Kryuchkov had either resigned or were also ill. According to Yazov, they had planned to meet twice that day, but met only once. In the evening, a curfew was suddenly imposed in Moscow, apparently to clear the streets in preparation for an assault on Yeltsin's White House. But the streets did not clear. Demonstrators ambushed tanks as they rolled through underpasses, throwing petrol bombs at them and tarpaulins over their visors to blind them.

The KGB's Alpha anti-terrorist unit refused orders to storm the Russian parliament. Another plan, to send helicopter gunships into action against the White House that night, was foiled by air force general Yevgeny Shaposhnikov (later named USSR defence minister), who told the plotters he would scramble fighters to down the helicopters.

The coup was crumbling. In street battles, three young men were killed by tanks, crushed or shot. The coup leaders' nerves now failed completely. The next morning, Wednesday 21st, Yazov ordered the troops to pull back.

In the afternoon, as the tanks rumbled out of Moscow, a column of black Zils laced its way through them at high speed, heading for Vnukovo airport. Inside were four of the conspirators – Yazov, Kryuchkov, Lukyanov and Baklanov – plus Vladimir Ivashko, the deputy leader of the Communist Party. They were on their way to the Crimea to beg the president, like an all-forgiving tsar, for mercy.

At the same time Boris Yeltsin, addressing an emergency session of the Russian parliament, announced that he was also sending a delegation to the Crimea – to rescue Gorbachev and bring him back to Moscow. This delegation consisted of Russian vice-president Alexander Rutskoi, Russian prime minister Ivan Silayev, former Soviet interior minister Vadim Bakatin, and a Gorbachev adviser, Yevgeny Primakov. They were accompanied by about 50 armed officers, under Rutskoi's command.

According to Bakatin, they decided to leave the officers at the airport, ten kilometres from Gorbachev's dacha, and to take no weapons with them. 'It was a warm Crimean evening, such a contrast with the rain in Moscow two hours before. We were very tense. We were afraid the plotters might have gone to take Gorbachev away. We had no idea what was happening. We drove to Foros, but then [security chief] Plekhanov ordered us to get out and walk the rest of the way to the dacha.'

The putschists got there first. At five o'clock, Chernyayev recalls, they filed through the entrance of Gorbachev's villa. 'All of them bore a battered look and a grim face, and they all bowed to me! I realised at once they had come to ask for pardon.'

Gorbachev, however, refused to see them. Bakatin recalls how he and the others in Rutskoi's delegation marched straight past the plotters, who were huddled in a group outside. 'There were bodyguards inside with submachine-guns – I'd never seen anything like it.' Gorbachev appeared, warmly embraced his saviours, and spent several hours telling and re-telling what he had gone through.

The president's communications were by now restored, and he used them to order the putschists' arrest, to retake control of the Kremlin, and to talk with President Bush.

In the early hours of Thursday morning Gorbachev, dressed in a sweater and open-necked shirt, flew back to Moscow. Still not entirely sure that the coup had been defeated, he flew in Rutskoi's plane rather than in the easily identifiable presidential plane in which the putschists had arrived. Yazov, Kryuchkov and Baklanov were all arrested by the Russian KGB as soon as they set foot in Moscow airport. The other conspirators were also quickly rounded up, Yanayev having to be woken from a drunken sleep on the divan in his Kremlin office. Boris Pugo, the interior minister, shot himself to avoid arrest.

The coup failed because it was misconceived, strategically and tactically. Its organisers had tried to give their actions a semblance of legality – by referring to articles in the Soviet Constitution, by not immediately rounding up opposition politicians, by declaring a state of emergency only in 'parts' of the country because by law only the Supreme Soviet had the right to declare one throughout the land. But the very premise on which their actions was based (Gorbachev's 'inability' to govern) collapsed as soon as Yeltsin and Western leaders demanded independent proof of Gorbachev's illness. The pretence that reforms would continue was laughable, since the Emergency Committee's first statement, justifying the coup, criticised just about everything Gorbachev had done. Crucially, the coup leaders failed to cut off communications with the outside world. Thanks to this, Western television viewers saw vivid pictures of the resistance to the putsch, including eyewitness reports from inside the White House, and Yeltsin was able to maintain telephone contact with Western leaders – who made it clear they recognised him, not 'acting president' Yanayev, as the country's legitimate leader in Gorbachev's absence.

Above all, the coup failed because of popular resistance to it. It was, in other words, defeated by the reforms introduced by Gorbachev since 1985 – *glasnost*, democracy, the liberation of the Soviet mind – things which the blinkered ideologues in the Emergency Committee had never accepted and could not comprehend. Their botched attempt to turn the clock back proved that *perestroika* had become irreversible.

DURING the flight from the Crimea back to Moscow in the early hours of 22 August, Gorbachev remarked to his aide, Chernyayev: 'We are flying into a new era.' He was right, but events were to show that he was only dimly aware of just how different the new era would be.

He misjudged two things: that authority had slipped out of his hands into Yeltsin's, and that the Communist Party was so discredited by the coup that it could no longer be reformed.

The dramatic shift of power began the moment Yeltsin delivered his tank-top denunciation of the coup and declared the conspirators guilty of treason. Suddenly, Gorbachev's greatest challenger became his defender. While many other Soviet politicians waited or wavered, Yeltsin instantly saw the coup for what it was, and unflinchingly opposed it. Gorbachev would owe him a huge debt of gratitude.

In the two-and-a-half days of the coup Yeltsin issued a stream of decrees that increased his own standing. On the Monday, he annulled the orders of the Emergency Committee on the territory of the Russian Federation (RSFSR). He ordered all officials to obey the RSFSR government, not the Committee, and called on army and KGB units involved in Gorbachev's overthrow to stand down. On the Tuesday he demanded a meeting with Gorbachev in the presence of Yanayev, and access to the president for World Health Organisation doctors. A presidential edict stated that he was taking control, with immediate effect, of all forces stationed in the RSFSR. He declared Yazov's and Kryuchkov's orders invalid. He instructed his deputy, Alexander Rutskoi, to set up a Russian National Guard, and appointed General Konstantin Kobets Russian defence minister. On Wednesday, it was Yeltsin's *Russian* KGB officers who arrested the coup leaders. He issued a decree transferring all state enterprises on Russian territory from Soviet to RSFSR jurisdiction. He even put Soviet radio and television into the hands of the Russian government, and sacked its chief, Leonid Kravchenko – something that was in fact the prerogative of the Soviet president.

Even after Gorbachev returned to Moscow on Thursday, Yeltsin continued to amass powers. He banned Communist Party cells in army units in the RSFSR. He announced that he and Gorbachev were *together* drawing up a list of candidates for a new government of national trust. He reinstated the Russian tricolour as the republic's official flag. *He* sacked the heads of the two Soviet news agencies, TASS and Novosti.

Gorbachev, for his part, seemed out of touch. At his first press conference, on the Thursday, he continued to talk about the possibility of 'reforming' the Communist Party and purging it of reactionaries in order that it should regain its position as the 'living force of *perestroika*'. It was entirely wrong, he said, to speak of the entire Party as reactionary.

That night ordinary Muscovites showed what they thought of that. A large crowd toppled the statue of Felix Dzerzhinsky, the founder of the Soviet secret police, and celebrated with fireworks and vodka all night in the middle of Lubyanka Square, right in front of the KGB headquarters. Other statues of revolutionary leaders were carted away over the next days. 'People power', which had first expressed itself on the barricades at the White House, was now much more decisive than Gorbachev's word. No longer would his term, *perestroika*, apply to what was happening: this was a real revolution, a merry, laughing revolution, sweeping away the Communist Party, its system, its values, its statues, and its leaders. It took Gorbachev another forty-eight hours to realise what was happening. His tardiness inflicted permanent damage on his position.

By Friday 23 August, Yeltsin's supremacy over Gorbachev was in full flight. Yeltsin chaired a session of the Russian Supreme Soviet, broadcast live on television, like a judge, while Gorbachev, standing at the rostrum, looked like a defendant in the dock. He faced a barrage of hostile speeches over his pro-Party remarks. Yeltsin, far from helping him out, almost bullied the Soviet president. At one point he strode across to the rostrum, jabbed his finger at him and forced him to read aloud the minutes of a Council of Ministers meeting that had been held on the first day of the coup, which demonstrated that several ministers had supported it.

A few minutes later Yeltsin announced, to thunderous applause and cheering in the hall, that the building of the central committee had been sealed up. 'Don't get carried away with emotions, we need a clear head', Gorbachev pleaded. But the momentum was relentless.

Interrupting Gorbachev's thoughts about the union treaty, Yeltsin suddenly declared that – 'to relieve the tension' – he was signing a decree suspending the activities of the Russian Communist Party. Gorbachev was left speechless, stammering: 'Boris Nikolayevich, Boris Nikolayevich. . . '

'There,' replied Yeltsin, flourishing his pen. 'It's signed!'

Gorbachev again revealed his impotence: 'I don't know what is written there. . . but if it resembles what Boris Nikolayevich said, then I don't think you should support him. Not all the Russian Communist Party participated in the plot or supported it. It will be a mistake to ban the Communist Party.'

There was uproar in the hall, and Yeltsin pedantically explained that what he had done was perfectly legal: 'We're not *banning* the Russian Communist Party – just suspending its activities pending the results of the investigation into its involvement in [the coup].'

In recognition of what had actually happened during the coup, the two men agreed on a plan (quite unconstitutional) for the transfer of each one's duties to the other in the event of disability. It put the men on an equal footing, but in reality Yeltsin now dwarfed Gorbachev. All new government appointments were made by Gorbachev only after consultation with Yeltsin. They included the selection of Vadim Bakatin, whom the conservatives had tried to get rid of the previous winter, as new head of the KGB, with a brief to turn it, for the first time in Soviet history, into an organisation not aimed against the Soviet people. Yeltsin's Russian government took control of all USSR economic ministries and government communications. He even took charge of all CPSU and KGB files, by turning them over to the Russian archives administration – though not before many secret documents were shredded by the last good communists left in the buildings before they were sealed up.

It was only on Saturday 24 August that Gorbachev finally changed tack. In the morning he spoke at the funeral of three young men killed defending the barricades on the last night of the coup. In the afternoon he had a meeting with two close advisers, Shakhnazarov and Bakatin, who patiently explained to him that all his thoughts about reforming the Communist Party were misplaced, and that it was time to recognise that he really had flown back 'to a new era'. Alexander Yakovlev, who joined them a little later, seemed to clinch the argument by declaring that discussing how to reform the Party was 'like looking for the best way to offer tea to a dead body.'

In the evening Gorbachev issued a historic statement. He announced that he was giving up the Party leadership, called on the central committee to disband itself, and ordered the nationalisation of all Party property and assets throughout the land. The brief statement on *Vremya*, the evening television news, spelt the end of communist rule in Russia after almost 74 years. The Party no longer had any property, nor a leader, nor even a central committee to convene a congress or conference to decide its future.

The final blow to the Party came the following week, when the Supreme Soviet voted to suspend the CPSU for the duration of the investigation into the coup. It was tantamount to a ban. Party offices all over the country, already under lock and key, began to be transferred to other purposes, and their officials were seen frequenting the recently created employment offices, looking for new jobs.

THE collapse of the Communist Party was quickly followed by the crumbling of the Soviet Union itself. All the old arguments about the proposed union treaty were now up in the air. A much more fundamental question had arisen: whether the Soviet Union was to continue as a *country*, albeit with a confederal internal structure, or whether it was to be transformed into an alliance or community of independent states.

When the Congress of People's Deputies met for an extraordinary session on 2 September, it was presented with a blueprint for a new state structure which left the final shape of the union unspecified. In an 'interim period', the country would be governed by a new State Council consisting of President Gorbachev and the leaders of the republics. The Congress of People's Deputies itself was abolished – though as a sop to resentful members they were allowed to retain their (now meaningless) status as people's deputies until the next general election. The new top legislative body was a revamped Supreme Soviet, in which the republics' voices would be paramount. And with the entire government having been sacked in the wake of the coup, an Inter-Republican Economic Council was to be formed to manage the economy and – at last – introduce a market system in the shortest possible time.

In the weeks following the failure of the coup, the republics became increasingly assertive. One by one, they declared 'independence', though each meant something different by it. On 6 September the new State Council, at its first meeting, recognised the three Baltic republics as independent states outside of the Soviet Union – ignoring the relevant Soviet laws to which Gorbachev had hitherto clung. Lithuania, Latvia and Estonia were immediately recognised by most foreign countries and accepted into the United Nations.

The remaining twelve republics of what now tended to be called 'the former Soviet Union' were rapidly growing apart. Few of them were interested in a new political union, and even those that accepted the need for a military-strategic alliance also demanded the right to have their own national guards or armies.

Only an economic union seemed feasible at this stage, but the republics could not agree on what powers should be given to what remained of the 'centre'. The man charged with the task of bringing the bickering republics together, at least economically, was Grigory Yavlinsky, author of the ill-fated 500 Days plan in the summer of 1990 and the 'Grand Bargain' of the spring. Even his credentials as a free-marketeer were not enough to persuade some republics that the new union would be sufficiently different from the old. Partly, this was because of fears that it would be dominated by Russia, which controlled most of the country's resources and assets.

These fears were strengthened by Yeltsin's behaviour immediately after the coup. On three occasions the Russian president seemed to overreach himself. He threatened to consider redrawing borders with any neighbouring republics which did not sign a treaty – his statement caused angry demonstrations in the Ukraine and Kazakhstan. He suspended communist newspapers – drawing criticism from leading liberals. And he tried to assert exclusive Russian control over all Soviet foreign-currency bank transactions. He had to retreat over each issue – in the last case after being firmly put in his place by Gorbachev, who told him that while it had been appropriate for Yeltsin to take supreme control during the coup, it was no longer so now that Gorbachev was back in charge.

On 18 October the first agreement governing the post-Soviet

order was finally signed – but by only eight of the former republics. The treaty provided for an economic zone covering all signatory-republics, with a single monetary and banking system, joint customs control and tariffs, and coordinated energy, transport and communications policies. Apart from the now independent Baltic states, the treaty was not signed by Georgia, Moldavia, Azerbaijan and – most importantly – the Ukraine, which was already designing its own banknotes and was intent on introducing its own currency.

In itself, the treaty could do nothing to solve the country's massive food shortages or reverse the huge slump in industrial production. The required shift to a market economy had still scarcely begun. As winter loomed, the perennial talk of hunger assumed a new urgency. But with the power vacuum only papered over, Western countries remained loath to pour more than token amounts of aid into what still looked like a 'black hole'.

FEW nations have endured such a tragic history as the Russians. Every attempt to introduce democracy, 'civilise' the country, or drag it into the Western world, failed. Enlightened despots alternated with benighted ones, whether tsarist or communist.

But only the communist autocrats dared to experiment on their subjects. For seventy years they tried to mould a new kind of human being, 'superior' to that which existed before the Revolution. The experiment went hideously wrong: it produced peasants who hated the land, workers who hated working, neighbours who denounced each other to the KGB, shop assistants who hid goods from their customers, journalists who were professional liars, and millions of petty bribe-givers.

In the course of one evening a Russian man told me about his life: how he threw bread to starving children crowding round his train as he passed through a famine area in the thirties; how he voted in class for 'foreign agents' to be shot; how his father, a Bolshevik, was shot in the Stalinist purges; how he had listened secretly to the BBC on a banned shortwave radio, in a communal flat shared with three other families; how he had wept over Stalin's death. He told me about the 'political education' sessions at work (this in the eighties); about his futile attempts to make a few common-sense suggestions to the bureaucrats who ran his publishing house; about that day's good fortune at his office, where some imported frozen chickens were delivered; and about the impossibility these days of buying boxes of chocolates – he needed a box to secure treatment from his doctor, and another for his dentist. . .

One cannot say that Russians have emerged unbroken from this degrading Orwellian nightmare. The experiment has inflicted lasting damage on their society, their environment, and on the people themselves. Vast tracts of the Soviet countryside may never recover from the ecological havoc wrought by planners. The economy itself has been stripped of the very mechanisms that make normal markets work: putting them back will be a painful, protracted process. Few Soviet bureaucrats – the people who have run the factories, farms and ministries until now – can be expected to turn themselves into businessmen capable of thriving in market conditions, and it will be decades before a new generation of entrepreneurs grows up, free of the suspicions, blind obedience and fear of innovation which were inculcated in their elders. It is hard to imagine where the farmers who might one day fill the food shops are to come from, since all successful peasants who cared about the land were exterminated by Stalin and replaced in the main by unmotivated 'collective farmers' who were mere labourers, hired by the state bureaucracy.

The Second Russian Revolution put an end to the biggest laboratory test in history. It required Gorbachev to declare the experiment a failure before the nation of 'guinea-pigs' could rebel. Now, humiliated and still reeling as though anaesthetised, they are retaking control of their destinies.

IN the new Soviet Union – under whatever title it emerges – the man who facilitated the revolution seems likely to play a much smaller part. If it is a mere community of independent states, Gorbachev's role may resemble that of the president of the European Commission, while real power resides with the presidents of those states – Yeltsin (or his successor) and his counterparts. Even if the former Soviet republics decide on a joint political future, there is no guarantee that Gorbachev will be chosen as its leader in a free election. His popular standing is so low that he is unlikely to outlive the transition period.

Both the successes and the failures of *perestroika* stemmed in large measure from Gorbachev's personality. During his first years in power, when he was the most radical member of the leadership, his brilliance (not to mention deviousness) as a seeker of compromise brought rapid step-by-step progress, as he persuaded the conservatives to agree to more and more liberal policies. But later, when the new political structures he created became dominated by more radical politicians, he found himself in the centre, no longer leading the reforms but acting as a conciliator between the conservatives and liberals who wanted to go much further than he did.

In all three main policy areas – the political system, the economy and inter-ethnic relations – Gorbachev's vision seemed to stop some way short of the measure needed to complete the revolution he began. Even the shock of the coup did not immediately change that.

In politics, he was a genuine reformer – and from about 1987 a radical one, who understood that real democracy necessarily implied a free, multi-party system. Being a committed socialist, however, he tried to engineer a transition which would give the Communist Party time to renew itself and become a force capable of winning a free election. It may be argued that Gorbachev had to introduce democracy in this way because the huge hardline mass of Party *apparatchiki* (whose power has been amply demonstrated) would not tolerate an immediate jump. Whatever his motivation, the structures and freedoms he created quickly brought about a situation which demanded that the transition be completed much faster than he – or the communists – wanted. At that point, Gorbachev was left behind.

In the economy, his judgment was clouded both by ideology and by his relatively poor grasp of the subject. He accepted the idea of the market system later than he did democracy – too late – and he always remained worried by its social consequences. His heart never seemed to be in it. As a socialist, he would have preferred to make the planned economy work if only it were feasible. He had a visceral fear of private ownership of the land, and as late as October 1990 he passed a decree setting limits on profits – the very engine of the market system. All the economists who advised him remarked on his brilliance at absorbing ideas, spotting their weaknesses, developing them, and directing the search for alternatives. But with no formal training in market economics (his new advisor, Nikolai Petrakov, put him through a series of 'tutorials' in early 1990), he tended, in the end, to muddle through. His eclectic approach, and inveterate desire to find compromises, repeatedly produced unworkable plans.

Perhaps Gorbachev's greatest flaw was his Russianness. The nationalities problem, of course, was truly intractable, for the Soviet 'colonies' were internal, and could not simply be 'set free'. But Gorbachev never appeared to understand the feelings or longings of the nations that had suffered for centuries under Russian or Soviet dominion, seeing their predicament at best only in economic terms. He had less sympathy for, say, the Lithuanians living under Russian rule than for the much smaller number of Russians who would find themselves a minority in an independent Lithuanian state. He sincerely believed that the peoples of the Soviet Union would live better together than separately, and pointed quite erroneously to the unifying processes in the European Community as proof of world trends, without appearing to understand the difference between the desire of free and sovereign states to come together, and his own efforts to preserve central control over non-Russian republics which still had scarcely any say in running their own economies. Radicals argued that the Soviet Union must first break up, so that market economies could be set up in its constituent parts (thus once and for all breaking the subordination to Moscow), before the free republics could voluntarily join together along the lines of the European Community. Yet it was only after the failed coup left him with no other choice that Gorbachev finally accepted the need for such a confederal structure.

In the light of the coup, one other tragic flaw must be added to the list: Gorbachev was a poor judge of character. He himself admits that he had fully trusted most of those who tried to overthrow him. His advisers had warned him, and even voted against several of the key appointments in the winter of 1990, when he fell under the spell of the right. Yakovlev and Shakhnazarov suggest he was gullible. He relied too much on the KGB as a source of information, even when it was run by Kryuchkov, who thrived on stories of Western subversion and leftwing 'plots'. According to Yakovlev, Gorbachev supported the huge display of military might in Moscow in March 1990 (which could easily have led to bloodshed) because he believed Kryuchkov's tales about demonstrators preparing to storm the Kremlin, using specially-prepared ropes and hooks to scale the walls.

Whatever Gorbachev's personal shortcomings, it is doubtful whether any other leader could have achieved more in such a short time. Over seven decades the system produced a ruling and administrative class – Party functionaries, state bureaucrats, ideologues, generals and secret policemen – whose main aim was self-preservation. By making constant concessions to them as he reformed (one step backwards, two steps forward), Gorbachev at least bought time for democracy to take root, to such an extent that it was able to defeat the hardliners' coup when it came. Had he given too much to the radicals at an earlier stage – and precipitated a coup before the public and the press had become radicalised – the result might have been quite different.

Gorbachev never regarded Boris Yeltsin's constant criticism and prodding as anything other than a nuisance. Yet it was Yeltsin who better understood the public mood, and used his well-earned popularity to defeat the August attempt at counter-revolution. After the coup, as he turned from opposition figure to leader, his actions became more confused and lost direction. He, too, may prove to be a transitional figure.

The Second Revolution, begun by Gorbachev, was carried to its logical conclusion by Yeltsin and by the Soviet people whom it released from seven decades of tyranny. Now it is up to the people, reborn as individuals and as nations, to produce a new generation of politicians and economists, capable of building a new society from the wreckage of communism.

# Notes to the Text

*SWB* = *Summary of World Broadcasts*, BBC Monitoring Service

*IRS* = Mikhail Gorbachev, *Izbrannye rechi i statyi* (Moscow, Politizdat, 1987–1990)

CHAPTER ONE:
## 'We cannot go on living like this'

**1.** Impromptu speech by Gorbachev to his former class mates, at the old Law Faculty of Moscow University, 16 June 1990. The 'Second Russian Revolution' team were there by special invitation.

**2.** They spoke in the following order: Gromyko, Tikhonov, Grishin, Solomentsev, Romanov, Kunayev, Aliyev, Vorotnikov, Ponomaryov, Chebrikov, Dolgikh, Kuznetsov, Shevardnadze, Demichev, Zimyanin, Kapitonov, Ligachev, Ryzhkov, Rusakov.

**3.** The Russian, apparently, was *'krasivaya ulybka, no zheleznaya khvatka'*, i.e., more accurately, 'Nice smile but an iron bite' (like that of an animal). For Gromyko's published speech, see *Materialy vneocherednogo Plenuma Tsentral -'nogo Komiteta KPSS, 11 marta 1985 g.* (Moscow Politizdat, 1985).

**4.** The magazine was *Khimiya i zhizn (Chemistry and Life)*. See also *Literaturnaya gazeta*, 22 Sept 1990.

**5.** Zores Medvedev gives a detailed description of the Ipatovo method, and discusses its shortcomings in *Gorbachev* (Oxford, Blackwelil, 1986).

**6.** *IRS*, Vol 1, pp. 180–200

**7.** *Pravda*, 20 March 1983.

**8.** Incidentally, the reason the author and purpose of the document was not at first known in the West was because it had been photocopied in the Soviet Union – and that could only be done if the

cover page, which contained the words 'For official use only', was first removed.

**9.** It has often been assumed in the West that the general secretary chaired the Tuesday meetings of the Secretariat, but all Politburo sources confirm that even under Brezhnev this was in fact the duty of the 'second secretary'. Indeed, they tend to *define* the 'second secretary' as 'the man who ran the secretariat', rather than by the usual Western definition – 'the man in charge of ideology'.

**10.** Boris Yeltsin, *Against the Grain* (London, Jonathan Cape, 1990), p.112.

**11.** See 'Rasplata', *Isvestiya*, 2 August 1984

**12.** It has not been possible to corroborate unconfirmed reports about Chebrikov's and Solomentsev's role from top-level sources.

**13.** In speech at class reunion, Moscow University, 16 June 1990.

**14.** *Pravda*, 8 April 1985.

**15.** *IRS*, Vol. 2, pp. 210–224.

**16.** Martin McCauley (ed.), *The Soviet Union under Gorbachev* (London, Macmillan, 1987), p. 21.

**17.** *Pravda*, 1 April 1985.

**18.** Agence France Presse, 15 April 1985.

**19.** *Trezvost' – zakon nashei zhizni*, (Moscow, Politizdat, 1985).

**20.** Mark Frankland, *The Sixth Continent* (London, Hamish Hamilton, 1987), p. 201.

**21.** The Politburo meeting was held around 14 May, but Romanov's resignation was announced officially at the

central committee plenum on 1 July 1985.
**22.** Ligachev was placed prominently in the line-up on Red Square on May Day and at a war anniversary meeting on 8 May. ON 13 May he presided over an ideology conference in the central committee, and in July he was appointed chairman of the foreign affairs commission of the Council of the Union of the Supreme Soviet – a post traditionally given to the Party's 'number two'.
**23.** This information was given by Roy Medvedev at the First Congress of People's Deputies. Cf. *Izvestiya*, 30 May 1989.
**24.** Tikhonov had defended the project at a central committee plenum in October 1984; see *Pravda*, 25 October 1984.
**25.** *Pravda*, 28 September 1985.
**26.** *Sovetskaya Rossiya*, 21 July, 18 August and 8 September 1985.
**27.** Boris Yeltsin, *op. cit.*, p. 89.
**28.** *IRS*, Vol. 2, p. 317.
**29.** *Izvestiya*, 23 May 1988.
**30.** *Pravda*, 13 February 1986.
**31.** *Pravda*, 28th March 1986.
**32.** *Literaturnaya gazeta*, 15 October 1986.
**33.** Moscow Radio (Mayak), 1 December 1986.
**34.** Decree: 29 March 1985. Ligachev: *Pravda*, 6 April 1986.
**35.** *Pravda*, 17 June 1986.
**36.** Speech in Tolyatti, 8 April 1986; *IRS*, Vol. 3, p. 346.
**37.** M. Lemeshev, '*AES – prestuplenie pered chelovechestvom*', *Cherez ternii*, p. 589, (Moscow Progress, 1990).
**38.** *Pravda*, 25 April 1988.
**39.** *Argumenty i fakty*, 33/1988.
**40.** *Izvestiya*, 2 November 1988.
**41.** *Literaturnaya gazeta*, 10 September 1986.
**42.** Mikhail Gorbachev, *Perestroika* (London, Fontana, 1988), pp. 81–82.
**43.** *Literaturnaya gazeta*, 10 September 1986.
**44.** *Pravda*, 16 August 1986.
**45.** *Sovetskaya Rossiya*, 26 June 1990.

CHAPTER TWO:
## Principles Betrayed

**1.** *IRS*, Vol. 4, pp. 121–138, 139–151.
**2.** Boris Yeltsin, *op. cit.* p. 121.
**3.** By 1989 the Kazakh population had grown to 6.5 millions, slightly larger than the Russian (6.2 millions). See Radio Liberty's *Report on the USSR*, 18/1990, p. 18–19.
**4.** A commission of inquiry set up by the Kazakhstan Supreme Soviet finally reported in September 1990. See *Kazakhstanskaya pravda*, 28 September 1990.
**5.** *IRS*, Vol. 4, p. 237.
**6.** *Pravda*, 18 February 1987.
**7.** *IRS*, Vol. 4, p. 400.
**8.** *Pravda*, 1 March 1987.
**9.** *Pravda*, 12 February 1987.
**10.** Meeting on 19 June 1986. Radio Liberty *Arkhiv samizdata*, No. 5785.
**11.** Meeting with journalists, 11 February 1987. *IRS*, Vol. 4, p. 373–4.
**12.** *Moscow News*, 18 January 1987.
**13.** *Druzhba naradov*, Nos 4–6, 1987.
**14.** Soviet television, 31 May 1987.
**15.** *Ogonyok*, 27 June 1987.
**16.** *IRS*, Vol. 4, p. 429.
**17.** See *Moscow News*, 37/1987.
**18.** Boris Yeltsin, *op. cit.*, p. 10.
**19.** *Pravda*, 13 November 1987.
**20.** Yeltsin, *op. cit.*, p. 106.
**21.** The proceedings of the October plenum were eventually published in *Izvestiya TsK KPSS*, 2/1089.
**22.** Author's notes from news conference.
**23.** *Moskovakaya pravda*, 13 November 1987.
**24.** Yegor Ligachev, *Izbranne rechi i statyi*, p. 11. (Moscow, Politizdat, 1989).
**25.** *Izvestiya*, 12 July 1990.
**26.** Christian Schmidt-Häuer, *Gorbachev: the Path to Power* (Pan Books, London), p. 194.
**27.** *Pravda*, 18, 19 February 1988.
**28.** See *Pravda*, 19 March 1988.
**29.** Pavel Demidov in *Zhurnalist*, 5/1988.

CHAPTER THREE:
## Revolution from Above

**1.** *SWB*, 4 August 1986.
**2.** *Pravda*, 4 June 1988.
**3.** *Izvestiya*, 10 June 1988.
**4.** *Pravda*, 2 June 1988.
**5.** *Sovetskaya Rossiya*, 1 June 1988.
**6.** *Pravda*, 6 June 1988.
**7.** *Izvestiya*, 9 June 1988.
**8.** *Vedomostio Verkhovnogo Soveta SSSR*, 31/1988.
**9.** All speeches published in *XIX Vsesoyuznaya konferentsiya Kommunist-*

cheskoi partii Sovetskogo Soyuza, 28 iyunya – 1 iyunya 1988 g: Stenograficheskii otchet (two volumes) (Moscow, Politizdat, 1988).

**10.** The size of the Supreme Soviet was later revised to 542.

**11.** The group included Alexander Yakovlev, Vadim Medvedev, Ivan Frolov, Antoly Chernyayev, Valery Boldin and Georgy Shakhnazarov.

**12.** Not three, as Yeltsin says in his memoirs.

**13.** SWB, 4 July 1988.

**14.** Komsomolskaya pravda, 23 July 1988.

**15.** Soviet television, 19 July 1988.

**16.** Soviet television, 5 August 1988.

**17.** Speeches in Riga, 10 August, and Vilnius, 12 August 1988.

**18.** Izvestiya TsK KPSS, 1/1989, pp. 81-86.

**19.** Izvestiya TsK KPSS, 1/1989, pp. 93-94.

**20.** SWB, 16 September 1988.

**21.** Izvestiya Tsk KPSS, 1/1989, pp. 48-51.

**22.** Pravda, 8 December 1988.

**23.** Soviet television, 11 December 1988.

CHAPTER FOUR:
## Revolution from Below

**1.** Officially known as 'constituency pre-election meeting'.

**2.** IRS, Vol. 7, p. 411.

**3.** See Elizabeth Teague, 'Gorbachev outfoxes the opposition', Report on the USSR (Radio Liberty, Munich), 109/1989, pp. 1-3.

**4.** See TASS interview with justice minister Boris Kravtsov, SWB, 2 November 1988; also interview with lawyer, Sofia Kelina, of the Academy of Sciences, in Izvestiya, 29 December 1988.

**5.** Izvestiya, 10 April 1989.

**6.** Pravda, 11 February 1989.

**7.** See Shevardnadze's speech to central committee plenum, 6 February 1990.

**8.** Interview with Ligachev.

**9.** Pravda, 11 April 1989.

**10.** Pravda, 27 April 1989.

**11.** Ogonyok, No. 26, June 1988.

**12.** Pravda, 13 May 1989.

**13.** The entire proceedings of the first Congress of People's Deputies were published in Izvestiya, starting on 27 May 1989.

**14.** Officially, the head of state was known as Chairman of the Supreme Soviet, but he was often referred to, especially abroad, as 'president'.

**15.** Decrees on demonstrations and interior troops, both dated 28 July 1988, in Vedomosti Verkhovnogo Soveta, 31/1988.

**16.** Boris Yeltsin, op. cit., p. 190.

**17.** A start had been made a little earlier – the theatre director Mark Zakharov had caused a storm on Lenin's birthday, 21 April, by suggesting on the controversial late-night television show, Vzglyad (Viewpoint), that Lenin's body should be removed from its mausoleum and reburied, and several short works by Solzhenitsyn had been reprinted – but the free speech heard at the Congress opened the floodgates.

**18.** Radio Liberty, Report on the USSR, No. 41, 1989, pp. 4–5.

**19.** Liternaya gazeta, 8 August 1990.

**20.** Moscow News, No. 34, 26 August, 1990.

**21.** Business in the USSR, May 1990.

**22.** Soviet television, 2 March 1989.

**23.** Soviet television, 11 March 1989.

**24.** Pravitelstvenny vestnik, 5/1990.

**25.** Komsomolskaya pravda, 14 July 1989.

CHAPTER FIVE:
## The Empire Cracks Up

**1.** Pravda, 5 July 1990.

**2.** Moscow News, 38/1990.

**3.** Isvestiya, 2 June 1989.

**4.** Pravda, 26 August 1990.

**5.** Pravda, 20 September 1989.

**6.** Pravda, 4 March 1989.

**7.** 'And the Walls Came Tumbling Down', Channel Four television, 5 November 1990.

**8.** In a speech to the founding congress of the Russian Communist Party; Sovetskaya Rossiya, 21 June 1990.

**9.** Materialy Plenuma Tsentral'nogo Komiteta KPSS, 11, 14, 16, marta 1990 g. (Moscow 1990), p. 91.

**10.** Shevardnadze at the 28th Congress of the CPSU; Pravda, 5 July 1990.

**11.** Pravda, 26 November 1989.

**12.** Transcript in Izvestiya TsK KPSS, 4/1990.

**13.** Sokolov tried to prevent a Popular Front from being formed in Belorussia. The Front had to hold its first congress in Vilnius.

**14.** Transcript of plenum in Izvestiya TsK KPSS, 6/1990.

15. Agence France Presse, 11 January 1990, and Vilnius Radio, see *SWB*, 15 January 1990.

16. The 'autonomous republic' of Nakhichevan is separated from Azerbaijan proper by a strip of Armenian territory, much as Nagorny Karabakh is separated from Armenia by Azerbaijani land.

CHAPTER SIX:
**The Climax of Perestroika**

1. *Moscow News*, 34/1990.

2. Igor Sedykh of Novosti press agency, in *The Independent*, 20 December 1990.

3. *Materialy Plenuma Tsentral'nogo Komiteta KPSS 11, 14, 16 marta 1990 g.* (Moscow, 1990), pp. 37–41.

4. *Izvestiya TsK KPSS*, 5/1990, pp. 32–59.

5. *The Guardian*, 14 March 1990.

6. *On the 'Lithuanian Problem' (White Book)*, p. 21, (Moscow, Novosti, 1990).

7. Law on Secession in *Pravda*, 7 April 1990.

8. *Sovetskaya Rossiya*, 21 June 1990.

9. *Ibid.*

10. *Materialy Plenuma Tsentral'nogo Komiteta KPSS 11, 14, 16 marta 1990 g.*, p. 53.

11. *Izvestiya TsK KPSS*, 3/1990, p. 101.

12. Stenogram of discussion in Izvestiya Ts KPSS, 3/1990, pp. 41–115.

13. *Liternaturnaya gazeta*, 2 May 1990.

14. See Georgy Arbatov in *The Financial Times*, 2 May 1990.

15. *Financial Times*, 29 May 1990.

16. *Izvestiya TsK KPSS*, 4/1990/ See Radio Liberty *Report on the USSR*, 18/1990, pp. 4–6.

17. *Pravda*, 3 July 1990.

18. The only published account of this meeting was by a Tver district secretary, V. Bragin, in *Argumenty i fakty*, 28/1990.

19. *Pravda*, 11 July 1990.

20. Gorbachev and Ivashko had evidently planned that the latter would become deputy general secretary and did not expect any hitches, because Ivashko gave up his position as Chairman of the Ukrainian Supreme Soviet (to which he had only just been elected) just days before this election.

21. A third candidate, a professor from Leningrad, later put his own name forward, so there were three candidates in the end.

22. *Pravda*, 10 October 1990.

23. *Izvestiya*, 16 August 1990.

24. *Izvestiya TsK KPSS*, 3/1990, p. 124; TASS, 30 January 1991.

CHAPTER SEVEN:
**The Old Order Fights Back**

1. From Yazov's testimony to investigators after August coup, *Der Spiegel*, 41/1991.

2. Sources for the events in the Crimea are: Anatoly Chernyayev's diary, in *Time*, 7 October 1991; Gorbachev's press conference, 22 August 1991; Gorbachev at Russian Supreme Soviet, 23 August 1991.

3. Details of the meeting on night of 18 August in statements by Yazov, Kryuchkov and Pavlov to interrogators, in *Der Spiegel*, 41/1991, by Vladimir Shcherbakov, first deputy premier (to Supreme Soviet, 28 August 1991, on Moscow radio, 25 August 1991) and in *The Guardian*, 29 August 1991.

# Soviet Political System in 1985

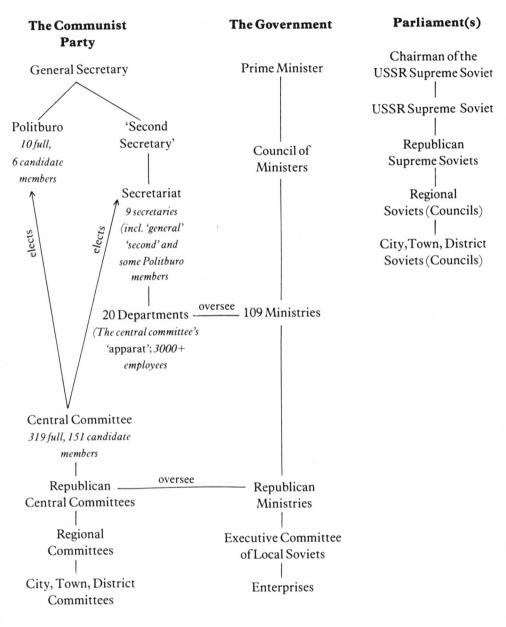

| The Communist Party | The Government | Parliament(s) |
|---|---|---|
| General Secretary | Prime Minister | Chairman of the USSR Supreme Soviet |
| | | USSR Supreme Soviet |
| Politburo *10 full, 6 candidate members* | 'Second Secretary' | Council of Ministers | Republican Supreme Soviets |
| | Secretariat *9 secretaries (incl. 'general' 'second' and some Politburo members* | | Regional Soviets (Councils) |
| | | | City, Town, District Soviets (Councils) |

elects    elects

20 Departments ——— oversee ——— 109 Ministries
*(The central committee's 'apparat'; 3000+ employees*

Central Committee
*319 full, 151 candidate members*

Republican ——— oversee ——— Republican
Central Committees    Ministries

Regional    Executive Committee
Committees    of Local Soviets

City, Town, District    Enterprises
Committees

227

# Political System after 1988 Reforms

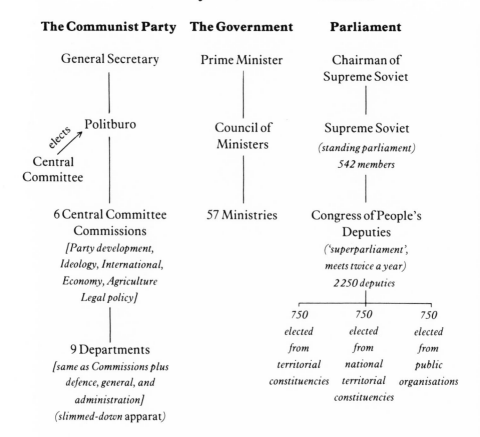

| The Communist Party | The Government | Parliament |
|---|---|---|
| General Secretary | Prime Minister | Chairman of Supreme Soviet |
| *elects* → Politburo | Council of Ministers | Supreme Soviet *(standing parliament)* 542 members |
| Central Committee | | |
| 6 Central Committee Commissions [*Party development, Ideology, International, Economy, Agriculture Legal policy*] | 57 Ministries | Congress of People's Deputies (*'superparliament', meets twice a year*) 2250 deputies |
| 9 Departments [*same as Commissions plus defence, general, and administration*] (*slimmed-down* apparat) | | 750 *elected from territorial constituencies* | 750 *elected from national territorial constituencies* | 750 *elected from public organisations* |

# Index

Abalkin, Leonid 92, 97, 198
  in charge of economic
    reform 146–7, 183–4,
    185
Abkhazia 151
Abuladze,Tengis 61
Afanasyev, Yuri 91, 104,
    138, 139, 153–4
Afghanistan 22, 49, 50,95
Aganbegyan, Abel 15, 16
  economic adviser 33–5,
    145, 198
agriculture 117, 197, 220
  collectivisation 38–9, 64,
    144–5
  Food Programme 14, 33
  Gorbachev initiatives
    14–15, 38–9
  Ipatovo method 12–13
Akademgorodok 33
Akhromeyev, Marshal Sergei
    158
alcoholism
  campaign against 27–9,
    116–17
Aleksandrov, Anatoly 42
Aliyev, Geidar 6, 13, 28
Ambartsumov, Yevgeny 33
Andreyeva, Nina 83–4, 86,
    87
Andropov, Yuri 9, 10, 16,
    21
  anti-alcohol campaign 14,
    27
  death 18
  and economy 14, 15
  relations with Gorbachev
    15–17
anti-semitism 103
Aral Sea
  siphoning off for irrigation
    projects, 47
Arbatov, Georgy 23, 33
*Argumenty i fakty* 44
armed forces *see* military
Armenia
  earthquake 121–4
  feuding with Azerbaijan
    82, 108–9, 152, 167–8
  arms negotiations 10, 42,
    51–2

Article Six 160, 162, 171,
    172
  amendment to 173–4
Article 7 (Article 70) 58, 131
Article 11–1 (Article 190–1)
    58, 131
Association of State
  Enterprises 198
Azerbaijan 13, 28, 219
  feuding with Armenia 12,
    81–2, 108, 122, 123,
    152, 167–8

Baibakov, Nikolai 35
Baikal-Amur Railway (BAM)
    11
Bakatin, Vadim 26, 137,
    199–200, 201, 202, 213,
    216–17
Baklanov, Grigory 92, 205,
    206, 208, 209, 213, 214
Baku, 82
  Soviet military assault 167
Baltic republics *see* Estonia;
  Latvia; Lithuania
BAM *see* Baikal-Amur
  Railway
Belinsky, Vissarion 109
Belorussia 40
Berlin Wall 158
Bessmertnykh, Alexander
    208, 209
black market 38, 197
Bocharov, Mikhail 144
Bogolyubov, Klavdii 5, 17
Boldin, Valery 205, 206,
    207, 208, 209
Bondarev, Yuri 81
books *see* literature
Brakov, Yevgeny 129
Brazauskas, Algirdas 119,
    162–4
Brezhnev, Leonid 10–12, 13,
    14, 58, 155
Brovikov, Vladimir 172–3
building standards 66
Bukharin, Nikolai 62
Bulgaria 158
*Bulletin of the Christian
    Community* 59

Bush, George 205, 214
Butec 144

Ceausescu, Nicolae 158
censorship 43–4, 45
Central Committee of the
    CPSU 70, 133–4, 192
  new commissions set up
    115–17
  Plenums
    Dec 1983 17
    April 1985 25, 26
    June 1986 39
    Jan 1987 55–6, 57
    Oct 1987 72–5
    Sept 1988 114–15
    Sept 1989 154–5
    Dec 1989 160–2, 163–6
    Jan 1991 202
    April 1991 204–5
    July 1991 204
  reforms 90, 115, 187,
    190–2
  *see also* CPSU
Chebrikov, Viktor 23, 116
  in charge of legal policy
    118, 131, 133, 154
  KGB chief 7, 26, 52–3
Chernenko, Konstantin 8,
    10, 16–17
  death 5,7, 34
  election as General
    Secretary 18
  health 20, 22, 23
  relations with Gorbachev
    5, 6
Chernobyl disaster 40–3, 66
Chernyayev, Anatoly 33, 49,
    50, 206, 207, 213
Chikin, Valentin 84, 85, 87
*Children of the Arbat*
    (Rybakov) 63
Chornovil, Vyacheslav 179
Churbanov, Yuri 58–9, 134
Churkin, Vitaly 49–50
Club for Social Initiatives
    103
Club Perestroika 103
Cold War
  diminish of 24, 120
  collectivisation 39, 144–5

229